NORTHSTAR 2
READING AND WRITING
THIRD EDITION

AUTHORS
Natasha Haugnes
Beth Maher

SERIES EDITORS
Frances Boyd
Carol Numrich

PEARSON
Longman

Dedication

Charlie, Emmet, Oliver, Niko, Toby, and Theo.

NorthStar: Reading and Writing Level 2, Third Edition

Copyright © 2009, 2004, 1998 by Pearson Education, Inc.
All rights reserved.

No part of this publication may be reproduced, stored in a retrieval system, or transmitted in any form or by any means, electronic, mechanical, photocopying, recording, or otherwise, without the prior permission of the publisher.

Pearson Education, 10 Bank Street, White Plains, NY 10606

Contributor credit: Robin Mills, Laurie Frazier, and Helen S. Solórzano contributed material to FOCUS ON WRITING in *NorthStar: Reading and Writing Level 2, Third Edition*.

Staff credits: The people who made up the **NorthStar: Reading and Writing Level 2, Third Edition** team, representing editorial, production, design, and manufacturing, are Aerin Csigay, Dave Dickey, Ann France, Françoise Leffler, Melissa Leyva, Sherry Preiss, Robert Ruvo, Debbie Sistino, and Paula Van Ells.

Cover art: Silvia Rojas/Getty Images
Text composition: ElectraGraphics, Inc.
Text font: 11.5/13 Minion
Credits: See page 233.

Library of Congress Cataloging-in-Publication Data

Northstar. Reading and writing. — 3rd ed.
  4 v. ; cm.
  Rev. ed. of: Northstar / Natasha Haugnes, Beth Maher, 2nd. ed. 2004.
  The third edition of the Northstar series has been expanded to 4 separate volumes. Each level is in a separate volume with different contributing authors.
  Includes bibliographical references.
  Contents: Level 2 : Basic Low Intermediate / Beth Maher, Natasha Haugnes — Level 3 : Intermediate / Carolyn Dupaquier Sardinas, Laurie Barton — Level 4 : High Intermediate / Andrew English, Laura Monahon English — Level 5 : Advanced / Robert F. Cohen, Judy L. Miller.
   ISBN-13: 978-0-13-240991-9 (pbk. : student text bk. level 2 : alk. paper)
   ISBN-10: 0-13-240991-7 (pbk. : student text bk. level 2 : alk. paper)
   ISBN-13: 978-0-13-613368-1 (pbk. : student text bk. level 3 : alk. paper)
   ISBN-10: 0-13-613368-1 (pbk. : student text bk. level 3 : alk. paper)
   [etc.]
  1. English language—Textbooks for foreign speakers. 2. Reading comprehension—Problems, exercises, etc. 3. Report writing—Problems, exercises, etc. I. Haugnes, Natasha, 1965– Northstar. II. Title: Reading and writing.
  PE1128.N675 2008
  428.2'4—dc22

2008024492

ISBN 10: 0-13-240991-7
ISBN 13: 978-0-13-240991-9

Printed in the United States of America
1 2 3 4 5 6 7 8 9 10—CRK—13 12 11 10 09 08

CONTENTS

Welcome to *NorthStar*, Third Edition..................................iv

Scope and Sequence..................................xvi

UNIT 1 Finding the Ideal Job..................................1

UNIT 2 Country Life or City Life?..................................23

UNIT 3 Making Money..................................45

UNIT 4 A Different Path to Justice..................................71

UNIT 5 Subway Etiquette..................................93

UNIT 6 Serious Fun..................................113

UNIT 7 The Best Produce There Is..................................133

UNIT 8 "I'll take the train, thanks."..................................155

UNIT 9 What's Your Medicine?..................................179

UNIT 10 Endangered Cultures..................................201

Research Topics..................................225

Grammar Book References..................................231

WELCOME TO NORTHSTAR
THIRD EDITION

NorthStar, now in its third edition, motivates students to succeed in their **academic** as well as **personal** language goals.

For each of the five levels, the two strands—*Reading and Writing* and *Listening and Speaking*—provide a fully integrated approach for students and teachers.

WHAT IS SPECIAL ABOUT THE THIRD EDITION?

NEW THEMES

New themes and **updated content**—presented in a **variety of genres**, including literature and lectures, and in **authentic reading and listening selections**—challenge students intellectually.

ACADEMIC SKILLS

More purposeful **integration of critical thinking** and an enhanced focus on **academic skills** such as inferencing, synthesizing, note taking, and test taking help students develop strategies for **success** in the **classroom** and on **standardized tests.** A **culminating productive task** galvanizes content, language, and **critical thinking skills**.

- In the *Reading and Writing* strand, a new, **fully integrated writing section** leads students through the **writing process** with engaging writing assignments focusing on various rhetorical modes.
- In the *Listening and Speaking* strand, a **structured approach** gives students opportunities for **more extended and creative oral practice**, for example, presentations, simulations, debates, case studies, and public service announcements.

NEW DESIGN

Full **color pages** with more **photos**, **illustrations**, **and graphic organizers** foster student engagement and make the content and activities come alive.

MyNorthStarLab

MyNorthStarLab, an easy-to-use **online learning and assessment program**, offers:

- Unlimited access to reading and listening selections and DVD segments.
- Focused test preparation to help students succeed on international exams such as TOEFL® and IELTS®. Pre- and post-unit assessments improve results by providing individualized instruction, instant feedback, and personalized study plans.
- Original activities that support and extend the *NorthStar* program. These include pronunciation practice using voice recording tools, and activities to build note taking skills and academic vocabulary.
- Tools that save time. These include a flexible gradebook and authoring features that give teachers control of content and help them track student progress.

THE NORTHSTAR APPROACH

The *NorthStar* series is based on **current research in language acquisition** and on the **experiences of teachers and curriculum designers**. Five principles guide the *NorthStar* approach.

PRINCIPLES

1 The more profoundly students are stimulated intellectually and emotionally, the more language they will use and retain.

The thematic organization of *NorthStar* promotes intellectual and emotional stimulation. The 50 sophisticated themes in *NorthStar* present intriguing topics such as recycled fashion, restorative justice, personal carbon footprints, and microfinance. The authentic content engages students, links them to language use outside of the classroom, and encourages personal expression and critical thinking.

2 Students can learn both the form and content of the language.

Grammar, vocabulary, and culture are inextricably woven into the units, providing students with systematic and multiple exposures to language forms in a variety of contexts. As the theme is developed, students can express complex thoughts using a higher level of language.

3 Successful students are active learners.

Tasks are designed to be creative, active, and varied. Topics are interesting and up-to-date. Together these tasks and topics (1) allow teachers to bring the outside world into the classroom and (2) motivate students to apply their classroom learning in the outside world.

4 Students need feedback.

This feedback comes naturally when students work together practicing language and participating in open-ended opinion and inference tasks. Whole class activities invite teachers' feedback on the spot or via audio/video recordings or notes. The innovative new MyNorthStarLab gives students immediate feedback as they complete computer-graded language activities online; it also gives students the opportunity to submit writing or speaking assignments electronically to their instructor for feedback later.

5 The quality of relationships in the language classroom is important because students are asked to express themselves on issues and ideas.

The information and activities in *NorthStar* promote genuine interaction, acceptance of differences, and authentic communication. By building skills and exploring ideas, the exercises help students participate in discussions and write essays of an increasingly complex and sophisticated nature.

THE NorthStar UNIT

1 FOCUS ON THE TOPIC

This section introduces students to the unifying theme of the reading selections.

> **PREDICT** and **SHARE INFORMATION** foster interest in the unit topic and help students develop a personal connection to it.
>
> **BACKGROUND AND VOCABULARY** activities provide students with tools for understanding the first reading selection. Later in the unit, students review this vocabulary and learn related idioms, collocations, and word forms. This helps them explore content and expand their written and spoken language.

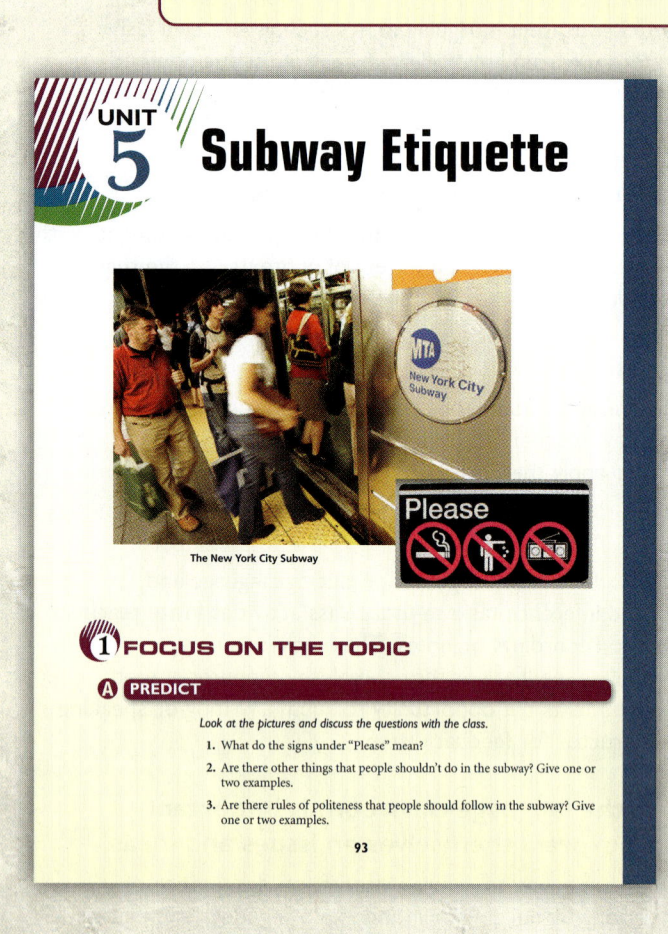

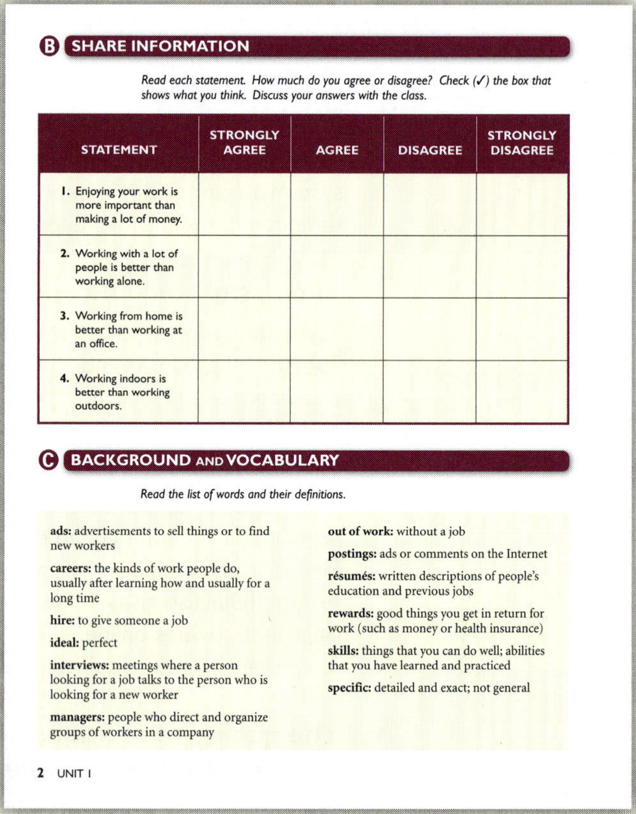

Welcome to **NorthStar**

2 FOCUS ON READING

This section focuses on understanding two contrasting reading selections.

> **READING ONE** is a literary selection, academic article, news piece, blog, or other genre that addresses the unit topic. In levels 1 to 3, readings are based on authentic materials. In levels 4 and 5, all the readings are authentic.
>
> **READ FOR MAIN IDEAS** and **READ FOR DETAILS** are comprehension activities that lead students to an understanding and appreciation of the first selection.

> Following this comprehension section, the **MAKE INFERENCES** activity prompts students to "read between the lines," move beyond the literal meaning, exercise critical thinking skills, and understand the text on a more academic level. Students follow up with pair or group work to discuss topics in the **EXPRESS OPINIONS** section.

Welcome to **NorthStar** vii

READING TWO offers another perspective on the topic and usually belongs to another genre. Again, in levels 1 to 3, the readings are based on authentic materials, and in levels 4 and 5, they are authentic. This second reading is followed by an activity that challenges students to question ideas they formed about the first reading, and to use appropriate language skills to analyze and explain their ideas.

INTEGRATE READINGS ONE AND TWO presents culminating activities. Students are challenged to take what they have learned, organize the information, and synthesize it in a meaningful way. Students practice skills that are essential for success in authentic academic settings and on standardized tests.

B READING TWO: Miles to Go Before You Eat

The following article is from *Sierra Magazine*. The writer tells about another way to look at produce in the United States.

Read the article and think about this question: "Is organic produce always best for the world?"

Miles to Go Before You Eat
By Paul Rauber

1 Your refrigerator is empty. You get on your bike to go grocery shopping. You bring your own bags so that you don't have to use plastic bags from the store. You buy organic bananas, a beautiful pineapple, and organic grapes, strawberries, and spinach. You are feeling good about feeding your family healthy food. You think about how lucky you are. You can buy all of these fruits and vegetables in November in Des Moines, Iowa!

2 You are doing good things for your family and for the environment, but you could do better.

3 Riding your bike saves gasoline. But the pineapple you just bought traveled to your town on an airplane from Hawaii. Your grapes traveled about 7,000 miles by boat and truck from Costa Rica. As a matter of fact, food in the United States travels an average of 1,500 miles from the farm to the dinner plate.

4 Buying organic food, riding a bike, and avoiding plastic bags are all good things to do for the environment. But if you are buying organic pineapples from Hawaii, you may not be seeing the whole picture. Maybe one of the best things we can do for the environment is to eat local produce. It uses less gasoline. It pollutes less. And it probably tastes better, too, since it is fresher.

5 Buying only local produce won't be easy at first. You will have to stop eating produce that doesn't grow nearby, like bananas. And you will be spending a little more on your food. But the world will be healthier, and so will you.

6 Take a look at how much gasoline each of these fruits uses to get to Des Moines, Iowa:

Pineapple (Costa Rica) 0.03 gallon of gasoline
Pineapple (Hawaii) 0.53 gallon of gasoline
Apple (Iowa) 0.10 tablespoon of gasoline
Apple (Washington) 1.92 tablespoons of gasoline

7 Pineapples use a lot of gasoline. But if you must buy one, notice that the Costa Rican pineapple makes more than half of its trip by boat. Boats don't use very much gasoline. Pineapples from Hawaii, however, travel by air.

8 Apples from Iowa travel only 60 miles in small trucks to Des Moines. The ones from Washington must travel 1,722 miles in large trucks.

140 UNIT 7

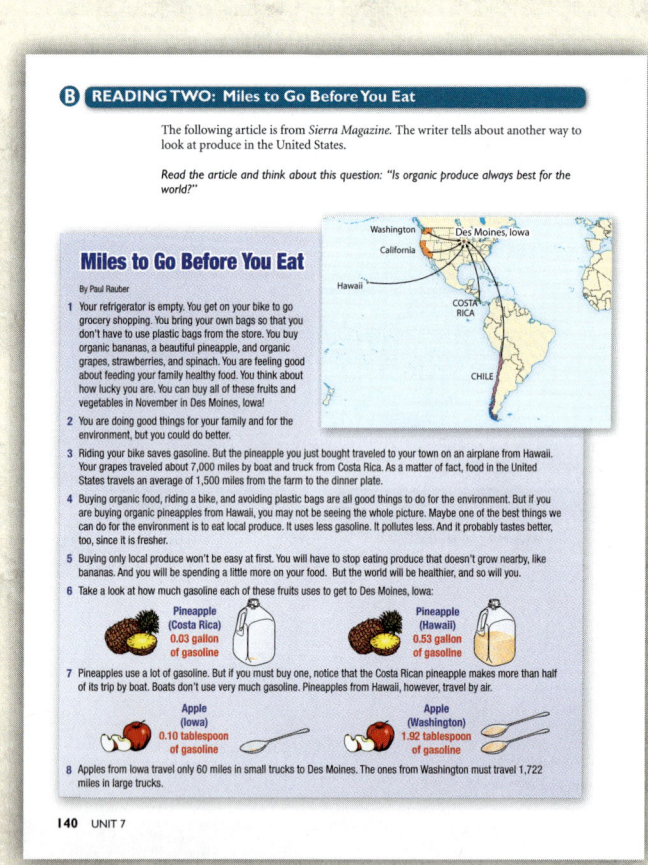

C INTEGRATE READINGS ONE AND TWO

STEP 1: Organize

Read the statements based on Readings One and Two. Then complete the chart with the advantages or disadvantages of different types of produce. Write the underlined words in each statement in the appropriate box in the chart.

Reading One
1. Sometimes organic produce <u>doesn't look as nice</u> as regular produce.
2. We can find most kinds of regular fruits and vegetables <u>all year long</u>.
3. Farming <u>chemicals cause cancer</u>.
4. Some farmers have gone back to growing produce the old-fashioned way—<u>without chemicals</u>.
5. Organic produce is <u>more expensive than regular produce</u>.
6. It is <u>usually fresh</u>.

Reading Two
7. It <u>uses less gasoline</u>.
8. It <u>pollutes less</u>.
9. It probably <u>tastes better</u> too, since it is <u>always fresh</u>.
10. You will have to <u>stop eating produce that doesn't grow nearby</u>, like bananas.
11. And you will be <u>spending a little more</u> on your food.
12. But the <u>world will be healthier</u>, and so will you.

	ADVANTAGES	DISADVANTAGES
Regular produce		
Organic produce		doesn't look as nice
Local produce		

142 UNIT 7

---

viii   Welcome to **NorthStar**

3 FOCUS ON WRITING

This section emphasizes development of productive skills for writing. It includes sections on vocabulary, grammar, and the writing process.

> The **VOCABULARY** section leads students from reviewing the unit vocabulary, to practicing and expanding their use of it, and then working with it—using it creatively in both this section and in the final writing task.
>
> Students learn useful structures for writing in the **GRAMMAR** section, which offers a concise presentation and targeted practice. Vocabulary items are recycled here, providing multiple exposures leading to mastery. For additional practice with the grammar presented, students and teachers can consult the GRAMMAR BOOK REFERENCES at the end of the book for corresponding material in the *Focus on Grammar* and *Azar* series.

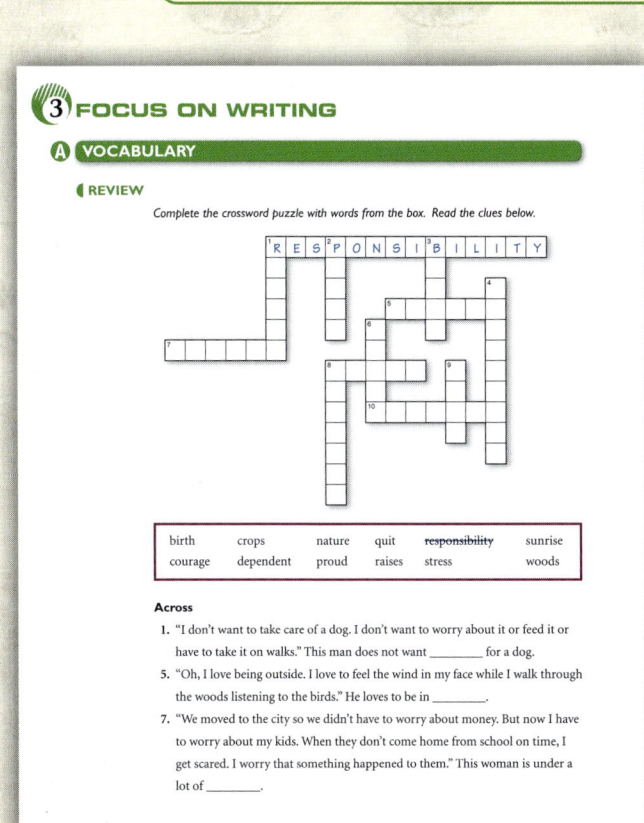

---

3 FOCUS ON WRITING

A VOCABULARY

REVIEW

Complete the crossword puzzle with words from the box. Read the clues below.

birth	crops	nature	quit	responsibility	sunrise
courage	dependent	proud	raises	stress	woods

Across

1. "I don't want to take care of a dog. I don't want to worry about it or feed it or have to take it on walks." This man does not want _____ for a dog.
5. "Oh, I love being outside. I love to feel the wind in my face while I walk through the woods listening to the birds." He loves to be in _____.
7. "We moved to the city so we didn't have to worry about money. But now I have to worry about my kids. When they don't come home from school on time, I get scared. I worry that something happened to them." This woman is under a lot of _____.

32 UNIT 2

B GRAMMAR: Simple Past Tense

1 Read the paragraph. Underline the verbs that tell about the past. Then answer the questions.

> Ben Holmes started the Farm School in Athol, Massachusetts, in 1991. Holmes, a city kid from California, spent summers on his uncle's farm in Ohio. There he learned to love working on the land. He created the school because he wanted to teach kids that work is about using your body and your mind together.

1. How is the simple past formed for most verbs (regular verbs)?
2. Which past tense verb is irregular? What is the base form of this verb?

SIMPLE PAST TENSE			
1. When we talk about things that happened in the past, we use the **simple past tense**.	Last summer, I **worked** on a farm. I **went** to the city yesterday.		
2. To form the simple past tense for **regular** verbs, add **-ed** to the base form of the verb. If the verb ends in **-e**, add only **-d**. If the verb ends in a consonant + **y**, change the **y** to **i** and then add **-ed**.	**Base Form** want talk live arrive study try	**Simple Past** want**ed** talk**ed** lived arrived studied tried	
3. Many verbs have **irregular** past tense forms. Here are some of these irregular verbs.	be do have eat get go make say	was / were did had ate got went made said	
4. In negative statements, use **didn't (did not)** + base form of the verb, except with the verb be.	need want be	didn't need didn't want wasn't / weren't	

Country Life or City Life? 37

Welcome to **NorthStar** ix

The **WRITING** section of each unit leads students through the writing process and presents a challenging and imaginative writing task that directs students to integrate the content, vocabulary, and grammar from the unit.

- Students practice a short **pre-writing strategy**, such as freewriting, clustering, brainstorming, interviewing, listing, making a chart or diagram, categorizing, or classifying.

- Then students organize their ideas and write, using a **specific structural or rhetorical pattern** that fits the subject at hand.

- Students then learn **revising techniques** within a sentence-level or paragraph-level activity to help them move towards **coherence and unity** in their writing.

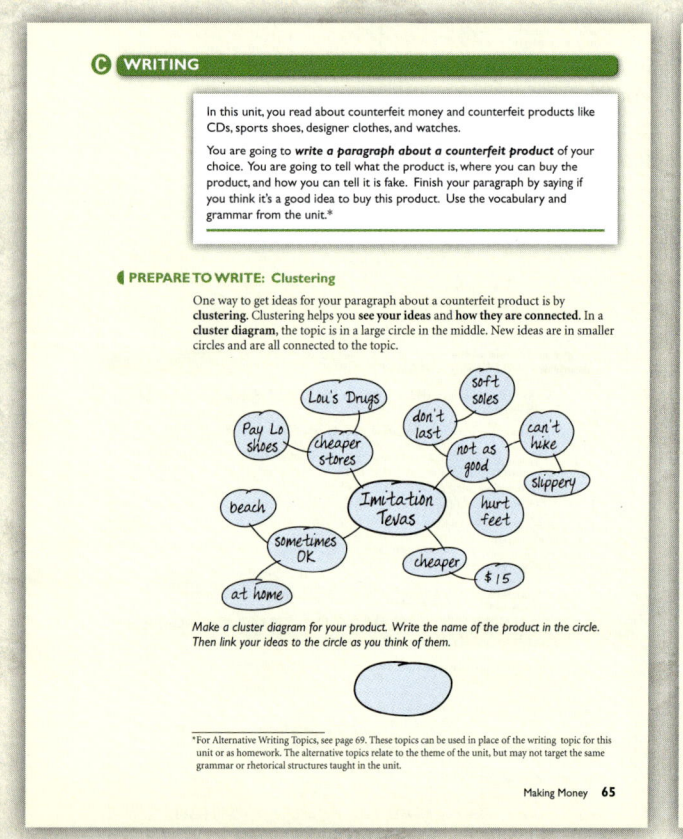

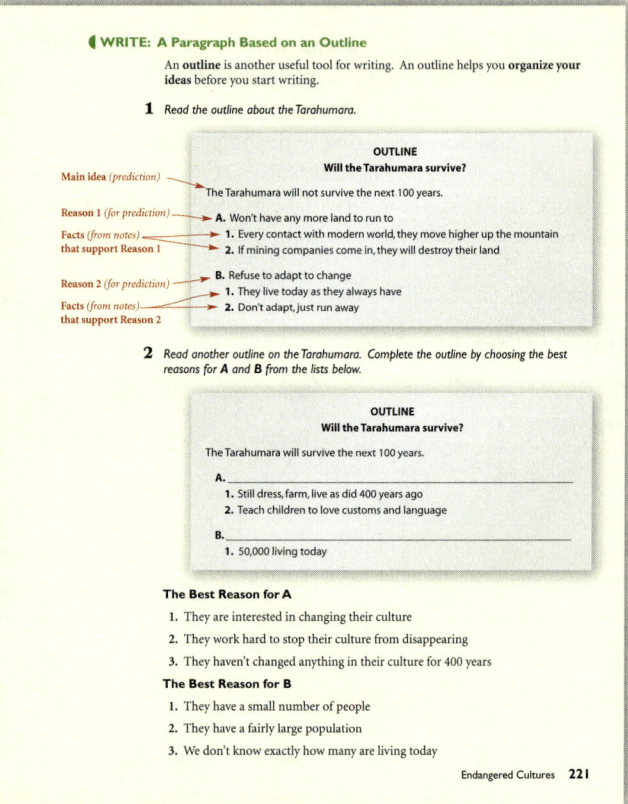

C WRITING

In this unit, you read about counterfeit money and counterfeit products like CDs, sports shoes, designer clothes, and watches.

You are going to *write a paragraph about a counterfeit product* of your choice. You are going to tell what the product is, where you can buy the product, and how you can tell it is fake. Finish your paragraph by saying if you think it's a good idea to buy this product. Use the vocabulary and grammar from the unit.*

PREPARE TO WRITE: Clustering

One way to get ideas for your paragraph about a counterfeit product is by **clustering**. Clustering helps you **see your ideas** and **how they are connected**. In a **cluster diagram**, the topic is in a large circle in the middle. New ideas are in smaller circles and are all connected to the topic.

Make a cluster diagram for your product. Write the name of the product in the circle. Then link your ideas to the circle as you think of them.

*For Alternative Writing Topics, see page 69. These topics can be used in place of the writing topic for this unit or as homework. The alternative topics relate to the theme of the unit, but may not target the same grammar or rhetorical structures taught in the unit.

Making Money 65

WRITE: A Paragraph Based on an Outline

An **outline** is another useful tool for writing. An outline helps you **organize your ideas** before you start writing.

1 Read the outline about the Tarahumara.

OUTLINE
Will the Tarahumara survive?

The Tarahumara will not survive the next 100 years.

- Main idea *(prediction)*
- Reason 1 *(for prediction)* — **A.** Won't have any more land to run to
- Facts *(from notes)* that support Reason 1
  - **1.** Every contact with modern world, they move higher up the mountain
  - **2.** If mining companies come in, they will destroy their land
- Reason 2 *(for prediction)* — **B.** Refuse to adapt to change
- Facts *(from notes)* that support Reason 2
  - **1.** They live today as they always have
  - **2.** Don't adapt, just run away

2 Read another outline on the Tarahumara. Complete the outline by choosing the best reasons for **A** and **B** from the lists below.

OUTLINE
Will the Tarahumara survive?

The Tarahumara will survive the next 100 years.

A. _____
1. Still dress, farm, live as did 400 years ago
2. Teach children to love customs and language

B. _____
1. 50,000 living today

The Best Reason for A
1. They are interested in changing their culture
2. They work hard to stop their culture from disappearing
3. They haven't changed anything in their culture for 400 years

The Best Reason for B
1. They have a small number of people
2. They have a fairly large population
3. We don't know exactly how many are living today

Endangered Cultures 221

In the final phase of the writing process, students **edit** their work with the help of a **checklist** that focuses on mechanics, completeness, enhancing style, and incorporating the vocabulary and grammar from the unit.

ALTERNATIVE WRITING TOPICS are provided at the end of the unit. They can be used as *alternatives* to the final writing task, or as *additional* assignments. RESEARCH TOPICS tied to the theme of the unit are organized in a special section at the back of the book.

x Welcome to **NorthStar**

COMPONENTS

TEACHER'S MANUAL WITH ACHIEVEMENT TESTS

Each level and strand of *NorthStar* has an accompanying Teacher's Manual with step-by-step **teaching suggestions**, including unique guidance for using *NorthStar* in secondary classes. The manuals include time guidelines, expansion activities, and techniques and instructions for using MyNorthStarLab. Also included are reproducible unit-by-unit achievement **tests** of **receptive** and **productive** skills, **answer keys** to both the student book and tests, and a unit-by-unit **vocabulary** list.

EXAMVIEW

NorthStar ExamView is a stand-alone CD-ROM that allows teachers to **create and customize** their own *NorthStar* tests.

DVD

The *NorthStar* DVD has **engaging**, **authentic video clips**, including animation, documentaries, interviews, and biographies, that correspond to the themes in *NorthStar*. Each theme contains a three- to five-minute segment that can be used with either the *Reading and Writing* strand or the *Listening and Speaking* strand. The video clips can also be viewed in MyNorthStarLab.

COMPANION WEBSITE

The companion website, www.longman.com/northstar, includes resources for teachers, such as the **scope and sequence**, **correlations** to other Longman products and to state standards, and **podcasts** from the *NorthStar* authors and series editors.

MyNorthStarLab

PEARSON LONGMAN mynorthstarlab — AVAILABLE WITH the new edition of **NORTHSTAR**

NorthStar is now available with **MyNorthStarLab**—an easy-to-use **online** program **for students and teachers** that saves time and improves results.

➤ **STUDENTS** receive **personalized instruction** and **practice** in all four skills. Audio, video, and test preparation are all in **one** place—available **anywhere, anytime**.

➤ **TEACHERS** can take advantage of many resources including online **assessments**, a flexible **gradebook**, and **tools for monitoring student progress**.

CHECK IT OUT! GO TO www.mynorthstarlab.com FOR A PREVIEW!

TURN THE PAGE TO SEE KEY FEATURES OF **MyNorthStarLab**.

Welcome to **NorthStar**

MYNORTHSTARLAB

MyNorthStarLab supports students with **individualized instruction**, **feedback**, and **extra help**. A wide array of resources, including a flexible **gradebook**, helps teachers manage student progress.

The MyNorthStarLab **WELCOME** page **organizes assignments and grades**, and **facilitates communication** between students and teachers.

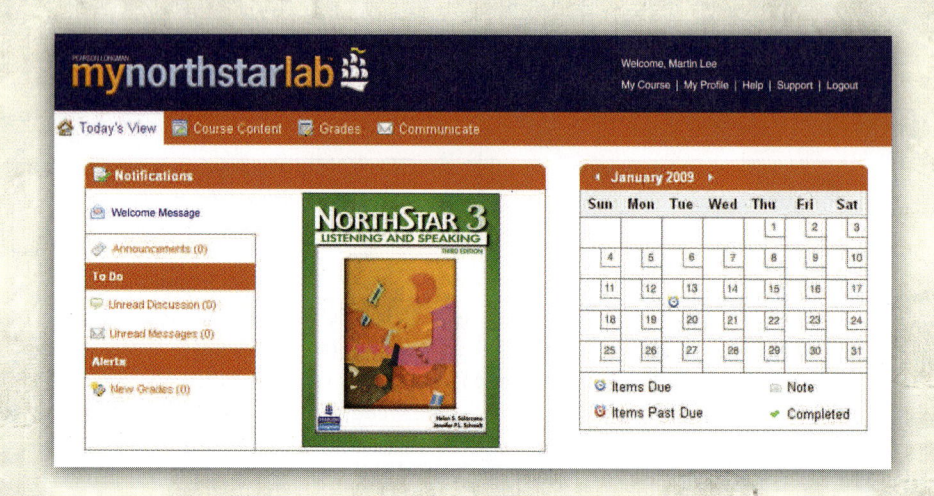

For each unit, MyNorthStarLab provides a **READINESS CHECK**.

➢ Activities **assess** student knowledge **before** beginning the unit and **follow up** with individualized instruction.

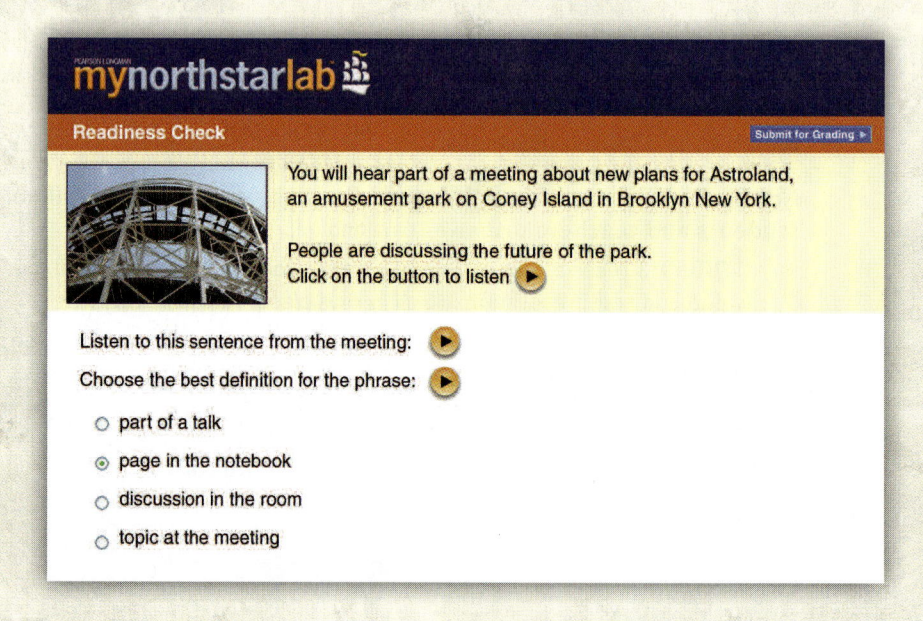

xii   Welcome to **NorthStar**

Student book material and **new** practice activities are available to students online.

➤ Students benefit from virtually unlimited **practice anywhere, anytime**.

Interaction with **Internet** and **video** materials will:
➤ Expand students' knowledge of the topic.
➤ Help students practice new vocabulary and grammar.

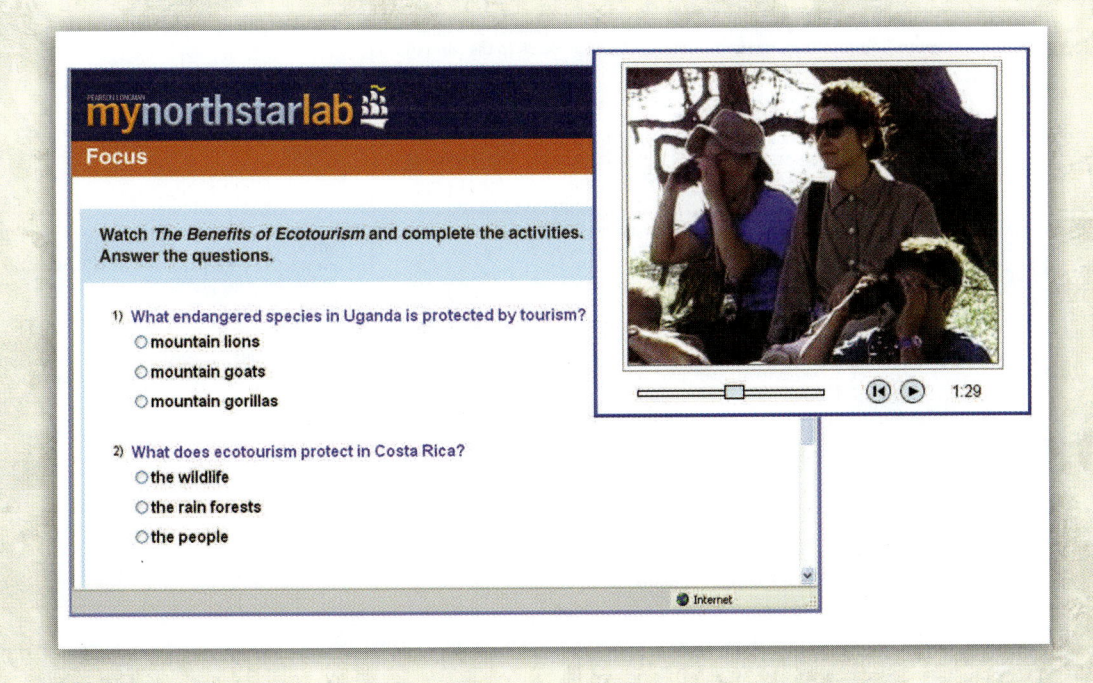

Welcome to **NorthStar**   xiii

INTEGRATED SKILL ACTIVITIES in MyNorthStarLab challenge students to bring together the **language skills** and **critical thinking skills** that they have practiced throughout the unit.

mynorthstarlab

Integrated Task - Read, Listen, Write

Submit for Grading ▶

THE ADVENTURE OF A LIFETIME

We at the Antarctic Travel Society <u>encourage</u> you to consider an excited guided tour of Antarctica for your next vacation.

The Antarctic Travel society carefully plans and operates tours of the Antarctic by ship. There are three trips per day leaving from <u>ports</u> in South America and Australia. Each ship carries only about 100 passengers at a time. Tours run from November through March to the ice-free areas along the coast of Antarctica.

In addition to touring the coast, our ships stop for on-land visits, which generally last for about three hours. Activities include guided sightseeing, mountain climbing, camping, <u>kayaking</u>, and <u>scuba diving</u>. For a longer stay, camping trips can also be arranged.

Our tours will give you an opportunity to experience the richness of Antarctica, including its wildlife, history, active research stations, and, most of all, its natural beauty.

Tours are <u>supervised</u> by the ship's staff. The staff generally includes <u>experts</u> in animal and sea life and other Antarctica specialists. There is generally one staff member for every 10 to 20 passengers. Theses trained and responsible individuals will help to make your visit to Antarctica safe, educational, and <u>unforgettable</u>.

READ, LISTEN AND WRITE ABOUT TOURISM IN ANTARCTICA
Read.
Read the text. Then answer the question.

According to the text, how can tourism benefit the Antartic?

Listen.
Click on the Play button and listen to the passage.
Use the outline to take notes as you listen.

Main idea:

Seven things that scientists study:

The effects of tourism:

Write.
Write about the potential and risks in Antarctica.
Follow the steps to prepare.

Step 1
• Review the text and your outline from the listening task.
• Write notes about the benefits and risks of tourism.

Step 2
Write for 20 minutes. Leave 5 minutes to edit your work.

xiv   Welcome to **NorthStar**

The MyNorthStarLab **ASSESSMENT** tools allow instructors to customize and deliver achievement tests online.

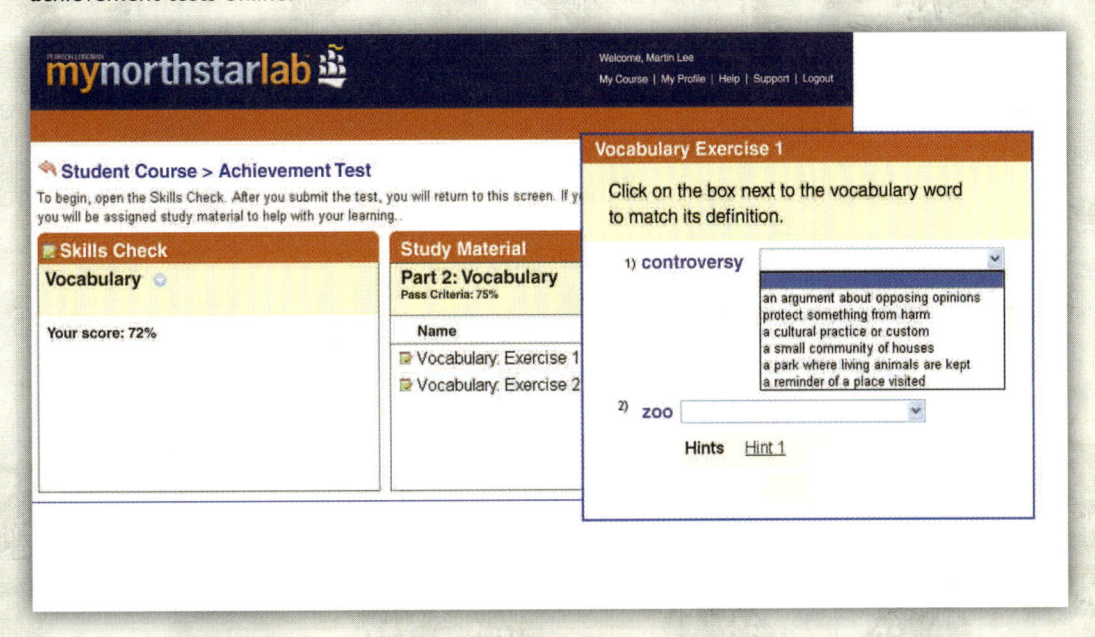

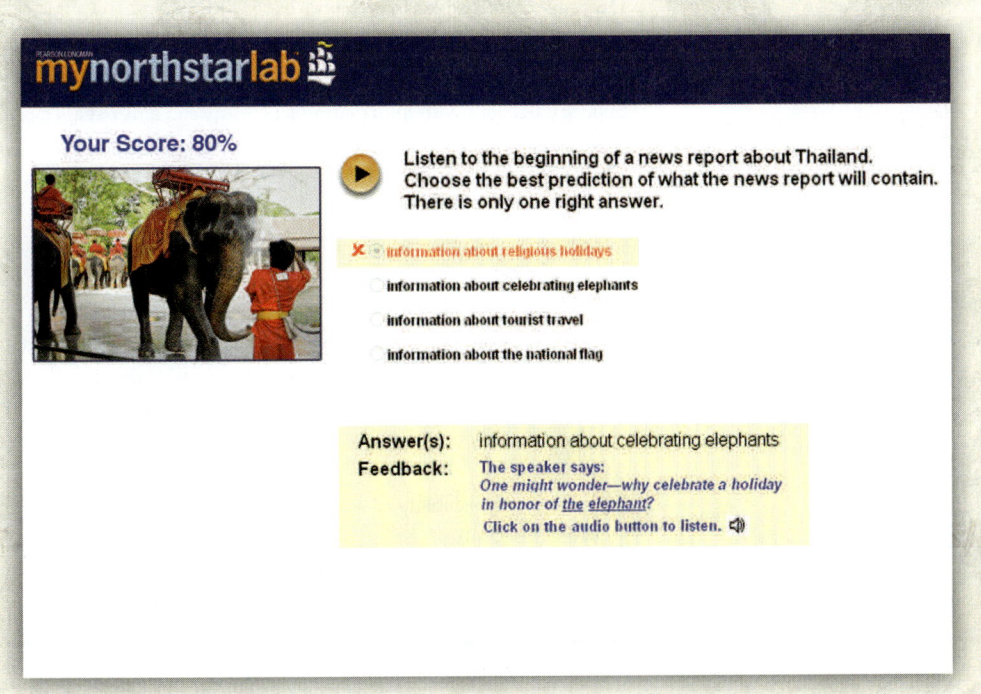

Welcome to **NorthStar**   xv

SCOPE AND SEQUENCE

UNIT	CRITICAL THINKING	READING
1 Finding the Ideal Job **Theme:** Work **Reading One:** *Finding the Ideal Job* A review of a book **Reading Two:** *The Ideal Job* A newspaper report	Interpret a cartoon Use prior knowledge Recognize personal attitudes and preferences Classify information Evaluate information according to criteria set forth in a text Infer word meaning from context Support opinions with reasons	Read and respond to an e-mail Read a book review Make predictions Read for main ideas Scan for details Relate personal experience to the readings Organize and synthesize details from the readings
2 Country Life or City Life? **Theme:** The Country and the City **Reading One:** *The Farming Life for Me* A letter to the editor **Reading Two:** *Leaving the Farm* A newspaper report	Compare family histories Use prior knowledge Infer word meaning from context Classify information Support opinions with reasons Evaluate advantages and disadvantages Compare and contrast city and country life	Predict reasons Identify main ideas Identify advantages and disadvantages Identify inaccurate details Relate the reading to personal opinions Organize and synthesize information from the readings
3 Making Money **Theme:** Money **Reading One:** *Making Money* A newspaper report **Reading Two:** *I Made It Myself* A true story of a counterfeiter	Identify personal values and assumptions Determine differences in two photos Infer word meaning from context Draw logical conclusions Support answers with information from the text Compare and contrast types of money and types of counterfeiters	Predict reasons Identify main ideas Search for and locate details Relate previous knowledge to the readings Read a newspaper report Organize and synthesize information from the readings
4 A Different Path to Justice **Theme:** Justice **Reading One:** *Vote for Restorative Justice* A pre-election flyer **Reading Two:** *Moving Past the Crime* A magazine article	Interpret a cartoon Identify personal values Infer word meaning from context Hypothesize about the points of view of others Support answers with information from the text Evaluate the applicability of a restorative justice program Compare reasons for and against restorative justice	Predict reasons Identify main ideas Identify inaccurate details Relate previous knowledge to the readings Classify descriptions and examples Organize and synthesize information from the readings

WRITING	VOCABULARY	GRAMMAR
Write sentences using descriptive and possessive adjectives Organize ideas in a list Identify topic sentences Use supporting sentences to add details Compose a paragraph	Use context clues to find meaning Define words	Descriptive and possessive adjectives
Rewrite inaccurate statements Write a personal letter Draw or use pictures for idea generation Write a descriptive paragraph Group similar ideas together Write supporting sentences with descriptive detail	Use context clues to find meaning Define words Identify word + preposition combinations	Simple past tense
Write a business memo Write sentences of comparison Organize ideas by clustering Write a well organized paragraph Provide clear explanations in a paragraph Analyze a paragraph to determine sentences that don't belong	Use context clues to find meaning Define words Find and use antonyms	Comparative form of adjectives
Write an e-mail Organize ideas into a chart Write a persuasive letter Provide specific reasons for one's opinion Evaluate the persuasiveness of one's reasons	Use context clues to find meaning Identify word associations Define words Use idiomatic expressions	*Should, ought to,* and *shouldn't* for giving advice

SCOPE AND SEQUENCE

UNIT	CRITICAL THINKING	READING
5 Subway Etiquette **Theme:** Etiquette **Reading One:** *A Civilized Suggestion* A newspaper editorial **Reading Two:** *Riding the Subway in Japan* A travel blog	Interpret public signs Identify and analyze personal values and assumptions Infer word meaning from context Hypothesize author's point of view Support opinions with reasons Compare and contrast rules in different places	Identify main ideas Identify details Make inferences Relate experiences to the readings Compare and contrast similar concepts between texts Organize and synthesize information from the readings Read a newspaper editorial
6 Serious Fun **Theme:** Games **Reading One:** *Serious Fun* A newspaper article **Reading Two:** *Saving the World with Computer Games* A magazine article	Infer word meaning from context Infer information not explicit in text Support responses with information from the readings Differentiate between main ideas and details Analyze and evaluate personal preferences	Identify main ideas Identify and match details Read a timeline Relate previous knowledge to the readings Compare concepts between readings Relate the readings to personal opinions Organize and synthesize information from the readings
7 The Best Produce There Is **Theme:** Food **Reading One:** *Organic Produce vs. Regular Produce* A newspaper column **Reading Two:** *Miles to Go Before You Eat* A magazine article	Establish criteria for choosing produce Evaluate and classify information Infer word meaning from context Hypothesize another's point of view Analyze advantages and disadvantages of buying different kinds of produce Support opinions with reasons	Read pricing labels Predict content Identify main ideas Scan for true details and correct false ones Relate personal values to the readings Organize and synthesize information from the readings Read a newspaper column

WRITING	VOCABULARY	GRAMMAR
Use new vocabulary in sentences Write responses to letters in an advice column Organize ideas in a list Write a travel web page Compose sentences in parallel structure Edit and evaluate letters to the editor	Use context clues to find meaning Define words Use idiomatic expressions	Imperative sentences
Complete a conversation Respond to an e-mail Brainstorm a list of games Write a review of a game Use words or phrases that show order of importance Edit and evaluate game reviews	Use context clues to find meaning Find synonyms Define words	Expressing habitual present with *when-* clauses
Write a response to a letter in an advice column Write opinions in response to a reading Write questions in the simple present Write a letter Get ideas for writing by asking yourself questions Write a brochure Acknowledge disadvantages in your writing piece and offer solutions	Use context clues to find meaning Define words Use idiomatic expressions	*Wh-* questions in the simple present tense

Scope and Sequence xix

SCOPE AND SEQUENCE

UNIT	CRITICAL THINKING	READING
8 "I'll take the train, thanks." **Theme:** Travel **Reading One:** *The Climate Train* A magazine article **Reading Two:** *On the Road with John Madden* A newspaper report	Interpret a map Evaluate best method of travel Infer word meaning from context Infer information not explicit in the text Hypothesize another's point of view Interpret people's motivations and values Correlate statements with possible speakers	Read a map Predict content Identify main ideas Scan for true details and correct false ones Organize and synthesize information from the readings Relate personal experiences to the readings
9 What's Your Medicine? **Theme:** Health problems and treatments **Reading One:** *Leech* An online encyclopedia entry **Reading Two:** *Gross Medicine* A magazine article	Compare and contrast different medical practices Infer word meaning from context Infer information not explicit in the text Classify information Support personal opinions with reasons Use prior knowledge	Predict content Identify main ideas Identify inaccurate details Organize and synthesize information from the readings Relate personal experiences to the readings Make inferences
10 Endangered Cultures **Theme:** Endangered cultures **Reading One:** *Will Indigenous Cultures Survive?* A magazine article **Reading Two:** *The Penan* A personal journal	Compare and contrast two photographs Infer word meaning from context Support inferences with information from the reading Contrast different cultural points of view Classify information Predict the future of cultures using information from the readings	Read a map Predict content Use prior knowledge Identify main ideas Locate supporting details in a text Draw examples from one reading to support general statements from another Read a personal journal Relate readings to personal opinions and experience

WRITING	VOCABULARY	GRAMMAR
Rewrite inaccurate statements Organize ideas into a chart Complete a conversation Write a persuasive e-mail Write a business e-mail Connect sentences with *and* and *but*	Use context clues to find meaning Define words Categorize words and phrases	Superlative form of adjectives
Rewrite inaccurate statements Organize ideas into a chart Complete a conversation Brainstorm a list of ideas Write a personal narrative paragraph Use time words to establish the order of events	Use context clues to find meaning Define words Make word associations	Adverbs of manner
Provide examples to support general statements Write a persuasive letter Formulate predictions Write interview questions Take notes Write an outline Write a concluding sentence	Use context clues to find meaning Define words Find correct word usage	Expressing predictions and future plans

ACKNOWLEDGMENTS

We would both like to thank Carol Numrich for her encouragement, coaching, and vision. Thanks also to Françoise Leffler and Debbie Sistino for their support in seeing this book through to the end.

Natasha thanks Professor Pat Porter and others at the San Francisco State University MATESOL program in the early 1990s for inspiration and great preparation for this project. She also thanks Jen Russell, Jen Pahlka, Shalle Leeming, and Ryan Detwiler for ideas, connections, research help, and feedback. And to John Tuttle, of course: Thanks for being my outside audience and number one support person, always.

Beth thanks her students of the past 15 years for providing her with the motivation to keep things clear and interesting. She wants to especially thank Tom Darci for providing a sounding board for every topic idea, proofreading every text, and generally cheering her through the entire process.

Natasha Haugnes and *Beth Maher*

Reviewers

For the comments and insights they graciously offered to help shape the direction of the Third Edition of *NorthStar*, the publisher would like to thank the following reviewers and institutions.

Gail August, Hostos Community College; **Anne Bachmann**, Clackamas Community College; **Aegina Barnes**, York College, CUNY; **Dr. Sabri Bebawi**, San Jose Community College; **Kristina Beckman**, John Jay College; **Jeff Bellucci**, Kaplan Boston; **Nathan Blesse**, Human International Academy; **Alan Brandman**, Queens College; **Laila Cadavona-Dellapasqua**, Kaplan; **Amy Cain**, Kaplan; **Nigel Caplan**, Michigan State University; **Alzira Carvalho**, Human International Academy, San Diego; **Chao-Hsun (Richard) Cheng**, Wenzao Ursuline College of Languages; **Mu-hua (Yolanda) Chi**, Wenzao Ursuline College of Languages; **Liane Cismowski**, Olympic High School; **Shauna Croft**, MESLS; **Misty Crooks**, Kaplan; **Amanda De Loera**, Kaplan English Programs; **Jennifer Dobbins**, New England School of English; **Luis Dominguez**, Angloamericano; **Luydmila Drgaushanskaya**, ASA College; **Dilip Dutt**, Roxbury Community College; **Christie Evenson**, Chung Dahm Institute; **Patricia Frenz-Belkin**, Hostos Community College, CUNY; **Christiane Galvani**, Texas Southern University; **Joanna Ghosh**, University of Pennsylvania; **Cristina Gomes**, Kaplan Test Prep; **Kristen Grinager**, Lincoln High School; **Janet Harclerode**, Santa Monica College; **Carrell Harden**, HCCS, Gulfton Campus; **Connie Harney**, Antelope Valley College; **Ann Hilborn**, ESL Consultant in Houston; **Barbara Hockman**, City College of San Francisco; **Margaret Hodgson**, NorQuest College; **Paul Hong**, Chung Dahm Institute; **Wonki Hong**, Chung Dahm Institute; **John House**, Iowa State University; **Polly Howlett**, Saint Michael's College; **Arthur Hui**, Fullerton College; **Nina Ito**, CSU, Long Beach; **Scott Jenison**, Antelope Valley College; **Hyunsook Jeong**, Keimyung University; **Mandy Kama**, Georgetown University; **Dale Kim**, Chung Dahm Institute; **Taeyoung Kim**, Keimyung University; **Woo-hyung Kim**, Keimyung University; **Young Kim**, Chung Dahm Institute; **Yu-kyung Kim**, Sunchon National University; **John Kostovich**, Miami Dade College; **Albert Kowun**, Fairfax, VA; **David Krise**, Michigan State University; **Cheri (Young Hee) Lee**, ReadingTownUSA English Language Institute; **Eun-Kyung Lee**, Chung Dahm Institute; **Sang Hyock Lee**, Keimyung University; **Debra Levitt**, SMC; **Karen Lewis**, Somerville, MA; **Chia-Hui Liu**, Wenzao Ursuline College of Languages; **Gennell Lockwood**, Seattle, WA; **Javier Lopez Anguiano**, Colegio Anglo Mexicano de Coyoacan; **Mary March**, Shoreline Community College; **Susan Matson**, ELS Language Centers; **Ralph McClain**, Embassy CES Boston; **Veronica McCormack**, Roxbury Community College; **Jennifer McCoy**, Kaplan; **Joseph McHugh**, Kaplan; **Cynthia McKeag Tsukamoto**, Oakton Community College; **Paola Medina**, Texas Southern University; **Christine Kyung-ah Moon**, Seoul, Korea; **Margaret Moore**, North Seattle Community College; **Michelle Moore**, Madison English as a Second Language School; **David Motta**, Miami University; **Suzanne Munro**, Clackamas Community College; **Elena Nehrbecki**, Hudson County CC; **Kim Newcomer**, University of Washington; **Melody Nightingale**, Santa Monica College; **Patrick Northover**, Kaplan Test and Prep; **Sarah Oettle**, Kaplan, Sacramento; **Shirley Ono**, Oakton Community College; **Maria Estela Ortiz Torres**, C. Anglo Mexicano de Coyoac'an; **Suzanne Overstreet**, West Valley College; **Linda Ozarow**, West Orange High School; **Ileana Porges-West**, Miami Dade College, Hialeah Campus; **Megan Power**, ILCSA; **Alison Robertson**, Cypress College; **Ma. Del Carmen Romero**, Universidad del Valle de Mexico; **Nina Rosen**, Santa Rosa Junior College; **Daniellah Salario**, Kaplan; **Joel Samuels**, Kaplan New York City; **Babi Sarapata**, Columbia University ALP; **Donna Schaeffer**, University of Washington; **Lynn Schneider**, City College of San Francisco; **Errol Selkirk**, New School University; **Amity Shook**, Chung Dahm Institute; **Lynn Stafford-Yilmaz**, Bellevue Community College; **Lynne Ruelaine Stokes**, Michigan State University; **Henna Suh**, Chung Dahm Institute; **Sheri Summers**, Kaplan Test Prep; **Martha Sutter**, Kent State University; **Becky Tarver Chase**, MESLS; **Lisa Waite-Trago**, Michigan State University; **Carol Troy**, Da-Yeh University; **Luci Tyrell**, Embassy CES Fort Lauderdale; **Yong-Hee Uhm**, Myongii University; **Debra Un**, New York University; **José Vazquez**, The University of Texas Pan American; **Hollyahna Vettori**, Santa Rosa Junior College; **Susan Vik**, Boston University; **Sandy Wagner**, Fort Lauderdale High School; **Joanne Wan**, ASC English; **Pat Wiggins**, Clackamas Community College; **Heather Williams**, University of Pennsylvania; **Carol Wilson-Duffy**, Michigan State University; **Kailin Yang**, Kaohsing Medical University; **Ellen Yaniv**, Boston University; **Samantha Young**, Kaplan Boston; **Yu-san Yu**, National Sun Yat-sen University; **Ann Zaaijer**, West Orange High School

UNIT 1
Finding the Ideal Job

1 FOCUS ON THE TOPIC

A PREDICT

Look at the cartoon and discuss the questions with the class.

1. What is the young man doing?
2. What kinds of work is he thinking of?
3. What do you think is the ideal job (the best job) for this young man?

1

B SHARE INFORMATION

Read each statement. How much do you agree or disagree? Check (✓) the box that shows what you think. Discuss your answers with the class.

STATEMENT	STRONGLY AGREE	AGREE	DISAGREE	STRONGLY DISAGREE
1. Enjoying your work is more important than making a lot of money.				
2. Working with a lot of people is better than working alone.				
3. Working from home is better than working at an office.				
4. Working indoors is better than working outdoors.				

C BACKGROUND AND VOCABULARY

Read the list of words and their definitions.

ads: advertisements to sell things or to find new workers

careers: the kinds of work people do, usually after learning how and usually for a long time

hire: to give someone a job

ideal: perfect

interviews: meetings where a person looking for a job talks to the person who is looking for a new worker

managers: people who direct and organize groups of workers in a company

out of work: without a job

postings: ads or comments on the Internet

résumés: written descriptions of people's education and previous jobs

rewards: good things you get in return for work (such as money or health insurance)

skills: things that you can do well; abilities that you have learned and practiced

specific: detailed and exact; not general

Now use the words from the list to complete this newspaper article about American workers and companies.

In 2005, only five percent of Americans were ____out of work____. That
                                                    1.
sounds like good news. But is it?

According to a 2005 survey, only 20 percent of American workers really love their jobs. Another 20 percent want to change jobs. This is a problem for workers, and it is also a problem for companies. Thirty-three percent of _____
                                                                                        2.
say that they don't care what happens to their companies—and those are the people who are supposed to be in charge[1]!

What do workers want? Usually we think that everyone wants more money, but today's workers are looking for other _____. They want health
                                                            3.
insurance and more vacation. They also want to know that they will learn new

_____ at a job. Older workers are usually happier with their jobs
      4.
than younger workers. This is probably because they have had time to think about

their _____ and find a job they like.
         5.

Many companies today try to make changes to keep workers happy. They ask

their workers _____ questions about what makes them really happy
                    6.
at work. If a worker loves his job, he will work harder and stay at the company. If

workers leave, companies have to _____ new people. And that takes
                                          7.
a lot of time. They have to write _____ and put _____
                                        8.   9.
on the Internet. They have to read hundreds of _____. They have to
                                                      10.
do _____ to meet people who want to work there. And even after all
     11.
that work, they might not find the _____ new worker.
                                          12.

[1] **be in charge:** be responsible for a group of people or an activity

2 FOCUS ON READING

A READING ONE: Finding the Ideal Job

Imagine you are not satisfied with your job. You decide to job hunt—that is, to look for a new job. With a partner, write a list of things you might do to find a job.

1. *I might ask someone in my family for a job.*
2. _____
3. _____
4. _____
5. _____
6. _____
7. _____
8. _____

Now learn what a professional has to say about this topic. Read a book review of a job-hunting manual.

The Book Review

FINDING THE IDEAL JOB

What Color Is Your Parachute? 2008:
A Practical Manual for Job-Hunters
and Career-Changers

by Richard Nelson Bolles, Ten Speed Press, $18.95.

1 You are **out of work**.
You hate your job.
You aren't satisfied with your **career**.
You are looking for your first job. Where do you start?

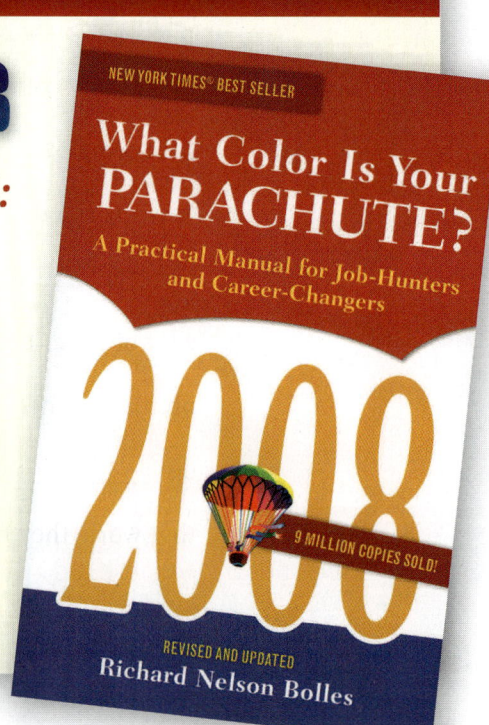

2   If you are like most Americans, you'll probably send your **résumé** to a lot of companies. You might search for job **postings** on the Internet or look for **ads** in the newspaper. But experts[1] say you won't have much luck. People find jobs only five to ten percent of the time when they use these ways. So what can you do?

3   One thing you can do is read Richard Bolles's *What Color Is Your Parachute?* [2] Bolles is an expert in job hunting. He has helped thousands of people find jobs and careers. This book is different from other job-hunting manuals. Bolles doesn't help you to find just another job. Instead, he helps you find your **ideal** job: a job that fits you, a job that makes you happy. What kind of job is ideal for you? If you don't know the answer, Bolles says, you can't find your ideal job. You need to have a clear picture in your mind of the job you want. The book has many exercises to help you draw this picture.

4   Bolles says that you must think about three things:
(1) YOUR SKILLS. What do you like to do? What do you do well? Are you good at talking to groups? Growing vegetables? Teaching? Drawing on the computer? Bolles asks you to think about all your skills, not only "work skills." For example, a mother of four children is probably good at managing people (children!). This woman may be a good **manager**.
(2) JOB SETTING. Where do you like to work? Do you like to work outside? At home? In an office? Alone or with others? What kinds of people do you like to work with?
(3) JOB REWARDS. How much money do you need? How much money do you want? What else do you want from a job? What makes you feel good about a job?

5   After Bolles helps you decide on your ideal job, he gives you **specific** advice on how to find that job. Bolles's exercises teach you how to find companies and how to introduce yourself. The chapter on job **interviews** is full of useful information and suggestions. For example, most people go to interviews asking themselves the question, "How do I get the company to **hire** me?" Bolles thinks this is the wrong question. Instead, he wants you to ask yourself, "Do I want to work here or not?"

6   Some people think that Bolles writes far too much and repeats himself. True, his book could probably have 100 pages instead of 456. But his writing style makes the book very easy to read, and a reader doesn't have to read the parts that seem less important. Other readers say that there is not enough space to write the answers to the exercises. But these are very small problems. *What Color Is Your Parachute?* is the best job-hunting manual you can buy.

7   *What Color Is Your Parachute?* was first written in 1970. Over nine million copies have been sold since then. The information is updated[3] every year. So, if you are looking for a job or if you have a job but want a new one, remember: Don't just send out copies of your résumé. Don't just answer ads. And don't wait for friends to give you a job. Instead, buy this book and do a job hunt the right way.

Barbara Kleppinger

---

[1] **experts:** people who know a lot about something
[2] **parachute:** something you wear when you jump out of a plane. When you jump, it opens up and it stops you from hitting the ground very hard.
[3] **updated**: changed to show new information

◖ READ FOR MAIN IDEAS

*Read each statement. Decide if it is true or false. Write **T** (true) or **F** (false) next to it. Compare your answers with a classmate's.*

_____ 1. *What Color Is Your Parachute?* is similar to other job-hunting manuals.

_____ 2. Bolles wants to help people find jobs on the Internet more quickly.

_____ 3. According to *What Color Is Your Parachute?*, job hunters should think about their skills, the job setting, and the job rewards they want.

_____ 4. *What Color Is Your Parachute?* includes specific advice on finding jobs.

_____ 5. The reviews of Bolles's book are all positive.

◖ READ FOR DETAILS

Look at the list of job-hunting methods. Decide where each one should go in the chart. Write each method in the correct column.

~~answer newspaper ads~~

decide what kind of job is ideal

decide what kind of place you want to work in

do exercises in *What Color Is Your Parachute?*

look on the Internet

send out lots of résumés

think about job rewards

think about your skills

FIND A JOB	
What Many People Do	**What Bolles Says Will Help You**
answer newspaper ads	

MAKE INFERENCES

Read each situation. Decide whether, according to Bolles, the person is making a mistake or doing the right thing. Circle your answer. Then discuss your decisions with the class.

1. Owen is a manager. He doesn't want to be a manager. But he's not looking for another job because he thinks he doesn't know how to do anything else. According to Bolles, Owen is _____.
   a. making a mistake
   b. doing the right thing

2. Amy studied to be a teacher. But now she's not looking for work as a teacher. Instead, she's thinking about whether teaching is really the right career for her. According to Bolles, Amy is _____.
   a. making a mistake
   b. doing the right thing

3. Bill is in a job interview. He is asking the person who is interviewing him some questions about the company. According to Bolles, Bill is _____.
   a. making a mistake
   b. doing the right thing

4. Kathy has a choice between a job that pays very well and a job that seems very interesting. She decides that for her, money is the most important thing. So she chooses the job that pays well. According to Bolles, Kathy is _____.
   a. making a mistake
   b. doing the right thing

5. Peter sent his résumé to many companies and he answered many Internet postings. Now he is waiting for someone to call him about a job. According to Bolles, Peter is _____.
   a. making a mistake
   b. doing the right thing

EXPRESS OPINIONS

Discuss the questions with a partner. Give your opinions. Then share your answers with the class.

1. The next time you look for a job, which of Bolles's ideas do you think you might use?

2. You are in an interview for a job with a very interesting company. What questions might you ask the interviewer about this company?

3. The title of the book is *What Color Is Your Parachute?* Why do you think the author chose this title?

B READING TWO: The Ideal Job

Read the stories about people who love their jobs.

THE IDEAL JOB BY ALEX FROST

1   Believe it or not, some people get paid—and well—for doing the things that make them really happy. Here are a few people who have the jobs of their dreams.

2   **"I get paid to make videos!"—Ryan**

When I was 14, my uncle gave me his old video camera and I started making videos. I didn't do so well at school, but I loved getting to know people and making videos about them. I taught myself to edit the videos on this simple computer program that my dad had. One day a friend of my mom's asked me to make a video of her family. She wanted to send it to her mother who lived in China. It was totally fun, and she paid me $150. Soon her friends asked me to make videos for them, and suddenly I had a business. That was 10 years ago. After awhile, I realized I had to learn more about video. So now I am studying video part-time and running my business. It's great!

3   **"I have the greatest job in the world."—Amanda**

I am a matchmaker with 41 years of experience. Because of me, 60 couples are now happily married or engaged. I have a very good eye for people. And I don't mean I match people on how they look. I mean, I can meet a person just once for 10 minutes, and I know for sure what kind of person he or she is. I get a feeling. And this feeling tells me, "Oh, he might be a great husband for Stephanie," or "Ah, now here is the woman for Timothy." I can't imagine a job that's more fun. I meet wonderful people. I work for myself. Nobody tells me what to do. I don't spend much time with a computer in an office—the whole city is my office! I make enough money to live a simple life. And I get so much joy from seeing what happens to my matches. A month ago, a couple stopped by on their way home from the hospital with their new baby girl. I'm so happy to think that I helped make that family!

4   **"I have a job with an incredible view."— Donna**

Teaching skydiving[1] is so exciting. I get to be outside, and I love seeing students on their first jump. They are all nervous and excited. When they get to the ground, they can't wait to call everyone they know and tell them they just jumped out of an airplane. Later, when they learn to turn and fly forward, they realize that they're not just flying stones. They realize that they're like birds—they can fly!

5   It wasn't easy to get this job. I had to have about 1,000 jumps and about two years of training. And the salary was only $15,000 for the first year. But I don't do it for the money. In fact, I don't need to get paid at all. I love it that much!

---

[1] **skydiving:** the sport of jumping out of airplanes with a parachute

Source: Based on information in Dave Curtin, "From Sky Diving Instructors to Fashion Consultants, Some Folks Just Love Their Jobs," Knight-Ridder/Tribune News Service, 11 March 1996.

Complete the sentences with the correct name from the reading.

1. _____Donna_____ made $15,000 her first year.
2. _____ helped 60 couples find each other.
3. _____ didn't do well in school as a child.
4. _____ has the same job she had 40 years ago.
5. _____ is studying to get better skills.
6. _____ loves teaching.
7. _____ studied and practiced for her job for two years.
8. _____ is in charge of a video business.

C INTEGRATE READINGS ONE AND TWO

STEP 1: Organize

Look at Reading One again. Reread Paragraph 4 about skills, setting, and rewards. Then look at this list of ideas from Reading Two and decide where each one should go in the chart. Write each idea in the correct column.

- ~~editing video~~
- making $15,000/year
- getting to know people
- working outside
- seeing people learn
- skydiving
- teaching
- understanding how people get along
- working in an office
- running a business
- working on a computer
- seeing happy couples who I introduced
- working with people

SKILLS	SETTINGS	REWARDS
editing video		

Finding the Ideal Job 9

STEP 2: Synthesize

How could the people in Reading Two answer the interview questions? Write answers for each person. Use information from the chart in Step 1.

1. **RYAN**

   a. What are your skills?

   <u>I have some video-editing skills. I am also learning more.</u>

   b. What kind of setting do you like working in?

   c. What rewards are important to you?

2. **AMANDA**

   a. What are your skills?

   b. What kind of setting do you like working in?

   c. What rewards are important to you?

3. **DONNA**

   a. What are your skills?

   b. What kind of setting do you like working in?

   c. What rewards are important to you?

3 FOCUS ON WRITING

A VOCABULARY

❰ REVIEW

Put the three sentences in each group in order. Write 1, 2, or 3 next to each sentence.

a. __1__ I saw a **posting** for an interesting job.

__3__ The company called and asked me to come in for an **interview**.

__2__ I sent my **résumé** to the company.

b. ____ Mr. Fredericks went to school for more **training**.

____ Mr. Fredericks lost his job after a 20-year **career**.

____ Mr. Fredericks realized he needed new **skills** to find another job.

c. ____ Myron **realized** that he needed to pay a higher **salary** because no one was interested.

____ Myron put **ads** in the paper and **postings** on the Internet for a new manager.

____ Myron's best **manager** quit.

d. ____ John was looking for someone with **specific** skills in photographing food.

____ John **hired** Karen.

____ John met Karen, who is **ideal** because she made ads for restaurants.

e. ____ Kelly quit because she wanted a job with different **rewards**.

____ Kelly is **running her own business**.

____ Kelly had a big **salary** at her last job, but she did not like the job.

❰ EXPAND

Each word or phrase in parentheses changes the meaning of the sentence. Cross out the word or phrase that does not make sense.

1. Kate's salary is (huge / pretty good / ~~expensive~~).
2. The rewards at my last job were (happy / great / not very good).
3. You will get some (teaching / technical / lazy) skills at this job.
4. Vladimir is a very (organized / long / unfriendly) manager.

(continued on next page)

Finding the Ideal Job   11

5. When Julie was 30, she realized (she wanted to own a restaurant / she needed a new job / she bought a new car).

6. Jen likes working in a (busy / quiet / short) office.

7. Sam works in a(n) (outdoor / delicious / beautiful) setting.

8. I want to work with (manager / smart / friendly) people.

9. For this job, you need to have very specific (abilities / skills / rewards).

10. Jake knows how to (design / write / build) very tall buildings.

11. Some workers really enjoy working (alone / on teams / in settings).

CREATE

Read the e-mail from Cristina to her friend Jenny.

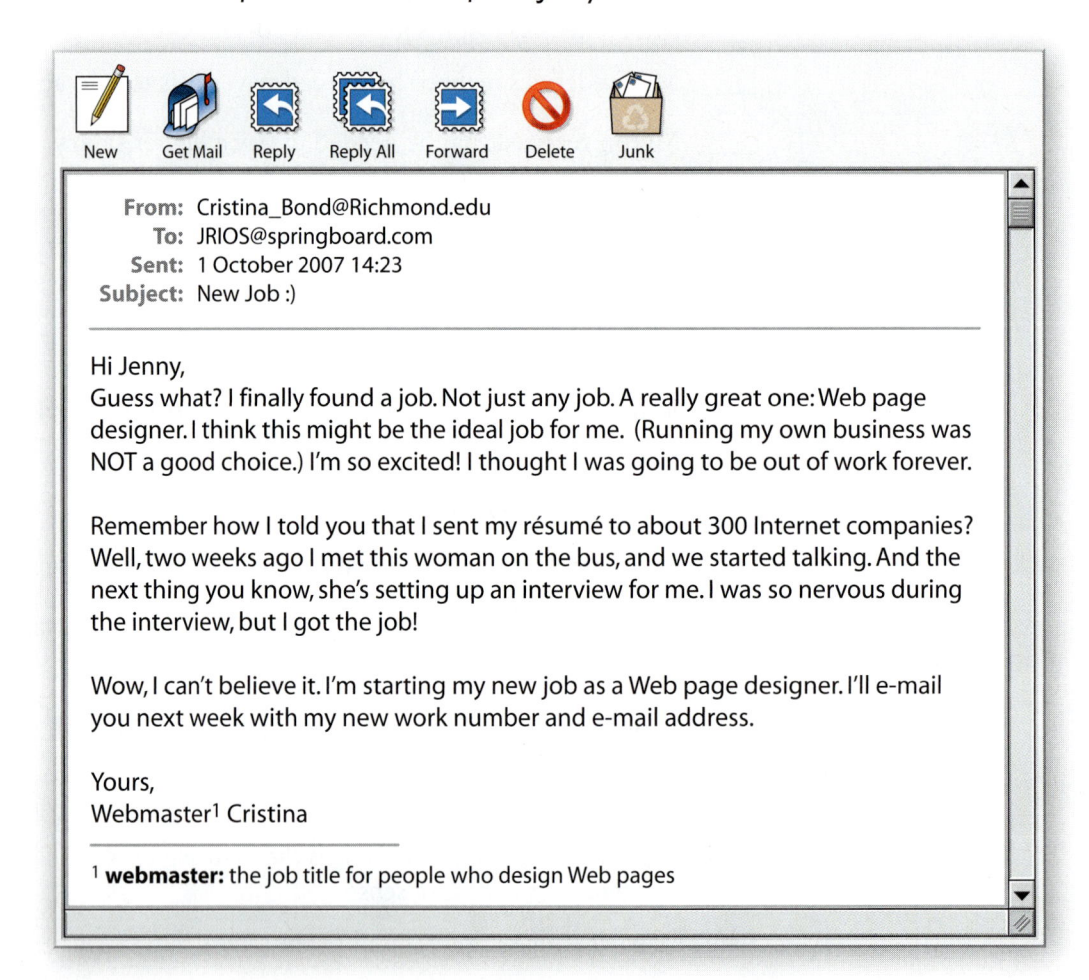

From: Cristina_Bond@Richmond.edu
To: JRIOS@springboard.com
Sent: 1 October 2007 14:23
Subject: New Job :)

Hi Jenny,
Guess what? I finally found a job. Not just any job. A really great one: Web page designer. I think this might be the ideal job for me. (Running my own business was NOT a good choice.) I'm so excited! I thought I was going to be out of work forever.

Remember how I told you that I sent my résumé to about 300 Internet companies? Well, two weeks ago I met this woman on the bus, and we started talking. And the next thing you know, she's setting up an interview for me. I was so nervous during the interview, but I got the job!

Wow, I can't believe it. I'm starting my new job as a Web page designer. I'll e-mail you next week with my new work number and e-mail address.

Yours,
Webmaster[1] Cristina

[1] **webmaster:** the job title for people who design Web pages

Now complete the e-mail from Jenny to Cristina. Use the words in parentheses to write the first five questions. Use other words from Review and Expand (pages 11–12) to write the remaining questions.

From: JRIOS@springboard.com
To: Cristina_Bond@Richmond.edu
Sent: 3 October 2007 11:16
Subject: Needing help

Hi Cristina,

Glad you finally found a job. Jobs are so difficult to find, or to keep. I just lost my job, and I need to find a new one very soon. How do you like Web design? Do you think a career in Web design might be for me? I have a lot of questions for you if you have time:

(salary) _What kind of salary do new Web designers get?_

(other rewards) _____

(specific skills) _____

(training in design) _____

(setting) _____

(office) _____

(your idea) _____

(your idea) _____

(your idea) _____

(your idea) _____

Thanks for your help. And best of luck in your new career. Can't wait to hear more about the job!

Love,
Jenny

Finding the Ideal Job

B GRAMMAR: Descriptive Adjectives and Possessive Adjectives

1 *Read the e-mail. Notice the boldfaced words. They are two kinds of adjectives: **descriptive adjectives** and **possessive adjectives**.*

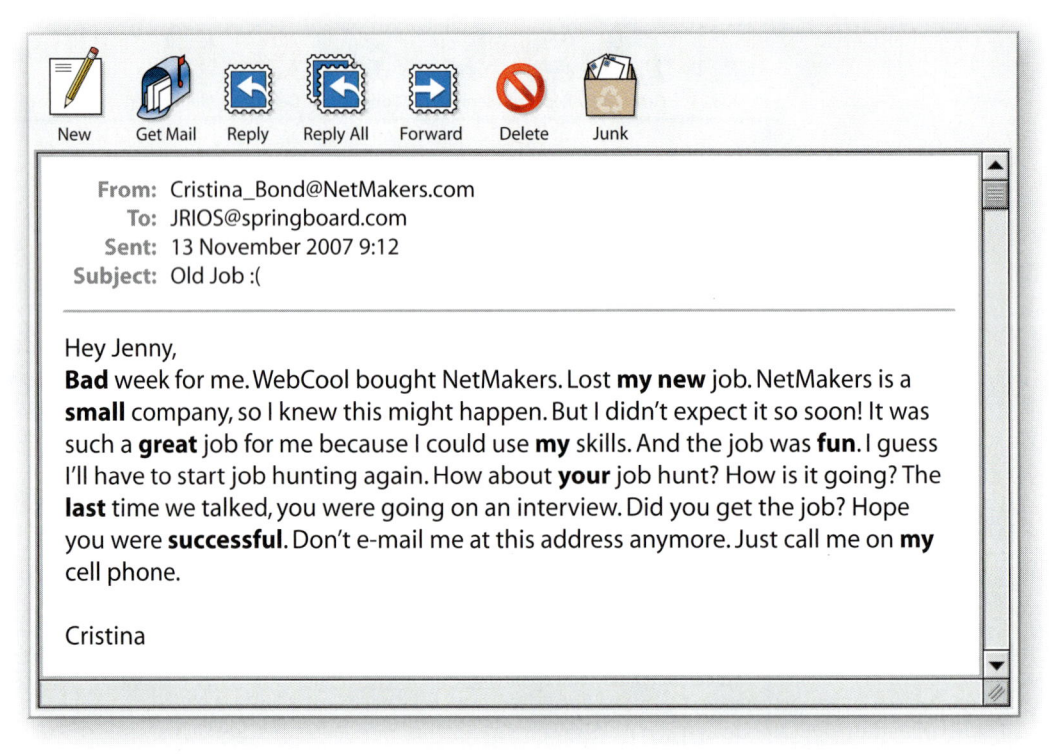

From: Cristina_Bond@NetMakers.com
To: JRIOS@springboard.com
Sent: 13 November 2007 9:12
Subject: Old Job :(

Hey Jenny,
Bad week for me. WebCool bought NetMakers. Lost **my new** job. NetMakers is a **small** company, so I knew this might happen. But I didn't expect it so soon! It was such a **great** job for me because I could use **my** skills. And the job was **fun**. I guess I'll have to start job hunting again. How about **your** job hunt? How is it going? The **last** time we talked, you were going on an interview. Did you get the job? Hope you were **successful**. Don't e-mail me at this address anymore. Just call me on **my** cell phone.

Cristina

List each adjective in the e-mail on one of the lines.

1. Descriptive adjectives: __bad,__
2. Possessive adjectives: __my,__

DESCRIPTIVE AND POSSESSIVE ADJECTIVES

1. Descriptive adjectives describe nouns. They can come after the verb **be**.	The teacher **is** *funny*.
They can come before a noun.	She is a *funny* teacher.
When a noun follows an adjective, use **a, an,** or **the** before the adjective. (*A* and *an* are used only with count nouns.)	She's **a** *funny* teacher. She's **an** *important* writer. **The** *new* teacher isn't here.
REMEMBER: Do not use **a, an,** or **the** when the adjective is not followed by a noun.	Gary is *smart*.

14 UNIT 1

> **2. Possessive adjectives** show belonging.
>
> A noun always follows a possessive adjective. When using possessive adjectives, do not use *a, an,* or *the.*
>
> Possessive adjectives have the same form before singular or plural nouns.
>
> **Possessive Adjectives**
>
> my   your   his   her   its
> our   your   their
>
> I have a job. **My job** is very interesting.
>
> **His boss** is nice.
>
> **Your office** is beautiful.
> **Your offices** are beautiful.

2 Use the words to write sentences.

1. for / Jenny / a / is / career / looking / new

    <u>Jenny is looking for a new career.</u>

2. like / She / job / didn't / old / her

    _____

3. Our / funny / manager / and / is / smart

    _____

4. Internet / job / his / Juan / new / found / on / the

    _____

5. sister / out / work / of / is / My

    _____

6. an / Richard Bolles / job / interesting / has

    _____

7. wife / has / office / David's / a / huge

    _____

8. Tom / Andrea / business / and / their / sold

    _____

9. pays / That / well / company / workers / very / its

    _____

10. résumé / has / a / Dee / great

    _____

Finding the Ideal Job   **15**

3 Describe the pictures. For each picture, write at least three sentences. Use at least one possessive adjective, one descriptive adjective before a noun, and one descriptive adjective after **be**. You can use the descriptive adjectives from the box.

| big | dirty | hungry | messy | sad | sleepy | young |
| curly | happy | long | old | short | straight | |

1. The man:
   The man is young. He has short hair. He is hungry.
   He drives an old truck.
   The truck:
   His truck is old. The old truck is dirty.

2. The woman:

   The desk:

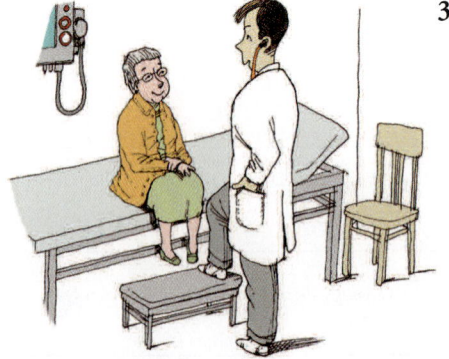

3. The doctor:

   The patient:

C WRITING

In this unit, you read about how to find your ideal job and about people who found their ideal job. Now think about *your* ideal job. Why is that job ideal for you?

You are going to **write a paragraph about your ideal job.** You will explain why this job is ideal for you. You will tell about the skills, setting, and rewards related to this job. Use the vocabulary and grammar from the unit.*

PREPARE TO WRITE: Listing

In order to help you think about the topic for your paragraph, you will do a prewriting activity called **listing**. Listing is **making a list of your ideas** before you begin to write. When you make a list, it is not necessary to write complete sentences *(see the list on page 9)*.

1 *Richard Bolles says that you need to know your skills, preferred settings, and rewards in order to find your ideal job. List these things in the chart. Then list some ideal jobs for you.*

SKILLS I HAVE	SETTINGS I PREFER	REWARDS I WANT

Possible Ideal Jobs for Me

_____

_____

_____

2 *Find a classmate who knows you well. Show your list to this classmate. See if he or she has any more ideas about jobs that might be good for you. Add them to the list, then choose an ideal job to write about.*

---

*For Alternative Writing Topics, see page 21. These topics can be used in place of the writing topic for this unit or as homework. The alternative topics relate to the theme of the unit, but may not target the same grammar or rhetorical structures taught in the unit.

Finding the Ideal Job

WRITE: A Paragraph and Its Topic Sentence

A **paragraph** is a group of sentences about one topic. The first sentence is the **topic sentence**. It states the **main idea** of the paragraph. For this assignment, the topic sentence will give the name of the writer's ideal job.

1 Read the paragraph. Then underline the topic sentence and circle the name of the writer's ideal job.

> I would like to be a mountain-climbing guide. I like this job for several reasons. First of all, mountain climbing is very exciting. Mountain-climbing guides get to climb tall, dangerous mountains. Second, I enjoy working outside. I like the fresh air much better than I like a stuffy office. Finally, I like to meet interesting people. Mountain-climbing guides travel to many different parts of the world and meet other adventurous people.

2 Each paragraph is missing a topic sentence. Choose the best one from the list and write it on the line. Remember that the topic sentence must give the name of the writer's ideal job.

Paragraph 1

> _____.
> There are many reasons why I like this job. First, I like animals. Animals bring a lot of joy to our lives, but they do not ask for a lot in return. I also enjoy helping animals and their owners feel better. Pet owners are happy when their pets are well. Finally, veterinarians get to work with other people who like animals. They can even bring their pets to work!

Topic Sentences

a. I would like a job working with animals.
b. I think I would like to become a veterinarian.
c. A veterinarian helps people and animals feel better.

Paragraph 2

> _____.
> Many people think accountants have boring jobs, but I think accounting is an interesting job. I like math, and I am good at it. I also like helping people manage their money. So I think I have the skills to be an accountant. Accountants mostly work alone. I like meeting people, but I prefer to work alone. Good accountants can earn a lot of money, and that is important for me.

Topic Sentences

    a. Accountants are very important for businesses and people.

    b. I would like to be a mathematician.

    c. My ideal job is to be an accountant.

3 *Write a topic sentence for the paragraph that you are going to write about your ideal job.*

Your topic sentence: _____

4 *Now write the first draft of your paragraph about your ideal job. Start with your topic sentence. Then write sentences that explain the idea in your topic sentence. Use the list you made on page 17 to help you write your paragraph.*

◀ REVISE: Adding Supporting Sentences

Sentences that come after the topic sentence are **supporting sentences.** They explain the main idea with specific **details and examples.**

1 *Read the paragraph. Underline the topic sentence. Then discuss with a partner what kind of information the writer could add to the paragraph.*

>   I would like to become an animator and make films like <u>Toy Story</u>, <u>Shrek</u>, and <u>Cars</u>. This job is ideal for me because I love to work on computers. It is important for me to work with fun people, and everyone I know in animation is really fun. Animators can make a lot of money, and that is important too.

Finding the Ideal Job

2 Read each paragraph and list of supporting sentences. Choose **two** sentences to add to the paragraph. Use an arrow to show where each sentence should go. Put the sentences about skills together, the sentences about setting together, and the sentences about rewards together. The first one has been done for you.

Paragraph 1

> I would like to become an animator and make films like Toy Story, Shrek and Cars. This job is ideal for me because I love to work on computers and I love to draw. It is important for me to work with fun people, and everyone I know in animation is really fun. Animators can make a lot of money, and that is important.

Supporting Sentences

a. I always buy a large popcorn when I go to the movies.

b. But the best reward is that I get to see films I helped to make in theaters.

c. I also know how to draw Manga animations.

d. Mickey Mouse was one of Walt Disney's first animations.

Paragraph 2

> Fashion designing is my dream job. I have good skills for designing clothes. Fashion designers have a lot of fun in their jobs. They can work alone at home or in a studio with others. One reward is that they get to see people wearing their designs. Designing clothes sounds like a lot of fun!

Supporting Sentences

a. I love wearing Dolce and Gabbana clothes.

b. I know how to sew, and I love to draw clothes.

c. Designing shoes could also be a fun job because I like shoes.

d. Fashion designers also get to travel, and I love to travel.

3 Now go back to the first draft of your paragraph. Do all your sentences support the topic sentence? If not, cross them out. Then add some more supporting sentences. Make sure these sentences explain the topic sentence with details and examples.

◀ **EDIT: Writing the Final Draft**

Write the final draft of your paragraph. Carefully edit it for grammatical and mechanical errors, such as spelling, capitalization, and punctuation. Make sure you used some of the vocabulary and grammar from the unit. Use the checklist to help you write your final draft. Then neatly write or type your paragraph.

✓ FINAL DRAFT CHECKLIST

- ○ Does your paragraph tell about your ideal job?
- ○ Does it tell about the skills, setting, and rewards related to this job?
- ○ Does it contain a topic sentence?
- ○ Are there enough supporting sentences to explain the topic sentence?
- ○ Do the supporting sentences give reasons why the job is ideal for you?
- ○ Do you use descriptive adjectives and possessive adjectives correctly?
- ○ Do you use new vocabulary that you learned in this unit?

ALTERNATIVE WRITING TOPICS

Write about one of the topics. Use the vocabulary and grammar from the unit.

1. Imagine your friend just finished college and doesn't know what to do for work. Write him or her an e-mail with advice. Use information from the review of *What Color Is Your Parachute?* Give at least three suggestions.

2. Do you know anyone who has his or her dream job? Write a paragraph about this person. Answer these questions:
   - Who is he or she?
   - What does he or she do?
   - How did he or she get the job?
   - What is most important to him or her about the job?

RESEARCH TOPICS, see page 225.

UNIT 2
Country Life or City Life?

1 FOCUS ON THE TOPIC

A PREDICT

Look at the pictures and discuss the questions with the class.

1. What are these people doing?
2. Where are they?
3. How do you think they feel when they do these things?

23

B SHARE INFORMATION

Work with a partner. Ask your partner the questions in the chart. Listen to each answer and check (✓) the right box. Share your partner's answers with the class.

Example

A: Where did your mother grow up?
B: (She grew up) In the suburbs[1].
A: Did she like it there?
B: Yes, she did. / No, she didn't. / No, she hated it.
A: *(to the class)* Mike's mother grew up in the suburbs. She liked that. / She didn't like that. / She hated that.

	IN A CITY	IN A SMALL TOWN	IN THE SUBURBS	IN THE COUNTRY
1. Where did *you* grow up?				
2. Your *mother*?				
3. Your *father*?				
4. Your *mother's mother*?				
5. Your *mother's father*?				
6. Your *father's mother*?				
7. Your *father's father*?				

---

[1] **suburbs:** places away from the center of a city, where a lot of people live

C BACKGROUND AND VOCABULARY

Read this article about a farm school. Try to guess the meanings of the boldfaced words.

> The Farm School in Athol, Massachusetts, is a working farm that teaches school children about farm life. The children stay at the farm for five days to learn about farming. For city kids, this visit to the Farm School is their first time being out in **nature**. With help from the Farm School teachers, the children do the daily work of farmers. They wake up before **sunrise** to milk the cows, clear the **fields**, plant the **crops**, collect the eggs, and brush Mac, the horse.
>
> The kids learn about taking **responsibility**. As the Farm School **raises** sheep, it's the job of each child to feed and take care of one of the sheep. The children learn what it feels like to have an animal **dependent** on them. If they are lucky, they may even see the **birth** of a baby sheep. In addition to the sheep, the children learn how to take care of the **woods** on the farm. The kids work hard at the Farm School but they all leave happy. They are **proud** of themselves for all the things they did and learned.

Now write the words next to their correct definitions.

| birth | dependent | nature | ~~raise~~ | sunrise |
| crop | field | proud | responsibility | woods |

1. _____raise_____ : to take care of children, animals, or crops
2. _____ : everything in the world that is not made by people, such as animals, plants, weather, etc.
3. _____ : something you have to do or take care of
4. _____ : the time in the morning when the sun comes up
5. _____ : needing someone or something to take care of you
6. _____ : an area of land used in farming
7. _____ : a plant or food grown by farmers
8. _____ : when a baby is born
9. _____ : pleased about yourself or someone connected to you
10. _____ : a place where a lot of trees grow together

2 FOCUS ON READING

A   READING ONE: The Farming Life for Me

The reading that follows is a letter to the editor of a magazine for young people. The writer is a teenage boy who lives on a farm. He explains why he thinks it's better to grow up on a farm than to grow up in the city.

Work with a partner. What do you think this boy's reasons are? Write a list of possible reasons.

1. _____
2. _____
3. _____
4. _____
5. _____

Now read the letter and see if your guesses were right.

Letters to the Editor • Letters to the Editor • Letters to the Editor • Letters to the Editor • Letters to the Editor

The Farming Life for Me

1   In the September 2007 issue of your magazine, you wrote that many farm kids wanted to live in the city. Well, I am a farm kid, and I don't want to live in the city. In fact, I want to explain exactly why I think it's better to grow up on a farm than to grow up in the city.

2   First, farm kids are too busy with farm work to get into trouble with drugs and alcohol like a lot of city kids do. We usually go home right after school to work on the farm and help our parents. We have to milk the cows, feed all the animals, drive the tractor in the **fields**, fix fences, help with watering the **crops** or any other kind of farm work. All these things keep us busy and out of trouble.

3   Second, farm kids understand at an early age what's really important in life. We help our parents when animals are born, and we take care of these animals until they die. I remember getting to pull my first lamb[1] when I was six. Watching the **birth** of an animal always makes

---

[1] **pull a lamb:** to help a mother sheep when she gives birth to a baby lamb

26   UNIT 2

me feel warm and happy. At the same time, I know why we **raise** these animals. They are going to be hamburgers and fried chicken. Like me, most farm kids learn a lot about life and death on the farm. That gives us an understanding of human life and death that city kids don't have.

4   In addition, farm kids have a much better understanding of **nature** than many city kids do. We work outside all year. We almost always get to watch the **sunrise**. We understand how heat or wind or snow can change our crops. We also understand how much water different crops need at different times of year. We can put our hands in the soil[2] and know how much water it needs. We know how to choose the best trees in our **woods** to cut down. Those are just a few of the many outdoor skills that farm kids learn young.

5   Finally, farm kids have a greater sense of **responsibility** than most city kids. We know that crops and animals are totally **dependent** on us. We know that they can die if we don't do our work. I learned at an early age to feed and water the animals on time and to water the crops regularly. Sometimes I'm tired or sick, or it's freezing cold or blowing snow. Even then, I know that I have to do these things because the animals, the crops, and my family depend on me.

6   For all these reasons, I think that it is better to grow up on a farm than to grow up in the city. My own experience growing up on a family farm in Colorado tells me this. I know that growing up on a farm made me the responsible, hardworking, and thoughtful young person my parents and community can be **proud** of.

Zachary Blaine, Colorado

---

[2] **soil:** the dirt or earth we plant our crops in

◀ READ FOR MAIN IDEAS

1 *Check (✓) the sentence that best describes Zachary's main idea in Reading One.*

_____ **a.** Zachary believes that growing up on a farm is great for children.

_____ **b.** Zachary explains why he thinks all children should grow up on farms.

_____ **c.** Zachary explains why he thinks it's great to grow up on a farm instead of in the city.

2 *Zachary gives four main reasons to support his idea. Choose the sentences that best express these four reasons. Label them 1–4 as they appear in the reading.*

_____ **a.** Farm children understand more about life and death than city kids.

_____ **b.** Watching the births of animals is good for farm children.

_____ **c.** Farm children understand soil better than city kids.

_____ **d.** Farm children are too busy doing farm work to get into trouble.

_____ **e.** Farm children learn to fix fences and drive tractors.

_____ **f.** Farm children understand more about nature than city children.

_____ **g.** Farm children have a greater sense of responsibility than city kids.

_____ **h.** Farm children are more comfortable being outside than city children.

READ FOR DETAILS

Read each statement. Part of the statement is incorrect; correct it. Then write the number of the paragraph in the reading where you found the information.

Paragraph

a. Farm kids have to do a lot of work on the farm such as milking the cows, watering the crops, and selling vegetables. _____

b. I feed and water the animals every day, and I water the crops every once in a while. _____

c. We know how to choose the worst trees in our woods to cut down. _____

d. At my house there is never enough work to do after school. _____

e. I remember the first time I saw a lamb born on our farm. _____

f. I'm comfortable seeing life and death on the farm. _____

MAKE INFERENCES

Read the statements and check (✓) the ones that you think Zachary Blaine probably agrees with. Discuss your answers with a partner.

____ 1. Farm kids would like to do the things that city kids do.

____ 2. Most city kids get into trouble with drugs and alcohol.

____ 3. Growing up with a lot of responsibility is good for kids.

____ 4. It's good for kids to visit places like museums, libraries, and theaters.

____ 5. Most city kids would like to grow up on a farm.

____ 6. City children might not get into trouble with guns, alcohol, and drugs if they had animals to take care of.

EXPRESS OPINIONS

Read the statements in Make Inferences again. Circle the number of each statement that you agree with. Discuss your choices with a partner. Give your opinions.

B READING TWO: Leaving the Farm

A hundred years ago, most farmers in the United States were small farmers. Now large farming companies do more and more of the farming. Because these companies are so big, they can sell their fruits and vegetables at a low price. This makes the small farms sell their crops at a low price too. As a result, most small farms don't make enough money. The farmers often have second and third jobs to bring in extra money. And sometimes these farmers decide to sell their farms and move their families to the city.

Read the article about a farm family in North Dakota who recently moved to the city.

Leaving the Farm
by Christopher Blum

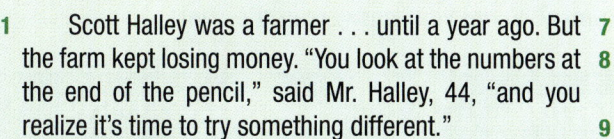

1. Scott Halley was a farmer . . . until a year ago. But the farm kept losing money. "You look at the numbers at the end of the pencil," said Mr. Halley, 44, "and you realize it's time to try something different."

2. With a heavy heart but a clear head, Mr. Halley became one of the thousands of American farmers who sell their land each year. What surprised Mr. Halley and others is that the move to the city was so easy. The farmers are finding jobs and their families are enjoying the city way of life.

3. Mr. Halley found a good job working as a scientist at North Dakota State University. His salary is now twice what it was when he was a farmer.

4. But even for those farmers who find good jobs, there is a price to pay in leaving farming.

5. "It's not just about making money but about the other rewards that farming can bring...working land your parent's parents worked, spending your days in nature, caring for animals," said Dr. Michael Rosmann, a farmer and psychologist who helps farmers. "For most of them, that grieving[1] lasts for the rest of their lives. To make the decision to quit farming, to do what's best for the family, takes an awful lot of courage." Mr. Halley feels the pull of the land every day. Once a week, he drives eight hours to work a small piece of his old farm, just to keep his connection to the land.

6. It was hard to leave, but Mr. Halley knows he did the right thing. For most families that leave the land, salary goes up and the stress from having little money goes down. Both parents and children are happier.

7. Halley's children love living in the city.

8. "The kids don't want to go back now," said Mr. Halley. "The telephone never stops ringing."

9. Megan Halley, 13, spoke with excitement about her new school. She especially likes art and computer technology. "Back on the farm," she said, "the old phone system took five minutes or more just to dial up the Internet."

10. "It's cool here," said Megan. She loves going to the nearby mall[2] to shop for new clothes and get the latest CDs of her favorite group. The closest store to the Halleys' farm was a 10-mile drive.

11. Before moving to the city, Megan worried about getting along with city kids.

12. "The boys here aren't any different than back in the country," she said. "There's just a lot more of them."

[1] **grieving:** feeling very sad when we have lost somebody or something we love
[2] **mall:** a large building with a lot of stores in it

Source: Based on information in "Leaving the Farm for the Other Real World," Dirk Johnson, *The New York Times*, November 7, 1999.

Now answer the questions. Check your answers with a partner.

1. Why does Mr. Halley drive back to his old farm once a week?
2. Is it easy for farmers to decide to leave farming and move to the city?
3. Are the Halleys happy they decided to sell the farm? Explain.

Country Life or City Life?

C INTEGRATE READINGS ONE AND TWO

STEP 1: Organize

Look at Readings One and Two again. What are the advantages and disadvantages of living in the city or living in the country? Write your answers in the chart.

	CITY LIVING	COUNTRY LIVING
1. Advantages	more money	understanding of nature
2. Disadvantages		

STEP 2: Synthesize

Imagine you are one of the children in the Halley family (Reading Two). Write a letter to Zachary Blaine (Reading One). Explain why you prefer the city to the country. Make sure to discuss at least two of his main points. Use information from the chart in Step 1.

Dear Zachary,

I read your letter to the editor last week, and I wanted to write you back. You make some good points about life in the country, but I still disagree with you. I want to explain why I think it's better for kids to live in the city.

First, you say that farm kids are too busy to get in trouble with alcohol and drugs. That makes it sound like all city kids have these problems. This is just not true. I think . . .

_____
_____
_____
_____

Second, you say that . . .

_____
_____
_____
_____

But, I think . . .

_____
_____
_____
_____

Even though both city and country living have their advantages and disadvantages, I still think it's better to live in the city. We can always come visit the country when we want to. So, I guess it's a good thing that there are people like you who continue to believe country living is best.

Sincerely,

_____

3 FOCUS ON WRITING

A VOCABULARY

REVIEW

Complete the crossword puzzle with words from the box. Read the clues below.

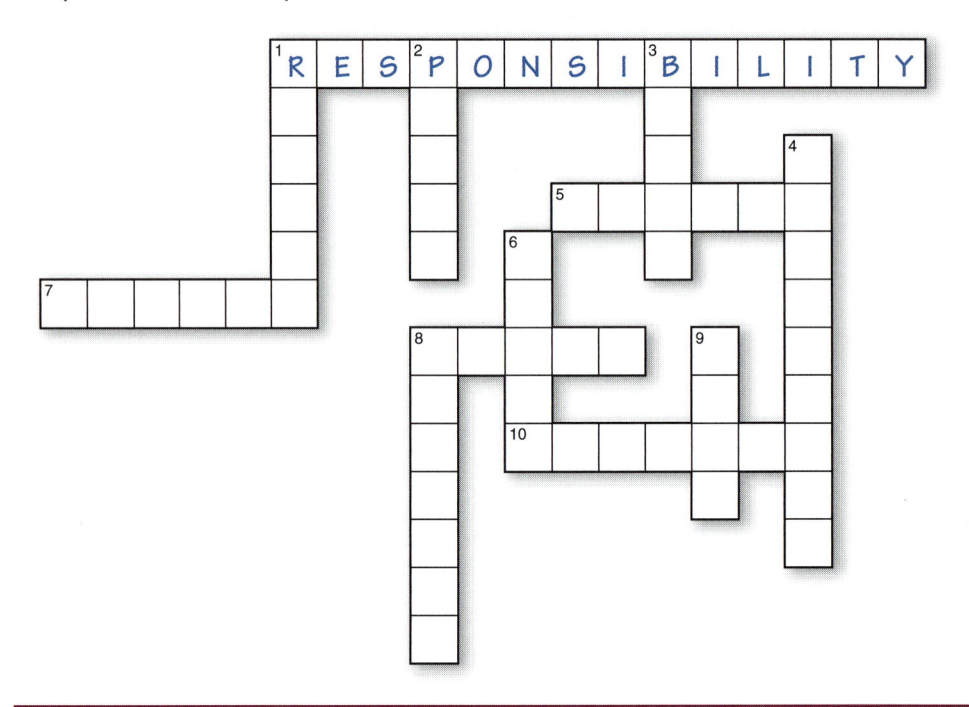

1. R E S P O N S I B I L I T Y

| birth | crops | nature | quit | ~~responsibility~~ | sunrise |
| courage | dependent | proud | raises | stress | woods |

Across

1. "I don't want to take care of a dog. I don't want to worry about it or feed it or have to take it on walks." This man does not want _____ for a dog.

5. "Oh, I love being outside. I love to feel the wind in my face while I walk through the woods listening to the birds." He loves to be in _____.

7. "We moved to the city so we didn't have to worry about money. But now I have to worry about my kids. When they don't come home from school on time, I get scared. I worry that something happened to them." This woman is under a lot of _____.

8. "Well, I already planted the corn. The tomatoes can't go in until April. I guess I could go out and plant the carrots and cucumbers today." This farmer is trying to decide which _____ to plant.

10. "I love this time of day. Most people are still asleep. I feel like I have the world and this beautiful view all to myself." The woman is watching the _____.

Down

1. "I've more chickens than you could count. I have black ones, brown ones, gray ones. I have young ones and old ones. What kind of chicken are you looking for?" This farmer _____ chickens.

2. "I'm so happy for you. You really did such a good job. I'm just so pleased." The mother is very _____ of her son.

3. "It was just amazing. I had never seen anything so beautiful! And to hold my baby son in my arms for the first time! I'll never forget it." This man is describing the _____ of his son.

4. "I just don't know what to do without my car. It takes me everywhere—to work, to the gym, to the store. I don't think I can live without it." This man is _____ on his car.

6. "I like to be in big open spaces. I don't really like tall buildings or even tall trees. In fact, I don't like any trees." This person would not like to walk in the _____.

8. "You are so brave to get a new job after being a farmer for 30 years. I just don't think I could do it." This farmer is talking to his neighbor. He thinks his neighbor has a lot of _____.

9. "I love the farm. I don't want to leave. But everyone tells me I'm losing money. They say I should sell the land and move to the city. But I'm not ready to give it up. I'm going to stay." This farmer doesn't want to _____ farming.

◀ EXPAND

It's important to pay attention to words that often go with the word you are learning. Choose the best phrase to complete each sentence. Circle your answer.

1. It's exciting to watch the _____ any animal. But to watch your own child come into this world is truly amazing.
   a. birth from
   b. birth to
   c. birth of

2. I think we should get a dog. It will teach the children about taking _____ an animal.
   a. responsibility for
   b. responsibility on
   c. responsibility of

3. It's important to do a good job when you know that someone is _____ you.
   a. dependent for
   b. dependent on
   c. dependent of

4. Michael's mother was very _____ him for taking care of their family cat when it got sick.
   a. proud for
   b. proud on
   c. proud of

5. For people _____, working hard in a garden can be relaxing.
   a. under a lot of stress
   b. in a lot of stress
   c. on a lot of stress

6. Every day I try to spend at least a few minutes _____.
   a. on nature
   b. in nature
   c. of nature

7. The view from my bedroom in the farmhouse was beautiful. I could see the flower garden. Then, past the fields, I could see the big old trees _____.
   a. in the woods
   b. under the woods
   c. on the woods

CREATE

You spent your vacation on your aunt's farm. Your friend visited a cousin in London. Read the letter from your friend. He asks you some questions about your vacation.

LONDON, ENGLAND

Dear Isaac,

I had a great time on my vacation. I loved London. My cousin has a great apartment. It's small, but it's on the thirteenth floor, and it has great views. From her windows I could see all the way to Big Ben and Parliament. I kept thinking of you on your aunt's farm. **(1) What kind of farm is it? What does she grow? Does she have animals?**

I saw five shows. I went to Westminster Abbey, London Bridge, and the Tower of London. Most nights, I went out to dinner and then went to a show or a movie or a concert. Or all three!

What about on the farm? **(2) What interesting things did you do or see?**

I had a super vacation. I think I really could live in a city like London! I love shopping all day and going out every night! What about you? **(3) Could you live on a farm?**

I hope you had a great time. I'll call you next week.

Talk to you soon,

Rogelio

(continued on next page)

Now reply to your friend. Answer his questions using as many of the words in parentheses as possible.

Dear Rogelio,

Thanks for your letter. It sounds like London was fantastic. It sounds so different from my vacation. I must say, though, I had a great time on Aunt Lisa's farm.

(1) It's a small farm, but . . .
_____
(fields / crops / woods / proud of / raise)
_____
_____

(2) I did some very exciting things. For instance, one day . . .
_____
(birth / sunrise / courage)
_____
_____

(3) Yes, I certainly could live on a farm. I love . . .
_____
(use / quit / responsibility)
_____
_____

Well, that's all I can think of for now. I can't wait to see you!

See you soon,

Isaac

36 UNIT 2

B GRAMMAR: Simple Past Tense

1 *Read the paragraph. Underline the verbs that tell about the past. Then answer the questions.*

> Ben Holmes started the Farm School in Athol, Massachusetts, in 1991. Holmes, a city kid from California, spent summers on his uncle's farm in Ohio. There he learned to love working on the land. He created the school because he wanted to teach kids that work is about using your body and your mind together.

1. How is the simple past formed for most verbs (regular verbs)?
2. Which past tense verb is irregular? What is the base form of this verb?

SIMPLE PAST TENSE	
1. When we talk about things that happened in the past, we use the **simple past tense**.	Last summer, I **worked** on a farm. I **went** to the city yesterday.
2. To form the simple past tense for **regular** verbs, add **-ed** to the base form of the verb. If the verb ends in **-e**, add only **-d**. If the verb ends in a consonant + **y**, change the **y** to **i** and then add **-ed**.	**Base Form** **Simple Past** want want**ed** talk talk**ed** live live**d** arrive arrive**d** study stud**ied** try tr**ied**
3. Many verbs have **irregular** past tense forms. Here are some of these irregular verbs.	be was / were do did have had eat ate get got go went make made say said
4. In negative statements, use **didn't (did not)** + base form of the verb, except with the verb *be*.	need **didn't** need want **didn't** want be **wasn't / weren't**

Country Life or City Life?

2 Read Toby's letter. Complete it with the simple past tense forms of the verbs in parentheses. Some of the verbs are regular and some are irregular.

Dear Ayla,

I just __got__ back from the fifth-grade class trip to the
         1. (get)
farm. It _____ great. I'm so tired. You wouldn't believe what we
         2. (be)
did in just three days. On the first day, the teachers _____ us
                                                         3. (show)
around the farm and we each _____ a chance to milk the cow
                             4. (get)
Daisy. After we _____ lunch, I _____ with some other
                 5. (eat)   6. (go)
students to the barn. There we _____ the horses. After dinner,
                                7. (brush)
the teachers _____ music and we _____ for hours.
              8. (play)   9. (dance)
We _____ really early the second day and _____
    10. (wake up)   11. (plant)
tomatoes all morning. After lunch, we _____ stones from the
                                      12. (carry)
field. That _____ hard! After dinner the second night,
            13. (be)
everyone _____ too tired to dance. We just _____
          14. (be)   15. (talk)
around the fire before bed.

I miss you and hope to hear from you soon.

Toby

C WRITING

In this unit, you read about life in the city and on a farm. Now what about you? When was the last time you visited the country? Went to a park?

You are going to **write a paragraph describing a farm or nature area** that you visited when you were a child or more recently. You will describe what this place looked like, what you did there, and how you felt. Use the vocabulary and grammar from the unit.*

---

*For Alternative Writing Topics, see page 43. These topics can be used in place of the writing topic for this unit or as homework. The alternative topics relate to the theme of the unit, but may not target the same grammar or rhetorical structures taught in the unit.

38   UNIT 2

PREPARE TO WRITE: Using Pictures

In order to help you think about the topic of your paragraph, you will do a prewriting activity using pictures. **Drawing a picture** of a place can help you **remember important details**.

Look at the photos. Then work with a partner and do the following.

1. Think of a farm or nature area that you have visited. The nature area can be a large place, such as a national park or a mountain, or it can be a small place, such as a city park or backyard garden.

2. On a separate piece of paper, draw a picture of the place. Don't worry about how good your drawing is. Just try to draw as many details as you can.

3. Show your picture to your partner. Using the picture to help you, describe the place to your partner and tell him or her what you did there.

4. After you talk about your picture, turn your picture over and write a list of all the things you said to your partner. You don't have to write in complete sentences.

Country Life or City Life?

WRITE: A Descriptive Paragraph

A good **description** is a **word picture** of a place or person. When you write a descriptive paragraph, you should **group similar ideas together** to help your reader imagine the place or person you describe. A paragraph about a place you visited should include the following parts:

> 1. the name of the place and where it is (its location)
> 2. what you saw there
> 3. what you did there
> 4. how you felt

1 Read the topic sentence for a paragraph about a trip to a small farm.

> Last summer I went on a trip to my friend's house near Adelaide, Australia.

The writer made a list of ideas for the rest of the paragraph. Group these ideas for her. Put an **S** next to those sentences that talk about what she saw. Put a **D** next to those sentences that talk about things she did. Put an **F** next to those sentences that talk about how she felt.

_____ 1. I had a great time and can't wait to go back for another visit.

_____ 2. I helped them feed the chickens and collect eggs.

_____ 3. We ate delicious fried eggs for breakfast every morning.

_____ 4. I also picked some of the vegetables from the garden for dinner.

_____ 5. They have a large vegetable garden and a small barn with chickens.

_____ 6. I tried to get up at sunrise every day.

2 Now write the first draft of your paragraph about the farm or nature area you visited. Start your paragraph with a topic sentence that gives the name and location of the place. Using your picture and your notes, write what you saw there and what you did there. End the paragraph with how you felt.

"Ten (five / two) years ago" OR "Last (week / month / year) I went to . . ."

_____
_____
_____
_____
_____

◀ REVISE: Adding Descriptive Details

Details help the reader **see a clear picture** of the place you are describing. You can add descriptive details by telling exactly where people and things are located, what they are doing, and what they look like.

1 Read each sentence. Check (✓) the three details that best add more detail to this sentence.

1. Next to the fields was a lake.
   _____ a. The barn was painted red.
   _____ b. It was pretty big and it had a small beach at one end.
   _____ c. It looked like the perfect place for a swim.
   _____ d. The water was a beautiful blue color.

2. I watched the sun come up every morning.
   _____ a. It was hard to get up so early.
   _____ b. The sky was full of reds and yellows.
   _____ c. After dinner we went for a walk.
   _____ d. The morning air smelled so clean and fresh.

3. There was a large oak tree in the middle of the garden.
   _____ a. It was at least 30 feet tall.
   _____ b. It had beautiful orange and red leaves.
   _____ c. Nobody ever used the back door of the house.
   _____ d. Lots of birds were sitting up in the branches.

2 Read the paragraph.

> Yesterday I went to visit my friend Lisa, and we sat in her garden all afternoon. Her garden is small. But it's very beautiful. We ate lunch and talked. I felt relaxed and happy.

Does it feel like something's missing? Turn to the next page and read the same paragraph with some details added.

Underline the added details. Notice how the details help make this paragraph more clear and interesting.

> Yesterday I went to visit my friend Lisa, and we sat in her garden all afternoon. Her garden is small. It's about the size of my living room. But it's very beautiful. It has a lot of different kinds of flowers. There are large pink ones and small blue ones. We ate lunch and talked about school and our friends. I felt relaxed and happy.

3 Now go back to the first draft of your paragraph. Add more descriptive details to make it clearer and more interesting.

EDIT: Writing the Final Draft

Write the final draft of your paragraph. Carefully edit it for grammatical and mechanical errors, such as spelling, capitalization, and punctuation. Make sure you used some of the vocabulary and grammar from the unit. Use the checklist to help you write your final draft. Then neatly write or type your paragraph.

✓ FINAL DRAFT CHECKLIST

- ❍ Does your topic sentence give the name and location of the place you visited?
- ❍ Do you group the details according to what you saw, what you did there, and how you felt?
- ❍ Do you use a lot of details?
- ❍ Do you use the simple past tense to describe past events?
- ❍ Do you use new vocabulary that you learned in this unit?
- ❍ Do you use vocabulary from this unit with the correct words such as *of, on, for,* etc.?

ALTERNATIVE WRITING TOPICS

Write about one of the topics. Use the vocabulary and grammar from the unit.

1. Look at the exercise Integrate Readings One and Two on page 30. Use the information in the chart to write two paragraphs. One paragraph should describe the advantages and disadvantages of city living. The other should describe the advantages and disadvantages of country living.

2. Which do you think is better, country life or city life? Write a paragraph to give your opinion.

3. Do you know a family who owned a farm in the past? Write a paragraph about that family. Describe their farm and why they left the farm. Where did they move to? Did they like it better or worse than living on the farm? Why?

RESEARCH TOPICS, see page 225.

UNIT 3
Making Money

U.S. $100 bill before 1996

U.S. $100 bill after 2004

1 FOCUS ON THE TOPIC

A PREDICT

Look at the bills and discuss the questions with the class.

1. Why do you think the $100 bill was changed?
2. What differences can you see between the two bills?

B SHARE INFORMATION

What do you think about the actions? Are they acceptable? Are they wrong? Some things may seem more wrong to you than others. For each action, check (✓) the box that shows what you think. Compare your answers in a small group.

ACTION	ACCEPTABLE	NOT SO WRONG	WRONG	VERY WRONG
1. A student doesn't want to buy a book he needs so he copies some chapters on a copy machine.				
2. A student copies a friend's paper and gives it to her teacher with her own name on it.				
3. A man finds a bag with $50 in it. He keeps the money.				
4. A man needs some money. He copies paper money on a copy machine.				
5. A girl needs some money. She takes $5 from her mother's wallet.				
6. A man borrows $10 from a friend and never repays him.				

C BACKGROUND AND VOCABULARY

When you read a story, there may be many words you don't know. Often you can still understand the story, and sometimes you can even understand these new words.

1 *Read the story. See if you can understand it even though some words are missing.*

One day last year, some New York City sanitation workers were very surprised when they emptied a garbage can. Along with the banana peels and empty Coke cans, they found $18 million in new _____.
1.

Who would throw out all that money? The workers felt that something was not right, so they called the United States Bureau of Engraving and Printing, the part of government that makes paper money. The Bureau employees said that the money looked real but that, in fact, it wasn't. It was _____—and not legal. The garbage must have belonged to
2.
_____, people who make money that is not real. They use both
3.
old and new _____, or ways to make money. For example, some
4.
make the money by using printing presses, big machines similar to those for making books or newspapers; others use _____ and other
5.
computer _____. These counterfeiters probably printed a lot of
6.
money and weren't happy with how it looked. Maybe the drawing wasn't good enough. Or maybe the _____ was not exactly the right color. So
7.
they threw it all out.

The people at the Bureau of Engraving and Printing were mad. Copying money is _____. Counterfeiters who get caught can go to prison
8.
for a long time. The people at the Bureau work very hard to _____
9.
people from making fake money.

The Bureau never caught these counterfeiters. Nobody knows if they were able to make another $18 million that looked _____ real.
10.

Making Money **47**

Now answer the questions. Then discuss your answers with a classmate.

1. What did the New York City sanitation workers find?
   _____

2. Who threw out all that money?
   _____

2 Read the story again. Work with a partner. Use information in the story to guess the meaning of the missing words. Write your guesses on the lines.

1. _____
2. _____
3. _____
4. _____
5. _____
6. _____
7. _____
8. _____
9. _____
10. _____

Now read the story with the vocabulary words filled in.

> One day last year, some New York City sanitation workers were very surprised when they emptied a garbage can. Along with the banana peels and empty Coke cans, they found $18 million in new __**bills**__.
> 1.
>
> Who would throw out all that money? The workers felt that something was not right, so they called the United States Bureau of Engraving and Printing, the part of government that makes paper money. The Bureau employees said that the money looked real but that, in fact, it wasn't. It was __**fake**__—and not legal. The garbage must have belonged to
> 2.
> __**counterfeiters**__, people who make money that is not real. They use both
> 3.
> old and new __**technologies**__, or ways to make money. For example,
> 4.

48 UNIT 3

some make the money by using printing presses similar to those for making books or newspapers; others use ___scanners___ and other computer ___equipment___. These counterfeiters probably printed a lot of money and weren't happy with how it looked. Maybe the drawing wasn't good enough. Or maybe the ___ink___ was not exactly the right color. So they threw it all out.

The people at the Bureau of Engraving and Printing were mad. Copying money is ___illegal___. Counterfeiters who get caught can go to prison for a long time. The people at the Bureau work very hard to ___prevent___ people from making fake money.

The Bureau never caught these counterfeiters. Nobody knows if they were able to make another $18 million that looked ___completely___ real.

Work with the class. Make a list of the new vocabulary words. Together write one definition that seems best for each word.

2 FOCUS ON READING

A READING ONE: Making Money

The following magazine article is about how some counterfeiters make fake money. It is also about how the U.S. government tries to stop counterfeiting.

Work in a small group. Make a list of things that you think the government might do to make money harder to copy.

1. _____
2. _____
3. _____
4. _____
5. _____

Now read the article. Were your ideas correct?

MAKING MONEY

BY AMELIA LAIDLAW

1. IT WAS SO QUICK AND EASY. A 14-year-old boy in Scottsdale, Arizona, pulled out a $50 **bill** and put it onto his school's new computer **scanner**. Then he printed ten copies of his $50 bill on a color copier. Within seconds he changed $50 into $550, and he was ready to shop.

2. Twenty years ago only a few people had the skills or **equipment** to make counterfeit money. Computer, copier, and printer **technology** is much better now, so today almost anyone can "make" money. With the new technology there is a new kind of **counterfeiter**: casual counterfeiters. These counterfeiters are called casual because they don't have special skills and don't need to plan much.

3. The number of **fake** bills made by casual counterfeiters on their home or office computer is growing fast. In fact, this number has doubled every year since 1989! There is no way to **completely prevent** counterfeiting. However, the government has a few new ways to make casual counterfeiting more difficult than ever before.

4. One way is to put very, very small words, called microprint, in hidden places on the bill. These words are only 6/1,000 inch. No one can read them without a magnifying glass, a special glass that makes things look bigger. And they are too small to come out clearly on a copier. If someone copies a bill that has microprint and you look at the copy through a magnifying glass, you will see only black lines instead of microprinted words.

5. Another way to prevent people from making **illegal** money on their home computers is to use special color-changing **ink**. Money printed with color-changing ink will look green from one direction and yellow from another. Home computers cannot use color-changing ink. So any copies from a home computer will have normal ink that is easy to notice.

6. Additionally, money is made on special paper with very small pieces of red and blue silk[1] mixed in. Only the U.S. government can buy this exact paper. And on each bill there is a special line that runs from the top to the bottom of the bill. Suppose, for example, that you hold a $20 bill up to the light. If you do this, you can see the line has the words "USA twenty." The line turns red if you put it under a special (ultraviolet) light. In 2004 the U.S. government started using different colors in the background of bills. These background colors, the line, and the special paper with red and blue silk are not easy for home computers to copy.

7. The Bureau of Engraving and Printing needs to keep changing the way it makes money because counterfeiters can learn to copy the changes. Today copiers can't copy microprinted words or color-changing ink. But in a few years, who knows?

---

[1] **silk:** a fine thread made by silkworms

◀ READ FOR MAIN IDEAS

1 *Each sentence tells the main idea of a paragraph in "Making Money." Read each sentence, then write the correct paragraph number next to it.*

Paragraph

a. Casual counterfeiting is becoming a big problem, and the government is fighting the problem. _____

b. Using color-changing ink is a way to prevent counterfeiting. _____

c. A child can easily copy paper money. _____

d. The government must always keep changing the bills to prevent counterfeiting. _____

e. Putting microprint on bills helps prevent counterfeiting. _____

f. New technology makes casual counterfeiting possible. _____

g. The special paper, line, and color on U.S. paper money help prevent counterfeiting. _____

2 *Check (✓) the sentence that best describes the main idea of the whole article.*

____ a. It's easier to counterfeit money today than it was 20 years ago, especially with the right equipment.

____ b. The government has several ways to try to prevent counterfeiting.

____ c. New technology makes counterfeiting easier, but the government changes bills every few years to make counterfeiting more difficult.

◀ READ FOR DETAILS

Complete the sentences with information from the article.

1. Twenty years ago, only a few people had the _____ or _____ to make fake money.

2. One way to prevent counterfeiters from making fake money on a _____ is to use microprinted words.

3. Bills have a _____ that you can see if you hold them up to the light.

4. Bills are printed on special paper that has pieces of _____ and _____ silk.

5. A boy in Scottsdale, Arizona, used his school's scanner to make _____ copies of a $ _____ bill.

6. Money printed with color-changing ink looks green from one direction and _____ from another.

Making Money **51**

◀ **MAKE INFERENCES**

*Which of these statements do you think are true? Write **T** (true) or **F** (false). Discuss your answers with a partner.*

_____ 1. Most casual counterfeiters make millions of dollars in bills.

_____ 2. The government is worried about casual counterfeiters.

_____ 3. The police catch most casual counterfeiters.

_____ 4. The government changes the way it makes money every few years.

_____ 5. Copiers will probably be able to copy microprint in just a few years.

◀ **EXPRESS OPINIONS**

Discuss the questions in a small group. Give your opinions. Then share your answers with the class.

1. Who gets hurt when people counterfeit? Who are counterfeiters stealing from?

2. What would you do if you saw someone copying money on a color copier?

B READING TWO: I Made It Myself

Before computers and copiers, counterfeiting was not easy. You needed the artistic skill to draw a copy of a bill, a large printing press, and the skill to use it. Counterfeiting often took a lot of time, planning, and hard work. Still the results were excellent. The counterfeit money looked and felt like the real thing. Today, professional counterfeiters still make fake money the old-fashioned way—on printing presses.

Now read the story of Michael Landress, who was once a professional counterfeiter.

I MADE IT MYSELF

1. It took months of planning, of trying to find the perfect paper, of mixing and remixing ink to get the right color, of printing and reprinting to get the right feel, but I did it. I made a perfect copy of a $100 bill.

2. During the days, I did regular print jobs at the shop. Then every evening at five o'clock, I sent my workers home, hoping no one would ask why I stayed late. I pulled out the paper, ink, and other equipment I hid away the night before and slowly, carefully worked until the sun came up. I didn't have time to sleep. I was too nervous to sleep anyway. As I worked, I worried about the Secret Service[1] agents coming to get me. In the beginning, as I prepared the paper, I said to myself, "I'm just printing little blue and red hair lines on paper. They can't arrest me for that. I'm not breaking the law." Then as I printed the numbers, I said, "I'm just printing small numbers in four corners of a page. They can't arrest me for *this*. What I'm doing isn't illegal." Finally, as I got closer and closer to printing something they could arrest me for, I began to wonder, "Is this really that bad? Who am I hurting? I'm making myself a few thousand dollars so I can take my boy and move to Puerto Rico. I'm just trying to do my best for my family. Is that so wrong?"

3. After about three weeks of slow work, I finally printed out a whole sheet of $100 bills. I took out the magnifying glass and studied my work. "No. Oh, Ben, no. Ben, you don't look right," I said aloud to the empty shop. The portrait[2] of Ben Franklin on the front of the bill just didn't look right. To most people, he probably looked like the one on the real bill. However, I could see that it wasn't a perfect copy. I needed it to be perfect. So, slowly, painfully, I started over.

4. A week later, I was printing the last of the bills. I didn't hear them come in because of the noise of the press. I just looked up from studying the now-perfect portraits of Ben Franklin to see a gun at my head and hear the Secret Service agent say, "Just like getting caught with your hand in the cookie jar, huh, Mike?"

---

[1] **Secret Service:** government agency that tries to find and catch counterfeiters
[2] **portrait:** a drawing or painting of someone's head

Source: Based on M. M. Landress with Bruce Dobler, *I Made It Myself* (New York: Grosset and Dunlap, 1973).

Now answer the questions. Check your answers with a partner.

1. The title of the story is *I Made It Myself.* What does "It" refer to?
2. In the third paragraph, Landress says, "No. Oh, Ben, no." Who is Ben? What was wrong? How does Michael feel?

3. In the fourth paragraph, Landress says, "I didn't hear them come in because of the noise of the press." Who does "them" refer to? What were they coming to do? Why?

4. The story ends with "Just like getting caught with your hand in the cookie jar, huh, Mike?" What do you think "getting caught with your hand in the cookie jar" means?

C INTEGRATE READINGS ONE AND TWO

◀ STEP 1: Organize

There are two kinds of counterfeiters: casual counterfeiters, like the 14-year-old boy in Scottsdale, Arizona, and professional counterfeiters like Mike Landress.

Based on Readings One and Two, compare the two kinds of counterfeiters. Look at the list of phrases. Then write each phrase in the correct box in the chart on the next page. Some phrases may be used twice.

~~artistic skills~~

printing presses

color-changing ink

paper does not have blue and red silk in it

special paper

computer printer ink

a print shop

know how to run a printing press

scanners

microprint looks like black lines

ink is not color-changing

home computer skills

computer printer paper

no special line

	CASUAL COUNTERFEITERS	**PROFESSIONAL COUNTERFEITERS**
1. What kind of skills do they need?		artistic skills
2. What tools, equipment, and materials do they need?		
3. How can you tell their bills are fake?		

◀ **STEP 2: Synthesize**

The U.S. government does a lot to prevent counterfeiting, but it has different ways of catching casual and professional counterfeiters.

Complete the two memos regarding counterfeit prevention. Use information from the chart in Step 1.

1.

U.S. Bureau of Counterfeit Prevention

To: Shopkeepers in the Washington, D.C., area
Re: Catching casual counterfeiters

We are finding many counterfeit bills in the Washington, D.C., area this month. These bills are made with home computer technology and are easy to recognize. Please help us to catch counterfeiters.

Tips for recognizing counterfeit bills:

1. (paper / feel) ____The paper feels different.____

2. (red and blue silk thread) _____

3. (line) _____

4. (*your idea*) _____

5. (*your idea*) _____

Making Money   **55**

2.

U.S. Bureau of Counterfeit Prevention

To: All U.S. agents
Re: Professional counterfeiter investigation

Professionally counterfeit bills are showing up in the New York, Philadelphia, and Boston areas. We cannot rely on shopkeepers to help us find these counterfeiters because the bills are very well done and difficult to recognize as counterfeit.

Very few people have the equipment, materials, and skills to counterfeit this well. We need to find out who has the special equipment and materials in order to find out who is counterfeiting these bills.

Here is a list of questions we need to answer in order to begin our investigation:

1. (printing presses) _Who owns printing presses?_
2. (ink) _____
3. (*your idea*) _____
4. (*your idea*) _____

3 FOCUS ON WRITING

A VOCABULARY

REVIEW

1 The sentences on the next page do not make sense. Replace the boldfaced word or phrase with its antonym (opposite) from the box so the sentences make sense.

arrested	completely	illegal	prevent
casual	~~counterfeiter~~	nervous	

56 UNIT 3

1. When I got the $100 bill, I noticed that the paper didn't feel right. "Is it possible that a ~~government worker~~ *counterfeiter* made this?" I asked myself.

2. Look at this bill. The ink is almost brown, not green. The paper feels like regular computer paper, not money. This must be the work of a **professional** counterfeiter.

3. The police officer took the woman by the arms, put her in the police car, and took her to the police station. He **set** her **free**.

4. His legs were shaking. His heart was going very fast. His lips were dry. He felt very **relaxed** as he gave the bank the counterfeit money.

5. The fire destroyed everything in the shop. The expensive designer clothing and all of the jewelry were **not at all** destroyed.

6. It's **not a problem** to make photocopies of money. Teachers should use real bills when they teach students about American money.

7. New Zealand, Brazil, and China now use special plastic instead of paper for their bills to **make** counterfeiting **easier**.

2 *Complete the sentences with the words from the box.*

| bill | equipment | fake | ink | scanner | technology |

1. Printing presses, copiers, scanners, and magnifying glasses are different kinds of _____ used in counterfeiting.
2. Even new printing presses use _____ that is over 500 years old.
3. I want to be able to put this magazine photograph on my computer screen. I need a(n) _____.
4. Don't be fooled by that "Rolex" watch. It's cheap because it's _____.
5. I need change. Can I have four quarters for a one-dollar _____?
6. Professor Porter always corrected my papers with purple _____ since she didn't like red.

Making Money 57

◀ **EXPAND**

1 Money isn't the only counterfeit product. Look at the pictures of other counterfeit products. How can you tell that these products are fake? Discuss with a partner.

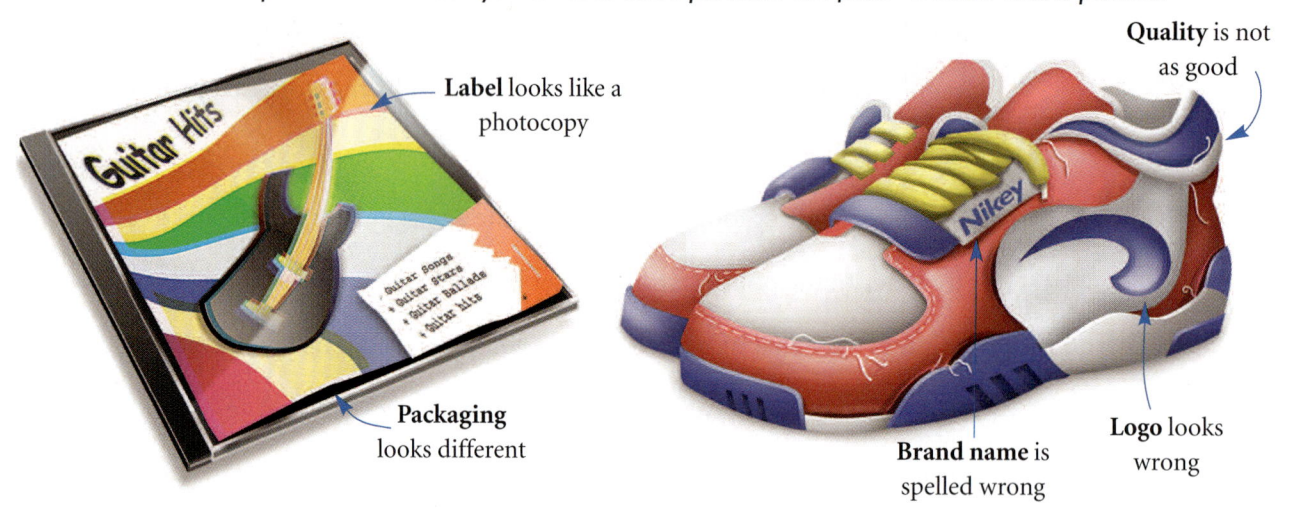

Label looks like a photocopy

Packaging looks different

Quality is not as good

Brand name is spelled wrong

Logo looks wrong

1. **Pirated** CD

2. **Imitation** sports shoes

2 Read about Nicole and Joe, and look at the picture.

Nicole and Joe are at the flea market, a market where people sell lots of cheap products. Nicole is surprised that there are so many cheap designer products. Joe knows that these products are all fake.

58   UNIT 3

Now complete the conversation with the words from the box.

| ~~brand name~~ | labels | packaging | quality |
| imitation | logo | pirated | |

NICOLE: Joe! Look at this! They have Rayban sunglasses for only $25!

JOE: Nicole, those aren't real. Those are *Raybams*—the __brand name__ is spelled wrong!
1.

N: Oh. But what about these bottles of perfume? It's Chanel!

J: Can't you tell that those are fake? They have different _____ and _____.
2. 3.

N: Oh, look! Here are some CDs of the Rolling Stones. I love the Rolling Stones!

J: These CDs are _____. Someone just copied the covers on their scanner.
4.

N: Well what about the shoes? These are Nikes, and they are really cheap!

J: You can tell that they are not Nikes because the _____ looks wrong . . . They are cheaper because the _____ is bad.
5. 6.
They will probably fall apart in one week!

N: What about those jackets? They look like Armani.

J: For $25? They are _____ Armani. Nicole, *everything* here is fake!
7.

Making Money 59

CREATE

Look at the picture and complete the conversation. Use as many of the words from the box as you can.

arrest	casual	counterfeiter	illegal	~~pirated~~
bills	completely	equipment	logo	prevent
brand name	counterfeit	fake	nervous	scanner

NICOLE: Well maybe *you* know that these products are all fake, but that kid over there is buying a lot of stuff. Look! He just bought some software.

JOE: Oh, that is __pirated__. You can tell because _____

_____.

N: And now he's buying _____.

How do you think he got all that money?

J: That's not real money. I think _____.

N: Really? _____.

J: It looks like he used _____.

N: You're right. He also seems _____.

J: Uh, oh. Look behind you! There _____.

N: Do you think _____?

J: I don't know, but I think we should leave before there is trouble!

60 UNIT 3

B GRAMMAR: Comparative Form of Adjectives

1 Read the advertisement. Underline all the words that end in **-er**. Then answer the questions.

COUNTERFEIT MONEY DETECTOR

Protect your business against counterfeit money!

Our new machine for checking bills is faster than the old machines. And our machine is easier than the old machines. All you do is put a bill in the machine. If the bill is counterfeit, an alarm bell will ring. It's as easy as that! Counterfeit protection is here. Buy the **Counterfeit Money Detector** today, and you can sleep well tonight.

You have to be smarter than the counterfeiters! Buy our machine.

Counterfeit Money Detector—$450
Call today. Call 1-800-12-MONEY

---

1. What three words did you underline?

   _____

   _____

   _____

2. What word follows each of these words?

   _____

The words you underlined are **adjectives in the comparative form**.

Making Money **61**

COMPARATIVE FORM OF ADJECTIVES

1. Use the **comparative** form of adjectives to compare two people, places, or things.	Our new machine is **faster** than the old machine. You have to be **smarter** than the counterfeiters.
2. If the adjective has **one syllable**, add **-er** to make the comparative. Add only **-r** if the word ends in **-e**.	fast fast**er** old old**er** large large**r**
3. When a one-syllable adjective ends in a consonant + vowel + consonant, **double the last consonant** and add **-er**.	big big**ger** hot hot**ter**
4. If a **two-syllable** adjective ends in **-y**, change **y** to **i** and add **-er**.	easy eas**ier** busy bus**ier**
5. Some adjectives have **irregular** comparative forms.	good **better** bad **worse**
6. For most adjectives that have **two or more syllables**, add *more* before the adjective to make the comparative.	In the past it was **more difficult** than it is today to counterfeit money.
7. Use **than** after the comparative form and before the second person, place, or thing. If the second person, place, or thing is understood, do not use **than**.	Dixon is **faster *than*** Amy. This machine is **more expensive *than*** that one. Bart doesn't like his bicycle. He wants to buy one that is **faster**.

UNIT 3

2 Two high school students are bored in class, so they are passing notes back and forth on a piece of paper. Complete the notes with the comparative form of the adjective in parentheses.

Can you believe how boring this class is? Aargh! This is even __more boring__ than Shoemaker's history class!
1. (boring)

Yeah. I'm almost asleep over here. Did you hear what Tom did last weekend? Wow. It's even _____ than any of the crazy things I did last summer at camp.
2. (bad)

No. What?

You know that old car of his? He really wanted to buy a _____ one. But he didn't have any money. So guess what he did?
3. (good)

He stole money from his parents?

No, he did something much _____ than that! He copied a $100 bill on his family's new scanner and printed it out with their color printer.
4. (crazy)

Wow! Doesn't he know counterfeiting is illegal?

I know. I told him. But he said he's _____ than most car salesmen. He says they won't even know the money is fake.
5. (smart)

This is _____ than anything he's ever done. He could go to jail!
6. (dangerous)

I know. I told him all that too. He just said making money this way is _____ and _____ than getting a job. Can you believe it?
7. (easy)   8. (fast)

Tom's crazy! He's really going too far this time!

Making Money 63

3 *Read the descriptions of two anticounterfeit machines. Then write sentences comparing the two machines. Use the adjectives from the box.*

Electronic Cash Scanner

$525

Will last for 10 years

TO USE: Place bills in machine and wait a few seconds for machine to electronically scan them.

If bills are counterfeit, a red light flashes and an alarm sounds.

Currency Validator Pen

$19.95

Will test up to 5,000 bills

TO USE: Make a small dot on each bill with the pen. Wait for the color to turn dark brown (counterfeit) or to turn yellow (good).

If bills are counterfeit, a dark brown spot appears on bill.

bad	difficult (to use)	expensive	good	slow
cheap	easy (to use)	fast	large	strong

1. The electronic cash scanner is stronger than the currency validator pen.
2. _____
3. _____
4. _____
5. _____
6. _____
7. _____
8. _____
9. _____
10. _____

C WRITING

In this unit, you read about counterfeit money and counterfeit products like CDs, sports shoes, designer clothes, and watches.

You are going to **write a paragraph about a counterfeit product** of your choice. You are going to tell what the product is, where you can buy the product, and how you can tell it is fake. Finish your paragraph by saying if you think it's a good idea to buy this product. Use the vocabulary and grammar from the unit.*

◀ PREPARE TO WRITE: Clustering

One way to get ideas for your paragraph about a counterfeit product is by **clustering**. Clustering helps you **see your ideas** and **how they are connected**. In a **cluster diagram**, the topic is in a large circle in the middle. New ideas are in smaller circles and are all connected to the topic.

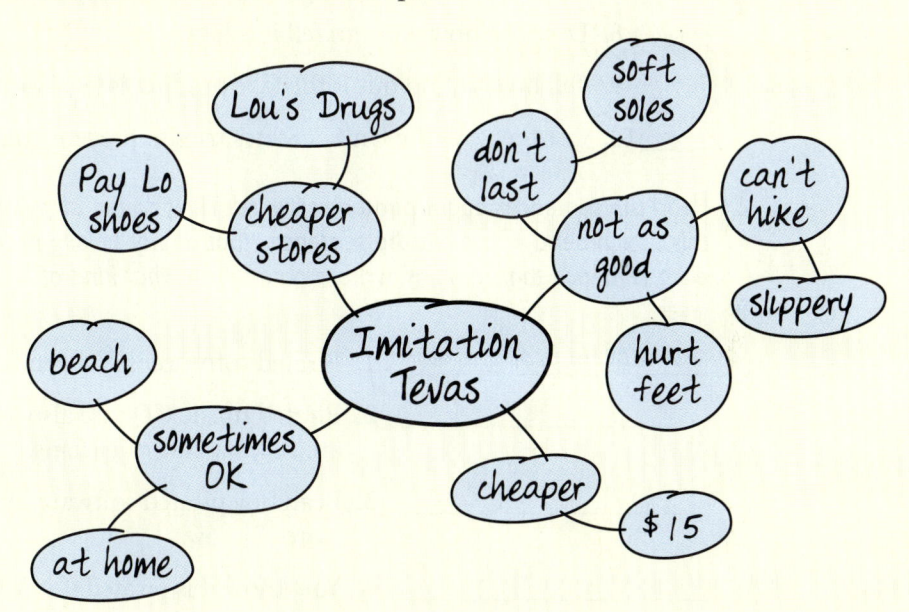

Make a cluster diagram for your product. Write the name of the product in the circle. Then link your ideas to the circle as you think of them.

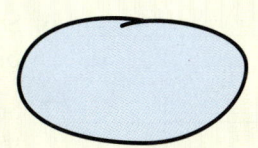

---

*For Alternative Writing Topics, see page 69. These topics can be used in place of the writing topic for this unit or as homework. The alternative topics relate to the theme of the unit, but may not target the same grammar or rhetorical structures taught in the unit.

WRITE: A Well-Organized Paragraph

To write a well-organized paragraph, you need to **select the right information**. Read the **directions** for your writing assignment carefully. They can often help you organize your ideas by telling you **what information to include**.

1 Go to page 65 and reread the directions for writing your paragraph about a fake product. Then read the list and check off the information you need to include. Cross out the things that you don't need to include in your paragraph.

_____ 1. ~~Describe counterfeit money.~~

_____ 2. Tell if you think it's a good idea to buy the product.

_____ 3. Tell exactly how much the counterfeit product costs.

_____ 4. Tell what the product is.

_____ 5. Tell about a time a store checked to see if the money you used was counterfeit.

_____ 6. Tell where to buy it.

_____ 7. Describe the people who make the product.

_____ 8. Describe how you can tell it is fake.

_____ 9. Tell how to find out if the fake product is legal or not.

_____ 10. List the ways the United States tries to prevent counterfeiting products.

2 Read the sentences about pirated software. They do not all belong in a paragraph for this assignment. Cross out the sentences that do not belong in this paragraph. Next to each sentence that remains, write a note telling what kind of information the sentence gives.

what the product is 1. Pirated software is one product that is counterfeit.

_____ 2. Pirated music CDs are also a big problem, and they are very bad for musicians.

_____ 3. I can buy pirated software in some small computer stores I know.

_____ 4. You know it is pirated if it is very cheap.

_____ 5. You can tell the software is pirated if the label is from a copy machine.

_____ 6. Sometimes the seller gives you a CD that has no printing on it.

_____ 7. Sometimes real copies of software cost more than a thousand dollars.

_____ 8. I think it is wrong to buy pirated software because it is like stealing from the company.

3 Now list the information you need to include in your paragraph. Then write the first draft of your paragraph.

1. Tell what the product is: _____
2. Tell where to buy it: _____
3. Describe how you can tell it is fake: _____
4. Tell if you think buying the product is a good idea: _____

REVISE: Giving Explanations

Can a reader actually tell the difference between the fake product you describe and the real product? A reader often needs **more information**, **more detail**, and **more explanations**.

1 Read the paragraph about Teva sandals. The reader wanted more information to really help him or her tell the difference. Look at the questions he or she wrote.

How can I tell?

Teva sandals are good sandals for hiking, but there are a lot of imitation Tevas in stores. It is easy to tell the difference. Real Tevas are stronger than fake Tevas. They are also more expensive. Real Tevas have the logo on them. Fake Tevas are OK to wear in your house, but if you plan to walk a lot, you should get real ones.

How much do real and fake ones cost?

What does the logo look like?

Now the writer has rewritten the paragraph. See how much clearer it is.

Teva sandals are good sandals for hiking, but there are a lot of imitation Tevas in stores. It is easy to tell the difference. Real Tevas are stronger than fake Tevas. If you pinch the soles with your fingers, Tevas will feel hard, but imitations will feel soft, like a pillow. Real Tevas are also more expensive. They cost about $85, but you can get them on sale for $40 sometimes. If you are paying only $25 or less, the sandals are probably not real Tevas. Real Tevas have the logo on them. The logo is a hand with a spiral in the middle. Fake Tevas are OK to wear in your house, but if you plan to walk a lot, you should get real ones.

2 With a partner, read the following paragraph and write questions where you need more detail, just as the reader of the Teva paragraph did.

> I like Chanel perfume, but I have to be careful to buy real Chanel and not fake. Guys sell fake Chanel perfume on the sidewalk in Los Angeles. The bottles are the same shape as real Chanel, but the label looks different. If you put the fake perfume on, it has the wrong smell. Fake Chanel is cheaper than real Chanel. But if you buy it, you waste your money because it smells very bad.

3 Share first drafts with a partner. Write questions on your partner's draft. The questions should help your partner give more information about how to tell the difference between the fake and the real product he or she describes.

4 Now look at your first draft and at your partner's questions. Give more information about how to tell the difference between the fake and the real product you describe.

EDIT: Writing the Final Draft

Write the final draft of your paragraph. Carefully edit it for grammatical and mechanical errors, such as spelling, capitalization, and punctuation. Make sure you used some of the vocabulary and grammar from the unit. Use the checklist to help you write your final draft. Then neatly write or type your paragraph.

✓ FINAL DRAFT CHECKLIST

- ○ Is your paragraph well organized? Does it have the right information?
- ○ Does your paragraph tell about a counterfeit product?
- ○ Does it tell where you can buy this counterfeit product?
- ○ Does it explain how you can tell that this product is fake?
- ○ Does it give your opinion about why it is or isn't a good idea to buy this product?
- ○ Do you use comparative adjectives correctly?
- ○ Do you use new vocabulary that you learned in this unit?

ALTERNATIVE WRITING TOPICS

Write about one of the topics. Use the vocabulary and grammar from the unit.

1. Write a paragraph comparing casual counterfeiters to professional counterfeiters. Use the information from the readings and from the exercises.

2. Suppose that you work in a store and that your boss asks you to choose an anticounterfeiting tool for the store and to write her an e-mail about it. You decide the store should buy the cash scanner.

   Look back at the exercise on page 64. Find one sentence you wrote that gives a reason why the pen is better. Find three sentences that give reasons why the scanner is better. Use these sentences to write your e-mail.

3. The word *counterfeit* applies to anything fake. For example, you can buy counterfeit Levi's jeans, counterfeit music CDs, or counterfeit computer software.

   Making counterfeit computer software is a crime. People copy expensive software and then sell it for less than it costs in the stores.

   Write a paragraph comparing counterfeiting computer software to counterfeiting money. Which one is more difficult? Which is a more serious crime? Explain.

RESEARCH TOPICS, see page 226.

Making Money **69**

UNIT 4
A Different Path to Justice

> Now I'm getting good at tagging. This one looks great!

> For tagging a storefront, first apologize to Mr. Kim. Second, go back to his store and repaint the wall you tagged.

Judge Williams

> I'm sorry.

1 FOCUS ON THE TOPIC

A PREDICT

Look at the comic strip and discuss the questions with the class.

1. Who are these people? What are they doing?
2. Do you agree with the judge?
3. How do you think the store owner feels about the teenager tagging his building? How do you think he feels about what the judge decided?

71

B SHARE INFORMATION

Look at the comic strip.

The Crime — mugger, victim — "Guilty! One year in prison!"
The Arrest
The Judgment — "One year for a mugging... It isn't fair!"
Prison — "There is no justice for people like us, my friend."

Now complete the chart and discuss your answers with the class.

STATEMENT	AGREE	DISAGREE
1. Mugging is a serious crime.		
2. Muggers should go to prison.		
3. They should go to prison for a long time (at least 10 years).		
4. They should do community service (cleaning the parks, for example).		
5. They should go to a psychiatrist for treatment.		
6. They should pay money to their victims.		
7. They should tell their victims, "I'm sorry."		
8. If they broke something, they should fix it.		

BACKGROUND AND VOCABULARY

Read the U.S. justice facts. Try to understand the boldfaced words without looking them up in a dictionary.

U.S. JUSTICE FACTS

- In 2004, two million people were in **prison** in the United States. These people lost their freedom because they broke the law[1].

- In 2003, the teenage **offenders** in prison were 15 percent female and 85 percent male. Of adults in prison, 23 percent were female and 77 percent were male.

- In the United States, **crime** is connected to money and jobs. People without jobs don't have money, and some will do things that are against the law to get what they need.

- The most common time for teenagers to **commit crimes** is during the first hour after school gets out. During school hours, teenagers are too busy to cause trouble.

- Some crimes hurt people. Other crimes hurt things such as cars, houses, or school buildings. Teenagers commit most of the crimes involving **damage** to things.

- People of all ages can have their cars or money stolen. People of all ages can be mugged. But teenagers are **victims** of crime more often than adults.

- To fight crime, people sometimes create **community** watch groups. In these groups, neighbors carefully watch what happens on their street and call the police when they see something unusual.

- In the U.S. justice system, the offenders may feel bad for what they did to the victims. But the offenders don't usually get to **apologize** to the victims for the pain they caused.

- Each year about 35 million people are hurt as a result of crime. Sixty-seven percent of these people will **heal** in body and mind within a month of the crime. Thirty-one percent will take 6–12 months to heal. A very small number of people will take years.

- Living in neighborhoods with a lot of crime **affects** people's health. A study shows that Americans who live in low-crime neighborhoods exercise 30–50% more than people who live in high-crime neighborhoods.

---

[1] **broke the law:** did something illegal or against the law

A Different Path to Justice

Now choose the best definition for each boldfaced word. Circle your answer.

1. **prison**	a. a locked place where criminals stay	b. a place where people study
2. **offender**	a. the person who did the crime	b. the person hurt by the crime
3. **crime**	a. dirt from the city	b. an action that is illegal or against the law
4. **commit a crime**	a. to do something against the law	b. to stop someone from causing a crime
5. **damage**	a. the thing that was stolen or taken	b. the harm that is done to something
6. **victim**	a. the person who did the crime	b. the person hurt by the crime
7. **community**	a. all the buildings in one place	b. all the people in one place
8. **apologize**	a. to say you are sorry for something you have done	b. to pay someone money
9. **heal**	a. to grow	b. to make something healthy again
10. **affect** (someone)	a. to make a change in someone	b. to hurt someone

2 FOCUS ON READING

A READING ONE: Vote for Restorative Justice

Before the last elections, the people of Littleton, Nevada, received a flyer telling them about a new program called "Restorative[1] Justice" and asking them to vote for it.

Read the title of the flyer and answer the questions. Then read the whole flyer. Were your guesses correct?

1. What kind of a program is "Restorative Justice"?
2. What is this flyer trying to do?

---
[1] **restorative:** bringing back to a whole or healthy state

74 UNIT 4

Restorative JUSTICE
- prevents **crime**   - supports **victims** of crime   - builds stronger **communities**

✓ *Vote YES for Restorative Justice for Littleton.*

1 What is Restorative Justice?
Crime hurts people. It hurts communities. Restorative justice helps people and communities **heal**. Victims get a voice. **Offenders** take responsibility for their actions.

2 How does Restorative Justice work?
STEP 1 : MEETING

In a face-to-face meeting, victim and offender take turns telling their story of the crime; what happened before, during, and after the crime; how the crime **affected** their lives; and how they feel about it.

STEP 2 : COMPENSATION[1]

The offender and the victim decide together how the offender will compensate for the **damages** caused by the crime. Sometimes offenders pay money to the victim. Sometimes they fix what was broken. Always they **apologize** for the pain they caused the victim, and sometimes that is all the compensation the victim wants.

3 Why do we need RJ?
We should stop filling our **prisons** with young men and women. Prison alone does not stop crime. Almost 50 percent of the men and women in U.S. prisons have been there before. And at the cost of $40,000 a year per person, prison is very expensive. We need to try something new.

4 How does RJ prevent crime?
When offenders go through RJ programs, they change. They feel differently about crime. They take responsibility for their actions. For the first time ever, many offenders begin to understand the victim's feelings. They work to make things right.

Seventy percent of offenders who go through restorative justice programs do not **commit crimes** again. They don't return to prison.

Restorative justice makes communities safer and saves money.

5 How does RJ help victims?
Victims get answers to their questions about the crime. They help decide what the compensation should be. Victims who go through RJ programs feel safer and less afraid than those who do not.

6 Won't RJ programs put dangerous criminals back on our streets?
NO. A restorative justice program is not *instead* of prison. It's *in addition* to prison. If an offender is in prison for 30 years, the restorative justice program won't change that. But both victim and offender can still meet and learn from each other. In all restorative justice programs, both offenders and victims must *choose* to be in the program. Usually really dangerous criminals won't. But many people who commit smaller crimes will. And most people who do enter restorative justice programs will not return to prison.

We don't need bigger prisons. We need Restorative Justice.

✓ *Vote YES for Restorative Justice.*

---

[1] **compensation:** money or services that someone receives because he or she has suffered injury, loss, or damage

◀ **READ FOR MAIN IDEAS**

Circle the best ending for each sentence.

1. The point of this flyer is _____.
    a. to tell people how bad the prison system is in their town
    b. to teach people what a restorative justice program is
    c. to convince people to vote for a restorative justice program in their town

2. Restorative justice _____.
    a. stops crime
    b. makes communities safer and stronger
    c. helps police put offenders in prison

◀ **READ FOR DETAILS**

These statements are false. Correct them. Change a word or phrase in each statement to make it true.

1. Restorative justice has ~~three~~ *two* main steps.

2. In the face-to-face meeting of a restorative justice program, the offender apologizes to the criminal.

3. The offender always pays money to the victim.

4. Most offenders who go through a restorative justice program are likely to commit a crime again.

5. Victims who go through a restorative justice program feel less safe than those who don't.

6. The victims and their families decide together what compensation the offenders should make for the crime.

7. Restorative justice programs work against the traditional justice system.

◀ **MAKE INFERENCES**

Read each statement in the chart. Decide who might say that statement. Check (✓) the box for the appropriate person.

STATEMENT	OFFENDER	VICTIM	PRISON WORKER
1. "It helped me understand why this happened to me."		✓	
2. "Now that we have that RJ program, I'm seeing fewer offenders back in prison."			
3. "I'm very sorry. I'll never do this again."			
4. "Until I heard his story, I really didn't understand how much pain I caused by doing what I did."			
5. "I thought I was going to hate her forever, but when I saw how young and scared she looked, I started to think maybe I could learn to stop hating her."			
6. "I wanted to ask him, 'Why me?'"			

EXPRESS OPINIONS

Discuss the questions with a partner. Then share your answers with the class.

1. In your opinion, restorative justice will work best for which kinds of crime?
2. Imagine your city tries to start a restorative justice program. Will you vote for or against such a program? Give your reasons.

B READING TWO: Moving Past the Crime

In Reading One you read a flyer describing how restorative justice works. Now you will read a magazine article about two people, one victim and one offender, who participated in a restorative justice program.

Read the article.

MOVING PAST THE CRIME
by Jack Billings

1 On May 30, 2006, 53-year-old Adam Carson was driving to work. While he was waiting at a stoplight, a truck crashed into his car. The driver of the truck was 21-year-old Lee Giron, and he was drunk[1]. Lee walked away from the crash, but Adam was killed.

2 Valerie Carson, Adam's wife, said, "I wanted to kill the man who killed my husband. I was so angry. So hurt. I wanted to scream at him—to tell him what it's like to have my whole life taken away. I didn't want him to *just* go to prison. I wanted him to *do* something to help me."

3 At 21, Lee was surprised and sad that the accident killed the older man. But in the months that followed, he mostly worried about going to prison. In the end, the court found Lee guilty of drunk driving, and he went to prison for one year. In prison, he didn't think about the accident or the Carsons. He thought only about what he wanted to do when he got out. When asked if he wanted to be in the restorative justice program at his prison, he was afraid. He felt terrible and didn't want to meet the wife of the man he had killed. What could he say to her? But finally he agreed. Valerie too was afraid to meet the man who had killed her husband. But she was still in so much pain, she thought maybe meeting him could change how she felt. She too agreed to be in the program.

4 At their first meeting, Valerie told her story. She described her anger, her sadness, and her fears. Lee listened, and at the end of her story he apologized to her. At their second meeting, Lee told his story. At their third meeting, Valerie and Lee decided what Lee could do to compensate for the damage. "Nothing could ever bring my husband back," Valerie says. "But I felt if people could hear Lee's story, another life might be saved." And so Lee and Valerie agreed to work together giving talks to young people about drunk driving. This is how Valerie found herself traveling around the country for four years, working with the man who killed her husband. "Restorative justice helped me to stop seeing Lee as a monster[2]. It helped me learn to forgive him."

[1] **drunk:** when someone has had too much alcohol
[2] **monster:** someone who is cruel and evil

Now answer the questions and discuss them with your class.

1. What was the crime that Lee committed?
2. What compensation did Valerie and Lee agree upon?
3. How did restorative justice help Valerie?

C INTEGRATE READINGS ONE AND TWO

◀ STEP 1: Organize

*Reading One (**R1**) gives descriptions of how restorative justice works and why it helps. Reading Two (**R2**) provides examples. Look at the list of sentences based on Readings One and Two. Then complete the chart, answering each question with the appropriate sentences.*

- Lee will probably never drink and drive again.
- Offenders come to understand the pain they caused the victim.
- Valerie learned to forgive Lee.
- Offenders and victims decide together what the offender can do to make things better for the victim.
- ~~Lee and Valerie share their stories of the accident, and Lee apologizes to Valerie.~~

QUESTION	DESCRIPTIONS (R1)	EXAMPLES (R2)
1. How does RJ work?	a. Offenders and the victims sit down together and share their stories of the crime. b.	a. Lee and Valerie share their stories of the accident, and Lee apologizes to Valerie. b. Lee agrees to travel around the country with Valerie giving talks to young people about drunk driving.
2. How does RJ help victims?	a. Victims can heal their pain from the crime.	a.
3. How does RJ prevent crime?	a. b. For many offenders, this understanding changes how they think and act.	a. Lee was able to say he was sorry. b.

A Different Path to Justice

STEP 2: Synthesize

Imagine you are Valerie Carson (Reading Two). A reporter would like to ask you a few questions for an article he is writing about the Littleton restorative justice program (Reading One). Use information from the chart in Step 1 to answer the questions.

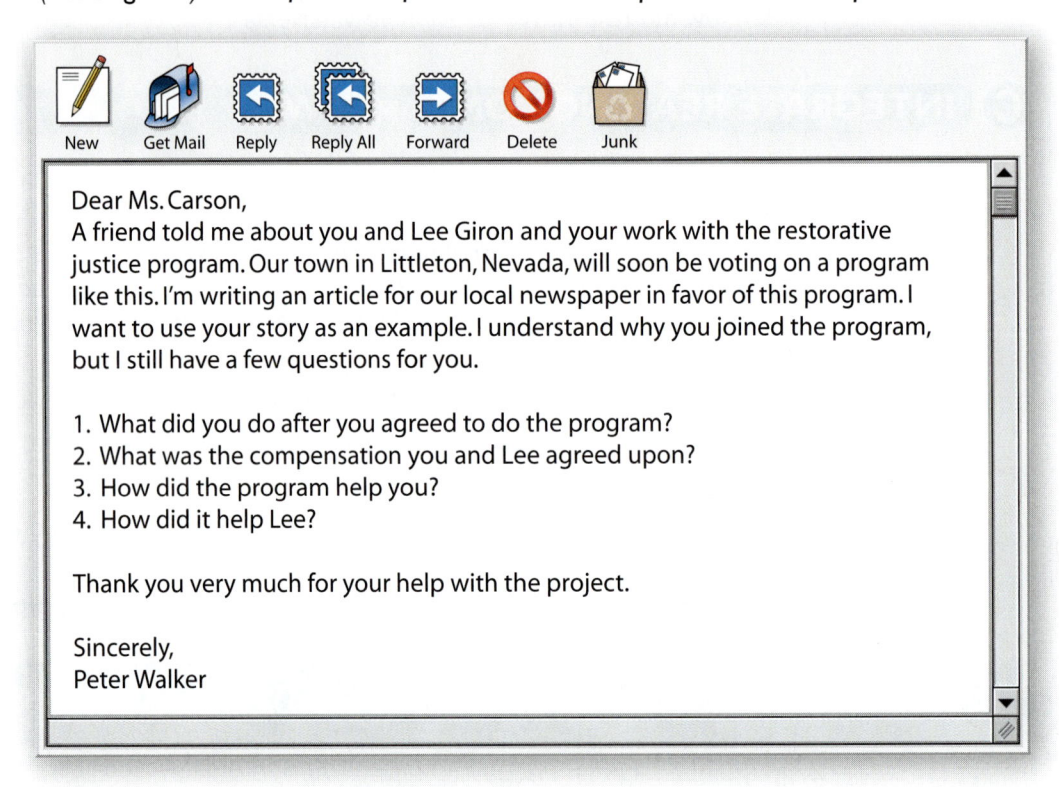

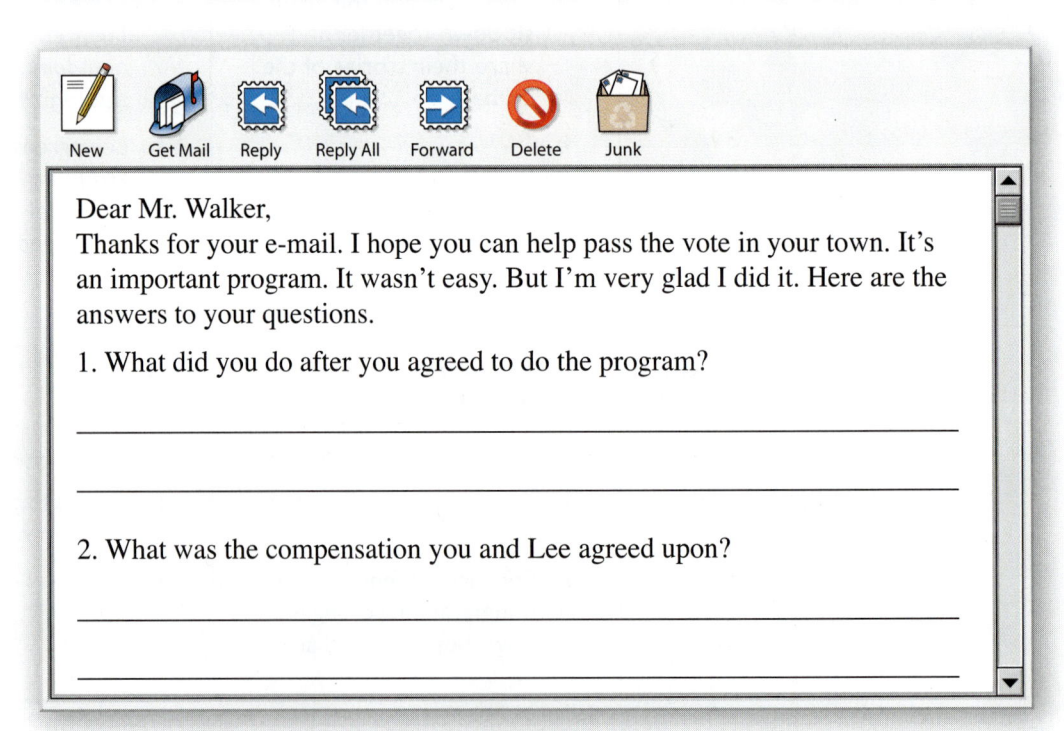

Dear Ms. Carson,

A friend told me about you and Lee Giron and your work with the restorative justice program. Our town in Littleton, Nevada, will soon be voting on a program like this. I'm writing an article for our local newspaper in favor of this program. I want to use your story as an example. I understand why you joined the program, but I still have a few questions for you.

1. What did you do after you agreed to do the program?
2. What was the compensation you and Lee agreed upon?
3. How did the program help you?
4. How did it help Lee?

Thank you very much for your help with the project.

Sincerely,
Peter Walker

Dear Mr. Walker,

Thanks for your e-mail. I hope you can help pass the vote in your town. It's an important program. It wasn't easy. But I'm very glad I did it. Here are the answers to your questions.

1. What did you do after you agreed to do the program?

_____

_____

2. What was the compensation you and Lee agreed upon?

_____

_____

3. How did the program help you?

_____

_____

4. How did it help Lee?

_____

_____

I hope this information helps. Good luck on the vote.

Sincerely,
Valerie Carson

3 FOCUS ON WRITING

A VOCABULARY

◖ REVIEW

Cross out the word or phrase that is not related to the boldfaced word.

1. **victim**: hurt, ~~house~~, offender
2. **crime**: law, police, medicine
3. **offender**: car, law, wrong
4. **community**: people, neighborhood, country
5. **affect**: change, cause, stop
6. **heal**: hurt, increase, get better
7. **damage**: tagged wall, beautiful car, broken window
8. **apologize**: happy, sorry, take responsibility
9. **prison**: school, criminals, justice
10. **forgive**: apology, sorry, gift
11. **guilty**: excited, responsible, wrong
12. **commit a crime**: go to prison, steal a wallet, mug a person

EXPAND

Read the statement on the left, paying attention to the boldfaced words. Then match the statement with the appropriate response on the right.

__e__ 1. You won't believe this. Some guy **beat up** my roommate last night on the way home from work.

____ 2. Did you hear? Someone **broke into** our neighbors' house yesterday. Luckily, they didn't take anything.

____ 3. Can you believe it? Someone **robbed** our house while we were away on vacation.

____ 4. This neighborhood is getting safer. Ten years ago we had a lot of **burglaries**. This year we haven't had one.

____ 5. I was mugged a couple weeks ago, and I'm having a hard time **getting over it**.

____ 6. My sister **changed her ways** when she became a mother. Before she had kids, she went out with her friends almost every night.

____ 7. My mother can't **make peace** with her brother after their big fight.

a. She must still be so angry at him.

b. That's great. I hear crime in general is down in your part of town.

c. But still, that's awful. Did they come through a window?

d. That's not surprising. I think people try to live better lives when they become parents.

e. That's terrible. Did he hurt him badly?

f. Well, of course you are. It was a terrible thing. You must still feel really scared.

g. That's awful. What did they take?

CREATE

A newspaper reporter is writing an article about crime in your hometown. She e-mailed you some questions.

Dear Residents of _____,
I'm writing to ask your opinions of crime in your hometown. I'm interested in your answers to the following questions:

- Who is involved in crime?
- What kinds of crime take place in your town?
- What does your community do to heal from the crimes in your town?
- What can people do to lower the amount of crime in your town?

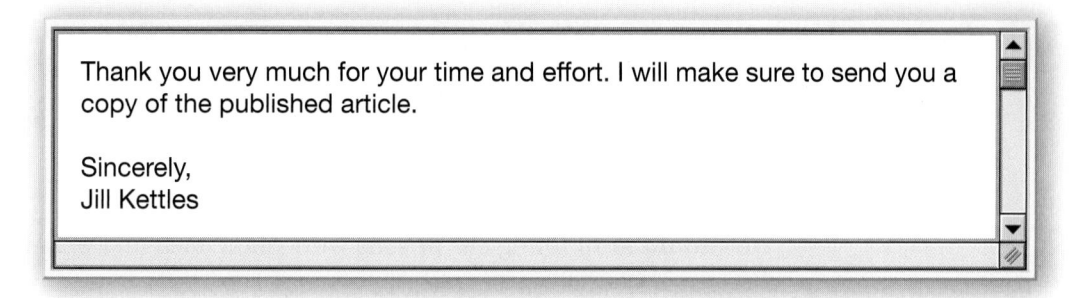

> Thank you very much for your time and effort. I will make sure to send you a copy of the published article.
>
> Sincerely,
> Jill Kettles

Now respond to Jill Kettles' e-mail. Use some of the words in parentheses in your answers to her questions.

Dear Ms. Kettles,

In general, crime in _____ is _____.
　　　　　　　　　　(name of your town)　　　*(not so bad / pretty bad)*

As for your questions, see my answers below:

Who is involved in crime?

_____
(victims / offenders)
_____

What kinds of crime take place in your town?

_____
(commit a crime / damage / break into / beat up / tagging / mugging / robbery / guilty)
_____

What does your community do to heal from the crimes in your town?

_____
(community / affect / heal / get over / make peace with)
_____

What can people do to lower the amount of crime in your town?

_____
(forgive / prison / get over / change one's ways)
_____

Sincerely,

_____
(your name)

A Different Path to Justice

B GRAMMAR: *Should, Ought to,* and *Shouldn't* for Giving Advice

1 *Read the excerpt from Reading One. Notice the boldfaced words. Then answer the questions below.*

> We **should stop** filling our prisons with young men and women. Prison alone does not stop crime.

1. Why did the writer of the flyer use *should*?
2. What form of the verb follows *should*?

SHOULD, OUGHT TO, AND SHOULDN'T FOR GIVING ADVICE

1. Use **should** or **ought to** to give advice or talk about what is a good thing to do.	In U.S. cities, you **should** always lock your car when you park. Women **ought to** hold their purses close to them when walking down busy streets.
2. Use **should not** or **shouldn't** to give advice or say that something is not a good idea. (**Ought to** is rarely used in the negative.)	Children **should not** talk to strangers. You **shouldn't** walk home from the subway alone after dark.
3. **Should** and **ought to** are used for both present and future.	You **should** call your mother now and tell her you arrived safely. You **ought to** fix that lock tomorrow.
4. Always use the **base form** of the verb with **should, shouldn't,** and **ought to.**	You **should lock** your doors at night. You **shouldn't give** your credit card number to people you don't know. You **ought to call** the police if you see someone committing a crime.

2 *Complete each statement with **should, ought to,** or **shouldn't** and the correct form of the verb in parentheses.*

Crime has become bad in your town. The police sent a list of simple things that you can do to avoid becoming the victim of a robbery or a mugging.

1. You _____ doors and windows when you leave your house.
   (lock)

2. You _____ your purse in your car.
   (leave)

3. You _____ the police if you see someone looking in your
   (call)
   neighbor's windows.

4. When walking to your car at night, you _____ someone to walk
   (ask)
   with you.

5. At night, you _____ around before getting out of your car.
   (look)

6. If you're the victim of a mugging, you _____ the mugger. You
   (fight)
   _____ him all your money.
   (give)

7. When walking alone at night, you _____ on your cell phone.
   (talk)
   When you talk on your cell phone, you don't look like you are paying attention.

8. You _____ into a car with someone you don't know.
   (get)

3 Friends from a faraway country are visiting you in your hometown. They will spend the day on their own as you go to work or school. Give them a list of things they **should, ought to,** or **shouldn't** do to keep safe in your town.

Example

When you ride the bus, you **should** keep your bags in front of you.

1. _____
2. _____
3. _____
4. _____

C WRITING

Imagine you received a pre-election flyer like the one in Reading One. Your hometown is trying to decide if it should spend public money on a restorative justice program.

You are going to **write a letter to the editor** of your local newspaper, **explaining why you think this program is or isn't good** for your town. You will try to persuade (convince) the reader to agree with your opinion. Use the vocabulary and grammar from the unit.*

---

*For Alternative Writing Topics, see page 91. These topics can be used in place of the writing topic for this unit or as homework. The alternative topics relate to the theme of the unit, but may not target the same grammar or rhetorical structures taught in the unit.

A Different Path to Justice **85**

PREPARE TO WRITE: Charting

Before writing, it can be helpful to **make a chart** of the **advantages and disadvantages** of the issue. To help you decide if you think your hometown should vote for a restorative justice program, you will complete a chart.

1 *To help you complete the chart, discuss the questions with a classmate.*

1. Does the justice system in your town help stop crime?
2. Does it help victims get over the crime?
3. Does it help offenders change their ways so they live better lives?

2 *Using information from your discussion, write at least two reasons **FOR** and two reasons **AGAINST** a restorative justice program in your hometown.*

REASONS TO VOTE *FOR*	REASONS TO VOTE *AGAINST*
1. Crime is high, and prison doesn't seem to help.	1. There isn't a lot of crime in my town. Our justice system seems to work well.
2.	2.
3.	3.
4.	4.

3 *Look at your chart carefully. Decide how you will vote. Write a clear statement of your opinion.*

WRITE: A Letter to the Editor

The purpose of a **letter to the editor** is to **persuade or convince** the newspaper reader to agree with your opinion. A letter to the editor has the following three parts:

> 1. introduction
> 2. statement of your opinion
> 3. reason(s) for your opinion

1 Read the letter to the editor. Then circle the introduction and underline the writer's statement of opinion and reason(s) for it.

> To the editor:
> I'm 18 years old, and I know a lot of teenagers. I know some kids at my school do things to this old lady on our street. They tag her garage or steal her mail. They don't think about her or how much these things affect her life. They just do it to joke with their friends. I think we should have a restorative justice program in this town because it would teach kids like these guys to understand and care about other people. I think it would make them stop.
>
> Sandy Slater
> Omaha, Nebraska

Introduction: In a letter to the editor, you are writing to people who don't know you. If you want to persuade people who don't know you, you must show them that **you have experience or knowledge** that makes your opinion important.

2 Read the two letters to the editor. Which person seems to know more about the topic: Nancy or Theodore? Check (✓) **A** or **B**. Discuss your answer with a partner.

A. ○

> To the editor:
> Ten years ago my son was arrested for drunk driving. He spent two months in prison. It changed his life forever. He hated being locked up. He was embarrassed and ashamed[1]. He promised himself he would never again do anything to get arrested. It made him a more responsible man. As a result, he has changed his ways and no longer drinks and drives. I think our current justice system works well. We don't need a new program in this town.
>
> Nancy Moore
> Carbondale, Illinois
>
> ───────────────
>
> [1] **ashamed:** feeling guilty or uncomfortable because of something you said or did

A Different Path to Justice

B. ○

> To the editor:
> I live in Seattle, but I grew up in Berlin, Germany. I think our police force is a good one. I always see them out on the streets. They are very friendly. I think they do a good job. We don't need to change anything with our justice system. It works well just as it is. We don't need a restorative justice program in this town.
>
> Theodore Ewing
> Bainbridge Island, Washington

3 Read the introduction in this letter to the editor. Cross out the information that does not help the reader believe this writer.

> To the editor:
> I grew up in Stanton. I've lived in Stanton my whole life. My mother and father used to live in Chicago. They moved to Stanton two months before I was born. Two years ago a man broke into my car and stole my purse and my radio. I know the guy was caught and arrested. But I don't know anything else. I have questions. Who was he? Why did he choose my car? Why did he take the money? I want to talk to him to get the answers to these questions. Also, I want to have a voice in what happens to him. I don't care if he goes to prison. I want him to buy me a new radio. That's why I will vote for the restorative justice program. I want victims to be included in the justice system.
>
> Amy Breslau
> E. Yarmouth, Maine

4 Write a sentence or two describing an experience you had that makes your opinion on restorative justice important. Your experience can be about a crime that happened to you or someone you know, or it can be about a crime you saw.

_____

_____

_____

5 Now write the first draft of your letter to the editor. Use your ideas from the previous sections. Be sure to include an introduction and a clear statement of your opinion.

REVISE: Providing Specific Reasons

When you try to persuade someone of your opinion, it's important to provide **specific reasons**. Often writers make the mistake of using reasons that are too general. Specific reasons will make your opinion **more persuasive**.

1 *Read the first draft of a letter to the editor. Underline the reason the writer gives for voting for the restorative justice program.*

A.

> To the editor:
> I moved to Oakland 25 years ago. Since that time, I've seen a lot of kids from my neighborhood sent to prison for small crimes. Most of these kids are good kids. But prison can make them hard. I'm voting for the restorative justice program. I think it will help these kinds of kids. We should all vote for the restorative justice program to keep our kids out of prison.
>
> Alicia Gonzalez
> Oakland, California

Now read the same letter with an improved reason. Underline the reason. Discuss with a partner why the reason in the revised letter is stronger than the reason in the first letter.

B.

> To the editor:
> I moved to Oakland 25 years ago. Since that time, I've seen a lot of kids from my neighborhood sent to prison for small crimes. Most of these kids are good kids. But prison can make them hard. I'm voting for the restorative justice program. I think it will give these kids the chance to learn how their actions affect other people. They will have to make peace with the person they hurt. We should all vote for the restorative justice program.
>
> Alicia Gonzalez
> Oakland, California

2 *Read the statement of opinion. Then check (✓) the reasons that best support the opinion. Discuss your answers with your class.*

> I think we should have a restorative justice program in our town.

_____ 1. I like the ideas in the restorative justice program. I think it will be a good thing for the people here in town.

_____ 2. The traditional system doesn't stop offenders from committing crimes again, and this new program will.

_____ 3. This program is better than the traditional justice system for the people of our town, and we need the best for our town.

_____ 4. Our current system doesn't help victims. This program helps victims heal from the pain of crime and gives them a chance to ask for compensation.

3 *Read the letter to the editor. Underline the reason for the writer's opinion. In the space provided, write a stronger reason with specific details.*

> To the editor:
> I've lived in this town a few years. I work for the police department. I see what happens to our town's criminals. Mostly, the criminals are teenagers who have nothing to do. They are bored and young. I think the restorative justice program will help kids. It is a great idea for a small town like ours.
>
> _____
> _____
> _____
> _____

4 *Now go back to the first draft of your letter to the editor. Look at your reasons. Rewrite them to make them as specific as possible.*

◀ EDIT: Writing the Final Draft

Write the final draft of your letter to the editor. Carefully edit it for grammatical and mechanical errors, such as spelling, capitalization, and punctuation. Make sure you used some of the vocabulary and grammar from the unit. Use the checklist to help you write your final draft. Then neatly write or type your letter.

> ✓ **FINAL DRAFT CHECKLIST**
>
> ○ Does your letter have the three main parts of a letter to the editor?
> ○ Does your introduction show that you know this topic well?
> ○ Do you give a strong statement of your opinion?
> ○ Do you give specific reasons for your opinion?
> ○ Do you use *should, ought to,* and *shouldn't* correctly?
> ○ Do you use new vocabulary that you learned in this unit?

ALTERNATIVE WRITING TOPICS

Write about one of the topics. Use the vocabulary and grammar from the unit.

1. Have you ever been the victim of a crime? In two or three paragraphs, describe the crime. Describe where it happened, what time of day it was, and what each person was doing before the crime. What happened to you after the crime? What happened to the offender? Do you think the traditional justice system worked well in this case?

2. Restorative justice offers victims the chance to forgive the offender. Do you think every victim can or should forgive the crime? Why or why not? Express your opinion in a letter to the editor.

RESEARCH TOPICS, see page 226.

UNIT 5
Subway Etiquette

The New York City Subway

① FOCUS ON THE TOPIC

A PREDICT

Look at the pictures and discuss the questions with the class.

1. What do the signs under "Please" mean?
2. Are there other things that people shouldn't do in the subway? Give one or two examples.
3. Are there rules of politeness that people should follow in the subway? Give one or two examples.

B SHARE INFORMATION

What happened the last time you took the subway, the bus, or the train? Were the other passengers polite? What did they do that was not polite?

Check (✓) the items that best complete the statement. Compare your answers with a partner.

On the subway, bus, or train, I think it is not polite when other passengers _____.

____ talk on a cell phone

____ take more than one seat

____ talk to me

____ don't talk to me

____ look at me

____ don't give their seats to elderly people

____ (*your idea*) _____

____ (*your idea*) _____

C BACKGROUND AND VOCABULARY

Inside a New York City subway car

Subway etiquette is the set of politeness rules for the people who ride (take) the subway. Other public transportation like buses or trains have similar rules. Some of these rules are written, like the ones shown by the signs on the previous page. But rules of etiquette are also often unwritten. Some examples of unwritten rules of etiquette in the New York subway are *Don't talk to people you don't know* and *Don't sit next to someone you don't know if there are other seats available.*

1 What do you do in the following situations? Take the quiz to see what kind of New York subway rider (passenger) you might be. Read each situation, then circle your answer. Pay attention to the boldfaced words.

SUBWAY ETIQUETTE QUIZ

1. You are trying to enter the subway station, but your MetroCard[1] doesn't work.
   - **A** You shout **rude** words and hit the turnstile[2] with your hand until a police officer comes to see what's going on.
   - **B** You quickly try two more times, then ask a subway employee for help.
   - **C** You try ten more times and say to the people waiting behind you: "You can never **rely on** these stupid machines! They are always broken!"

2. Your train arrives. As the doors open, you see that there are several people who want to get off the train.
   - **A** You stand to the side so that you don't **block** the way.
   - **B** You push through the doors as fast as you can to find a seat.
   - **C** You stand in front of the door and let people go around you to get off.

3. An **elderly** woman gets on the train. She looks for a seat, but there are no more seats left. You have a seat.
   - **A** You pretend to be asleep so that you don't **make eye contact with** her.
   - **B** You stay where you are and tell her to hold on to the **pole** when the train starts moving.
   - **C** You stand up and give your seat to the woman.

4. You have a cold and begin to **sneeze** on a crowded train. Someone hands you a tissue[3].
   - **A** You take it, say thank you, and **blow your nose**.
   - **B** You pretend not to notice.
   - **C** You ask, "Is there a 'no sneezing' rule? Is it your job to **enforce** it?"

---

[1] **MetroCard:** name of the card you need to have to ride the subway or the bus in New York City
[2] **turnstile:** a gate that spins around and only lets one person through at a time
[3] **tissue:** a paper handkerchief for wiping noses

Add up your points using this key.

1. Your score:	2. Your score:	3. Your score:	4. Your score:	Your total score:
A—0 points	**A**—2 points	**A**—1 point	**A**—2 points	_____
B—2 points	**B**—0 points	**B**—0 points	**B**—1 point	_____
C—1 point	**C**—1 point	**C**—2 points	**C**—0 points	_____

If your score is:

8 points: New York is proud to have you riding its subway. Thank you for being an excellent example of **civilized** behavior.

6-7 points: You have a few things to learn about how to behave in New York's subway. Watch other riders more carefully to learn about subway **etiquette**. And study the NYC Transit rules of conduct.

5 points or less: Please get a car. Or move to an island in the middle of the Arctic Ocean. Learn some **manners**.

Subway Etiquette

2 Look back at the boldfaced words in the quiz. Then match the words on the left with the definitions on the right.

__j__ 1. rude
____ 2. rely on (something)
____ 3. block
____ 4. elderly
____ 5. make eye contact with (someone)
____ 6. pole
____ 7. sneeze
____ 8. blow your nose
____ 9. enforce (something)
____ 10. civilized
____ 11. etiquette
____ 12. manners

a. to make sure that people do something that they are supposed to do
b. to blow air through your nose suddenly (saying "Aaaaatchoo!")
c. polite ways of behaving (*That child has no ___!*)
d. to expect something to work right
e. a long round piece of metal for holding onto
f. to stand in the way
g. old
h. to look someone in the eyes
i. to clean your nose with a tissue when you have a cold
j. not polite; hurtful
k. organized so that people are nice to each other and take care of each other
l. a set of politeness rules

2 FOCUS ON READING

A READING ONE: A Civilized Suggestion

Editorials are articles in newspapers where writers give their opinions. The following editorial is from the City section of a New York newspaper.

Read the title and the first paragraph of the editorial. What do you think the writer's suggestion might be about? Check (✓) your answer.

____ 1. good places to visit on the subway
____ 2. the restaurants with the best service in New York
____ 3. how to make the subway nicer to ride
____ 4. how to get around New York without riding the subway

Now read the editorial and see if your guess was right.

96   UNIT 5

A CIVILIZED SUGGESTION

BY DAN FORMAN

1. There is a very long list of rules for the New York City subway. Don't put your feet on a seat, don't carry open cups of coffee or soda, don't take more than one seat, don't ride while drunk ... Those are just a few of the rules. There are hundreds more.

2. So with this many rules, why is it still so unpleasant to ride the subway?

3. Some people think that the problem is that no one **enforces** the rule s. There aren't enough subway police, and the ones we have are too busy catching people who don't pay. Other passengers sometimes try to enforce rules. But you can't **rely on** them because New Yorkers have unwritten rules of **etiquette** against talking to strangers and **making eye contact with** strangers. How can you tell someone to take her shopping bags off the seat and throw away her Coke without talking to her or looking at her? It is difficult.

4. There are other New Yorkers who think that the subway is unpleasant because there are not *enough* rules. One rider wrote a letter to *The New York Times* a couple of weeks ago suggesting a few more subway rules. Here are some of the rules that she would like to see:

   - Don't lean[1] on the **poles**. You prevent other people from holding on. They can fall down.
   - Talk quietly. The trains are already too noisy.
   - Cover your mouth and nose when you **sneeze** or cough. Other riders don't want to catch your cold.
   - If your MetroCard doesn't work after three tries, ask a subway employee for help. Don't **block** the entrance.
   - Give your seat to **elderly** passengers or to parents with small children.

5. Of course, anyone who knows the subway probably agrees that those are great ideas for rules. But polite people already do all of those things. If those unwritten rules of etiquette are written down, will the **rude** people be more likely to follow them? Will anyone enforce them? It doesn't make sense to make more rules that no one will enforce.

6. The real problem is that we are forgetting how to be nice to each other. It is embarrassing that we need a rule to tell us to give our seat to elderly passengers. Nobody should need to be reminded to do that.

7. I say we stop talking about the rules and try to remember our **manners**. Let's be nice to each other not because a police officer might tell us to get off the train, but because it is the right thing to do. *Then* New York City would be more **civilized**—both above ground and below.

[1] **lean:** to support yourself against a wall or other surface

READ FOR MAIN IDEAS

Check (✓) the sentence that best describes the main idea of Reading One.

_____ 1. The New York subway has plenty of rules, but police officers need to work harder to enforce them.

_____ 2. People have lots of ideas about how to make the New York subway more pleasant to ride, but I think that we all need to just remember our manners.

_____ 3. Elderly passengers often have to stand up on the New York subway. All passengers need to work to enforce the etiquette rules about this.

_____ 4. New York has many etiquette rules, such as *Don't make eye contact* and *Don't talk with people you don't know.*

READ FOR DETAILS

Circle the best ending for each sentence.

1. The New York subway has _____.
   a. a long list of rules
   b. only a few very important rules
   c. no rules

2. The writer thinks that riding the New York City subway is _____.
   a. always a good experience
   b. very difficult
   c. not pleasant

3. Some people think that _____ should enforce the rules more.
   a. strangers
   b. police and other passengers
   c. passengers who take more than one seat

4. *Don't make eye contact* and *Don't talk to strangers* are examples of _____.
   a. general etiquette in New York City
   b. rules that one rider would like to have on the subway
   c. New York subway rules

5. *Don't lean on the poles* and *Talk quietly* are examples of _____.
   a. rules that one rider would like to have on the subway
   b. New York subway rules
   c. rules that police officers enforce

◀ **MAKE INFERENCES**

Read the opinions. Which ones do you think the writer of "A Civilized Suggestion" might have? Check (✓) them and discuss your answers with a partner.

_____ 1. It is more important to do things that you know are right than to let a police officer tell you what to do.

_____ 2. The problem is that the subway doesn't have enough etiquette rules.

_____ 3. We need more police on the subway system.

_____ 4. A civilized city should not need a lot of rules about good manners.

_____ 5. People used to be more polite.

_____ 6. Everyone knows what good manners are if they just think about it a bit.

◀ **EXPRESS OPINIONS**

Discuss the questions with a partner. Give your opinions. Then share your answers with the class.

1. Do you think that public transportation (buses, subways, trains) where you live is unpleasant to ride?

2. After reading "A Civilized Suggestion," do you think that New York's subway is less pleasant than the subway or bus in other cities? What makes you think so?

3. Which opinion do you agree with? Why?

   _____ a. We need more police to make people more polite.

   _____ b. We need more rules to make people more polite.

   _____ c. We just need to remember our manners.

B READING TWO: Riding the Subway in Japan

Read this blog from a San Francisco woman about subway etiquette in Tokyo.

http://www.shellystravelingblogspot.net

Riding the Subway in Japan

1 I was riding the 30 Stockton bus today through Chinatown, watching a group of young American women. They got really annoyed at the Chinese women who were pushing their way onto the bus. It made me think of an experience I had in Japan a few years ago, when *I* was living in a culture I did not grow up in.

Shelly is an English teacher who has traveled and taught in many countries, including Japan.

About Shelly

(continued on next page)

Subway Etiquette   **99**

2 I was in my second year of living in Tokyo. I thought I was a real expert in Japanese etiquette and culture.

3 I knew that I had to push gently onto the subway cars. I knew that I shouldn't make eye contact with people. I knew that blowing my nose loudly "American style" was very rude. And I knew that I shouldn't talk to people on the subway. That wasn't a problem, because my Japanese wasn't that good.

4 But one day, I was riding home from work on the subway and I remembered that I needed to call a friend about meeting for dinner. I took out my new cell phone and called her. Of course, if you know the Tokyo subway, you know that there are "no cell phones" signs everywhere. But I also noticed that many passengers used their phones on the subway. I thought that the no cell phones rule in Japan was like the no food rule on the New York City subway. It's a rule, but no one follows it, and no one enforces it.

5 As I was talking, other passengers looked at me sideways like Japanese people do when they think you are being rude. One elderly woman shook her head and looked straight at me.

6 I finished my conversation, and I got off the train. I was very confused. Japanese people use their phones. Why can't I do the same? I asked myself.

7 Later that evening, I told my friend about the experience. She smiled. "The sign says *no talking*," she said. "The others are all text messaging[1] or playing games on their phones. Sometimes they check their voicemail. Occasionally they whisper[2] a very short message to someone on a cell phone. But they never have whole conversations on their phones in the subway."

8 I was embarrassed.[3] I still had a lot to learn. Even though I knew a lot of Japanese habits, I was still American.

---

[1] **text messaging:** sending a written message on a cell phone
[2] **whisper:** speak very quietly
[3] **embarrassed:** feeling ashamed; feeling like you did something stupid

Circle the best answer to complete each statement.

1. The writer _____ in Japan.
   a. went on vacation
   b. lived

2. The writer thought that she understood _____.
   a. Japanese subway etiquette
   b. the Tokyo subway system

3. One thing that she did not understand was _____.
   a. how to use her cell phone
   b. when it is OK to use a cell phone on the subway

4. The other passengers looked at her when she _____.
   a. had a conversation on her cell phone
   b. tried to speak Japanese

5. When Japanese people use their cell phones on the subway, they are _____.
   a. having long conversations with their friends
   b. text messaging or playing games

C INTEGRATE READINGS ONE AND TWO

STEP 1: Organize

Read the list of rules (written and unwritten) mentioned in the two readings. Which rules are for the New York City subway, and which are for the Tokyo subway? Which rules are for both New York City and Tokyo? Check (✓) the correct column.

SUBWAY ETIQUETTE RULES	NYC SUBWAY	TOKYO SUBWAY
1. Don't put your feet on a seat.		
2. Don't carry open cups of coffee or soda.		
3. Push gently when getting on crowded subway cars.		
4. Don't ride while drunk.		
5. Don't make eye contact with strangers.		
6. Talk quietly.		
7. Don't take more than one seat.		
8. Don't talk to strangers.		
9. Don't blow your nose loudly.		
10. Don't talk on your cell phone.		

◀ **STEP 2: Synthesize**

Complete the conversation between Shelly, the blogger from Reading Two, and her friend Rachel. Rachel just got a job in Tokyo. Use information from the chart in Step 1.

RACHEL: I am a little nervous about riding the Tokyo subway. I have seen pictures of those guys who push you into the train cars. Do you have any advice?

SHELLY: Don't worry about the pushers. They are only at a few stations and only at the busiest times. But there are a couple of other things you should know about riding the Tokyo subway.

RACHEL: Like what?

SHELLY: Well, some rules of etiquette are different from the ones we have here in the New York subway. For example, _____
_____
_____ .

RACHEL: That's good to know. Anything else?

SHELLY: No, most of the other rules are the same as here in New York. For example, _____
_____ .

RACHEL: OK! Well thanks for the tips. I am sure they will be helpful.

SHELLY: No problem. Have a great time!

3 FOCUS ON WRITING

A VOCABULARY

◀ **REVIEW**

Read "An Open Letter to Subway Riders." Decide what kind of word (noun, adjective, or verb) you need to fill each blank. Look at the lists in the box. Choose the correct word from the appropriate list and write it in the blank.

Nouns	Adjectives	Verbs	
eye contact	civilized	blocking	rely on
manners	elderly	blow your nose	sneeze
pole	rude	enforce	

102 UNIT 5

An Open Letter to New York Subway Riders

Being a New York subway rider like you, I know that in our subway it is _____ to talk with strangers, and I also
                                                1.
know that we should not make _____ with each other.
                                    2.
But I think that we, New York subway riders, are forgetting some basic rules of etiquette.

Yesterday, I was on the A Train when a very _____
                                                        3.
man got on the train. As the train started to go, the poor man had to hold on to a _____ so that he didn't fall down. There
                    4.
were young people sitting in the seats around him. None of them moved. There was no one to _____ the "give your seat
                                                5.
to elderly passengers" rule, so I stood up. I was far from the old man, so I called to him and he started to come my way. He certainly wanted a seat. But there was a woman who was
_____ the way. So the poor man had to stand there. To
       6.
make things worse, there was a kid next to him who seemed to have a terrible cold. He started to _____ on the old
                                                        7.
man. I wanted to hand that kid a tissue and tell him "Just
_____," but I didn't.
       8.

I thought that New York was a _____ city, but I
                                        9.
guess I was wrong. You can't _____ anyone here to
                                    10.
have good _____ anymore.
              11.

◀ EXPAND

What is the correct response to each of the statements? Match each statement with a response from the list below. Each response can be used more than once.

Statements

__a__ 1. I gave my seat to a woman with three small children yesterday. It felt like the **polite** thing to do.

____ 2. My newspaper blew out of my hands when the train came. I didn't want to **litter**, but I couldn't pick the paper up off the tracks.

____ 3. I did not have a MetroCard, and I didn't have time to **wait my turn** at the MetroCard machine, so I just jumped over the turnstile.

____ 4. I know that it is **impolite** to talk on a cell phone on the bus. But I just found out that my father was in the hospital.

____ 5. Where I come from, it's polite to say hello to other people on a long bus ride. So I **greeted** everyone when I got on the bus to Chicago.

____ 6. I felt bad that I didn't **tip** the taxi driver. But my wallet was stolen earlier today, and I only had enough money for the taxi ride.

____ 7. I **stood in line** to wait for the train in London, since that was what everyone else seemed to be doing.

Responses

a. Good, you **followed the rules**. That was the right thing to do.

b. You **broke the rules**. You shouldn't do that.

c. What you did is **against the rules** of etiquette in the United States. These are unwritten rules, but they are still rules that you should learn.

d. Well, that's an **exception**. In unusual situations it is OK not to follow the rules.

◀ CREATE

Read the letters to an advice column about public transportation etiquette. Write a response to each letter. Try to use the words in parentheses for each one.

1.
> I am always annoyed when I take a taxi and I pay the driver, and he asks if I want change. Is that rude or am I crazy?
> — John, Chicago

Dear John: (against the rules of etiquette / tip)

Asking "Do you want change?" is not against the rules of etiquette. The driver is trying to save you time. You can simply say "Yes, I want change" and then decide how much money you want to tip the driver.

104   UNIT 5

2.

> I take the train to work every morning. I always buy a newspaper to read on the train, and then I leave it on my seat for someone else to read. My husband says that I should throw it away. I think other people might want to read it. What do you think?
> — Michelle, Washington D.C.

Dear Michelle: (follow the rules / litter / impolite)

_____
_____
_____

3.

> I just arrived here in New York from Togo, West Africa, to study for a year. I ride buses everywhere. But sometimes I get a little lost. I am afraid to ask the bus drivers for help because there are big signs on all the buses that say *Do not talk to the driver*. I am afraid to even say hello to the driver. How can I ask if I am on the right bus without breaking the rules?
> — Aliou, New York City

Dear Aliou: (apply / manners / greet / exception)

_____
_____
_____

4.

> Yesterday I was coming home from the airport on the airport bus. There were two guys who did not wait their turns to get on. They just pushed ahead of everyone else. Then they started smoking. Smoking!! Can you believe it? I had to sit right in front of them. They were speaking some other language and laughing. I was so mad I couldn't speak to them. They are not civilized at all! What can we do about people like this?
> — Sage, Seattle

Dear Sage: (break the rules / enforce / stand in line / rude)

_____
_____
_____

Subway Etiquette

B GRAMMAR: Imperative Sentences

1 Underline the verbs in the list of suggestions from Readings One and Two. Then answer the questions.

- Don't lean on the poles.
- Talk quietly.
- Cover your mouth and nose when you sneeze or cough.
- Don't block the entrance.
- Give your seat to elderly passengers or to parents with small children.
- Please don't talk on your cell phone.

1. Is there a subject in any of the sentences above?
2. Who is expected to do the things listed above?

IMPERATIVE SENTENCES

1. Use the **imperative** when you want to give clear **directions** or **orders**.	**Cover** your mouth and nose. **Talk** quietly. **Don't block** the entrance.
2. To form the imperative, use the **base form** of the verb.	**Take** your feet off the seat. **Push** gently.
3. In the **negative**, use **don't** before the **base form** of the verb.	*Don't lean* on the pole.
4. The **subject** of an imperative sentence is always **you**. We never state the subject unless we are addressing someone in particular.	CORRECT: **Talk** quietly. INCORRECT: **You talk** quietly. **Mario**, talk quietly.
5. To make a **polite request**, use the imperative with *please* at either the beginning or end of the sentence. If *please* is at the end of the sentence, there is a **comma** before it.	*Please* don't talk on your cell phone. Be quiet, *please*. Don't push, *please*.

106 UNIT 5

2 *Make imperative statements. Use the correct form of the verbs in parentheses.*

1. _____ on airplanes.
   (smoke / not)
2. _____ your cell phone at the movies.
   (turn off)
3. _____ your iPod in class, please.
   (take off)
4. _____ at a concert.
   (sing / not)
5. _____ in a red zone.
   (park / not)
6. _____ your taxi driver at least 10 percent.
   (tip)

3 *Rewrite the rules or suggestions for polite behavior, using the imperative. Remember that you can use "please."*

1. People shouldn't play loud music on the bus.

   _____

2. There is no smoking on the bus.

   _____

3. You should always say hello to your driver.

   _____

4. Shawn, you know that it's against the rules to talk to the driver.

   _____

5. Making eye contact with strangers is against New York's rules of etiquette.

   _____

C WRITING

In this unit, you read about subway etiquette in New York and Tokyo. Now think about a city you know well. What kind of etiquette does it have on its public transportation (subway, buses, taxis, trains, etc.)?

You are going to **write a Web page about etiquette on a type of transportation** in that city. First, you will give some information about the type of transportation you chose. Then you will give a list of important rules of etiquette for this type of transportation. Use the vocabulary and grammar from the unit.*

---

*For Alternative Writing Topics, see page 111. These topics can be used in place of the writing topic for this unit or as homework. The alternative topics relate to the theme of the unit, but may not target the same grammar or rhetorical structures taught in the unit.

PREPARE TO WRITE: Listing

Listing is making a **list of your ideas** before you begin to write. When you make a list, it is not necessary to write complete sentences.

1 *Choose a type of public transportation that you know well. Fill in the city or town and type of transportation you are writing about. List all of the rules that you can think of.*

City or Town: _____

Type of Transportation: _____

Rules of Etiquette: _____

_____

_____

_____

_____

_____

2 *Look at your list and cross out the rules that are less important. Keep the rules that are the most important. You should list about five rules.*

WRITE: A Web Page

A **Web page** is a place on the Internet that **gives information** about a particular subject. So, writing a Web page is writing to inform. When you write to inform people about something, you often write **in the "second person"** (using *you*, not *I*). This is not the place to tell your own stories. You should include only **general information** about the subject you are writing about.

1 *Look at the two introductions to a Web page about the Portland streetcars. Check (✓) the one that gives you the clearest information about streetcars in Portland.*

A. ○

www.portlandcares.org

Remember Your Manners Month: Portland, Oregon
A Civilized Way to Ride the Streetcars

Streetcars in Portland are very easy to use. The system is very new, so the cars are nice and clean. The best thing about them is that they are free in the center of town. You can ride through downtown as much as you want, and you don't have to pay. If you go outside of the downtown area, you can buy a ticket.

108 UNIT 5

B. ○

Remember Your Manners Month: Portland, Oregon
A Civilized Way to Ride the Streetcars

I thought the streetcars in Portland were very easy to use. I've never been on such clean streetcars! They were much nicer than the streetcars where I live. I went downtown every day, and I never paid any money at all. The only time I paid was when I went to the airport.

2 *Look at this introduction to a Web page about the London Tube. Rewrite each sentence so that it is not about the writer.*

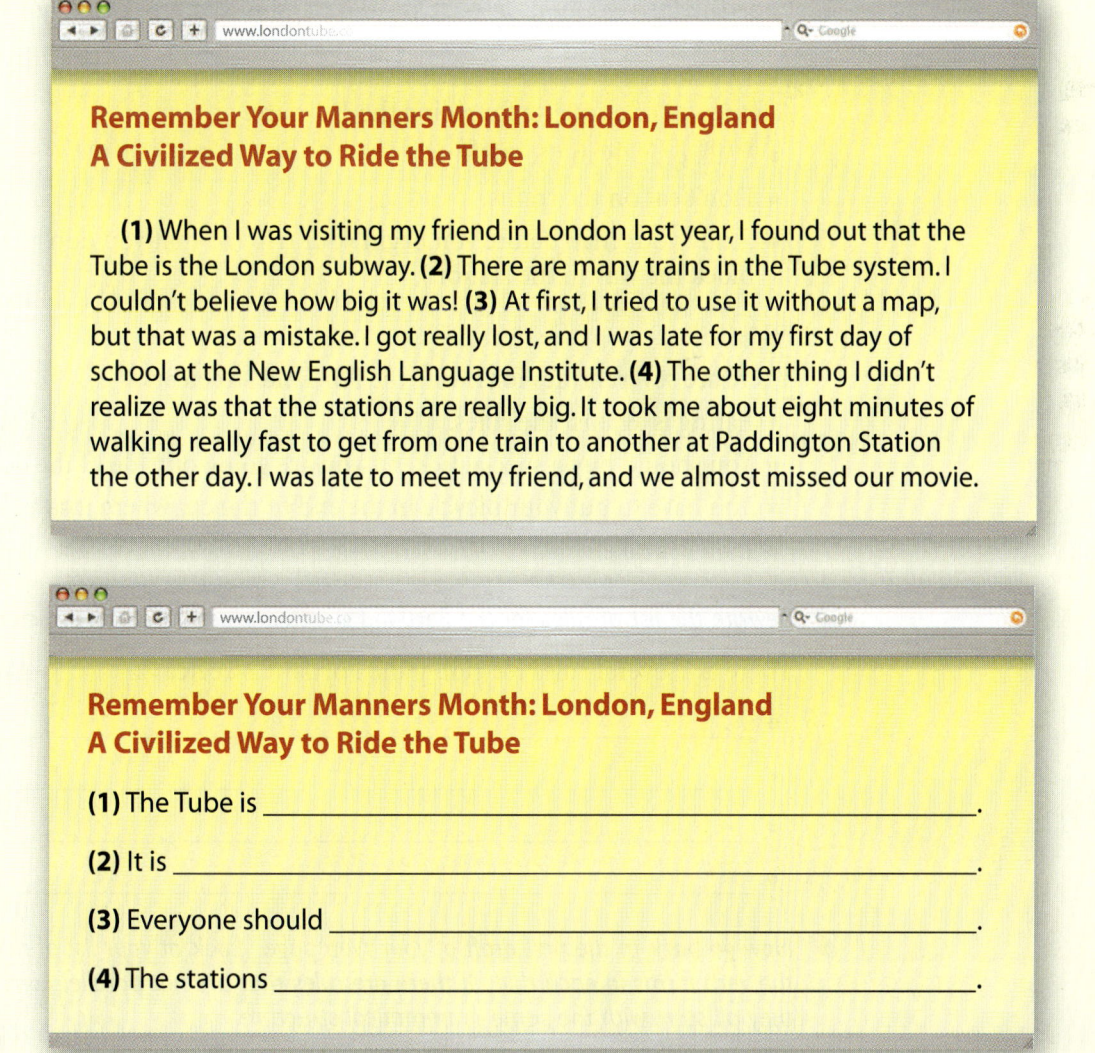

Remember Your Manners Month: London, England
A Civilized Way to Ride the Tube

(1) When I was visiting my friend in London last year, I found out that the Tube is the London subway. **(2)** There are many trains in the Tube system. I couldn't believe how big it was! **(3)** At first, I tried to use it without a map, but that was a mistake. I got really lost, and I was late for my first day of school at the New English Language Institute. **(4)** The other thing I didn't realize was that the stations are really big. It took me about eight minutes of walking really fast to get from one train to another at Paddington Station the other day. I was late to meet my friend, and we almost missed our movie.

Remember Your Manners Month: London, England
A Civilized Way to Ride the Tube

(1) The Tube is _____.

(2) It is _____.

(3) Everyone should _____.

(4) The stations _____.

Subway Etiquette   **109**

3 Now write the first draft of your Web page about etiquette on a type of transportation in the city of your choice.

1. Use the following type of title:

   Getting Around in _____ OR **Riding the** _____

2. Write an introduction where you give some important information about the type of transportation that you are writing about.

3. List a few rules (written or unwritten) that riders should know about.

◀ REVISE: Using Parallel Structure

When you write a **list**, it is a good idea to make all of the items in the list **parallel**, that is **starting with the same grammatical structure** (noun, verb form, gerund, etc.). This makes them clearer and easier to read. Lists that use different grammatical structures at the beginning of each item can be difficult to read.

1 *Underline the verb forms in each list. Which list is clearer? Check (✓) **A** or **B**.*

A. ○

A few rules of etiquette for riding the Tube are:
- Walk quickly in the stations.
- Don't eat on the trains.
- Study your map before you begin your trip (so that you don't have to stop and block the way in the station).

B. ○

There are several rules for riding the Portland streetcars:
- Eating is against the rules.
- You should buy a special ticket if you are going outside of the downtown area.
- You have to put your bicycle in the end of the car where it says "Bikes."
- Don't smoke.

2 *Rewrite the list of rules for the Portland streetcars, using parallel structure.*

There are several rules for riding the Portland streetcars:

- _____
- _____
- _____
- _____

3 *Now go back to the first draft of your Web page. Look at your list of rules and underline the verb forms in each rule. If there are rules that are not parallel, correct them so that they all start with the same grammatical structure.*

◀ **EDIT: Writing the Final Draft**

Write the final draft of your Web page. Carefully edit it for grammatical and mechanical errors, such as spelling, capitalization, and punctuation. Make sure you used some of the vocabulary and grammar from the unit. Use the checklist to help you write your final draft. Then neatly write or type your Web page.

✓ FINAL DRAFT CHECKLIST

- ○ Does the title of your Web page tell where and what kind of transportation you are writing about?
- ○ Does it give general information about this kind of transportation?
- ○ Does it avoid stories from your own personal experience?
- ○ Does it give information that would be useful to a reader who is going to visit this city and take this type of transportation?
- ○ Does your Web page tell about rules for riding this type of public transportation?
- ○ Do the rules in the list all follow parallel structure?
- ○ Do you use the imperative correctly?
- ○ Do you use new vocabulary that you learned in this unit?

ALTERNATIVE WRITING TOPICS

Write about one of the topics. Use the vocabulary and grammar from the unit.

1. What is the best way to get people to be polite to each other? Should there be more police to enforce rules? Should there be more rules? Should there be a general suggestion to remember manners? Or should there be something else? Write a blog giving your opinion. Include examples from your experience to support your opinion.

2. Your newspaper is asking for suggestions for new rules for the public transportation system in your town. Write an e-mail giving your suggestions for rules you would like to see. Be sure to explain what type of public transportation you are writing about.

3. Sometimes people from one culture think that people from another culture are rude. In reality, they are just following different rules of etiquette. Write two paragraphs comparing etiquette in two cultures you know that are very different. What rules might help people in those two cultures get along?

RESEARCH TOPICS, see page 227.

Subway Etiquette

UNIT 6　Serious Fun

1 FOCUS ON THE TOPIC

A　PREDICT

Look at the picture and discuss the questions with the class.

1. What are the children doing?
2. Is this a good way to spend time or not?
3. Can they learn things doing this?

B SHARE INFORMATION

What games do you like? Why are they fun?

Write the name of a game you like. It can be a computer game or a traditional game. Check (✓) the phrases that describe why you think it is fun. Be sure to add some of your own descriptions as well.

A game I like is _____. It is fun because . . .

____ it goes quickly

____ it is very easy

____ it is very difficult

____ it has nice pictures

____ it has a good story

____ it makes me laugh

____ it makes me think

____ it teaches me about _____

____ (your idea) _____

____ (your idea) _____

Discuss the games you like in a small group. Do you all agree on the things that make a game fun?

C BACKGROUND AND VOCABULARY

1 Read the timeline about the history of computer games. Try to understand the boldfaced words without looking them up in a dictionary.

1950–1960s	*OXO*, *TENNIS FOR TWO*, and *SPACEWAR* are the first **digital** games. Only the scientists who have computers can play these games.
1972	*PONG* is invented. It is like tennis on a computer. People stand in line for hours to try out this new kind of **entertainment** at Andy Capp's bar in Sunnyvale, California.

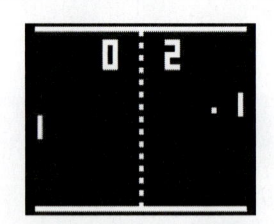

114   UNIT 6

1985 — The Japanese company Nintendo starts selling *SUPER MARIO*. Shigeru Miyamoto is the **designer** of the game. Miyamoto thought about the mountains where he grew up as he created the places where Mario goes.

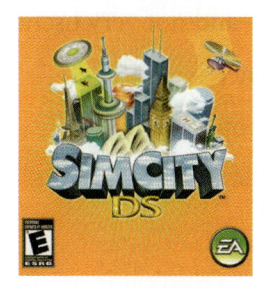

1989 — Will Wright's *SIM CITY* is released. Players in *Sim City* build cities. People who played *Sim City* found out that they were learning **serious** skills from the game. They were learning how to plan cities and buildings. They learned that bad planning can cause many things to go wrong in a city. Some *Sim City* players became architects[1].

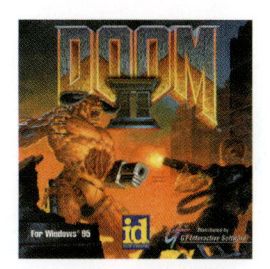

1993 — John Carmack and John Romero **combine** very real-looking computer art with a game to create *DOOM*. In *Doom*, players have to kill monsters and other creatures in order to survive or stay alive. It's a **survival** game. Like all games of this type, it is quite **violent**.

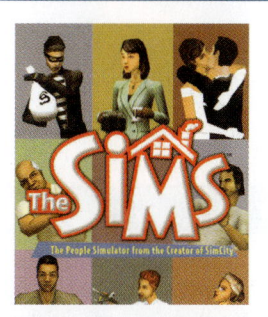

1993 — Will Wright shares his new idea for *THE SIMS* with people at his company. In *The Sims*, players take care of a family and manage their daily activities such as going to school, paying bills, and working. The people Wright works with think the game sounds **childish** and that adults won't be interested in it. They don't **take his idea seriously**. (Another company liked the idea. *The Sims* went on sale in 2000. It earned over $1 billion from 2000 until 2006.)

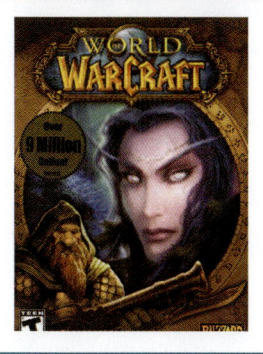

2004 — *WORLD OF WARCRAFT* (*WOW*) is released. *WoW* is an Internet game. It is very **complex** because you play against thousands of other people, not against the computer. When you play against the computer, you can usually see the computer's **pattern** after a while. You know what the computer is going to do. You understand how it thinks. But it is much harder to **figure out** what another person will do.

---

[1] **architects:** people who make the plans for houses or other buildings

Serious Fun

2 *Circle the best synonym¹ for each boldfaced word or phrase.*

1. **digital:** sports / (computer) / competition
2. **entertainment:** interesting food / delicious drink / fun thing to do
3. **designer:** person who created the product / person who drew the picture on the box / person who sells the product
4. **serious:** very sad / important and useful / funny and not very useful
5. **combine:** draw carefully / win easily / put together
6. **survival:** dying / staying alive / helping other people
7. **violent:** full of ugly monsters / full of loud music / full of guns and killing
8. **childish:** for girls / for children / cold
9. **take** (something) **seriously:** think it is important / think it is funny / sell it for a lot of money
10. **complex:** full of new ideas / slow and boring / complicated with lots of parts
11. **pattern:** solution / thing that repeats / big problem
12. **figure out:** understand / listen to / make a problem for

---

¹ **synonym:** a word with the same meaning as another word

2 FOCUS ON READING

A READING ONE: Serious Fun

The following article was in the *Los Angeles Times* the week before the E3 (a big game design meeting and show). The author, Raph Koster, is a game designer.

What do you think the title of the article might mean? Check (✓) all of the answers you think are possible.

Serious Fun might mean:

_____ 1. Computer games are fun, not serious.

_____ 2. Fun is important and useful for our lives.

_____ 3. The E3 is serious but not really fun.

_____ 4. Games can be both fun and serious.

_____ 5. Serious people never have fun.

Now read the article to see if your answers were correct.

116 UNIT 6

Serious Fun

by Raph Koster

1. STARTING ON WEDNESDAY, tens of thousands of visitors will come to Los Angeles to kill **digital** dragons[1] and shoot digital guns. They are gamers, and they will be here for the Electronic Entertainment Games Expo (E3), where game **designers** show what is new in the business.

2. Gaming is **serious** business. Seventy-five percent of American homes now have video and computer games, and gaming now earns as much money as the film business each year. Yet most people still think that computer games are **childish** and **violent**. They think that they are just silly **entertainment**.

3. Let me tell you why serious people should **take** gaming **seriously**.

4. Recent studies show that the brain[2] is really good at finding **patterns** and then doing something called "chunking"—**combining** several steps or pieces of information into one. For example, we don't need to remember all the steps of how we get dressed in the morning. Over time, we see a pattern to the steps and chunk them together. Gradually, we learn to do these things without thinking.

5. Do you remember locking your door this morning? Do you remember putting your keys away? Probably not, because your brain "chunked" these steps into "the things you do every morning." This is a good thing because if you really have to think about locking the door, your brain doesn't have the energy to notice other things (for example, the banana peel that your neighbor's three-year-old dropped in front of your door!).

6. Finding patterns and chunking information are so important for human **survival** that our brains make us feel good when we do it. Our word for this feeling that our brain sends us is "fun." Unfortunately, most people think that fun cannot be serious, when it is actually the reward we get for learning.

7. This is where games come in. Games are all about learning. Games let us practice seeing patterns, which is why they are so much fun.

8. "But some games are boring!" you say? Of course, as soon as we **figure out** the patterns in a game, the fun ends. Six-year-olds love playing tic tac toe[3]. Adults don't because they already know the pattern. Well-designed games have **complex** patterns. We can figure these complex patterns out little by little, so they stay fun for a long time.

9. There will be some very well-designed games at E3 this week. But most games will be teaching the same old things. There will be a lot of dragons. We won't be seeing too many games about living with climate change[4] or curing[5] cancer. Yet as game designers begin to understand the power of games, I believe they will start working with more serious subjects.

10. For this to happen, however, we all need to take games seriously. We all need to understand that they could one day help us solve some of the world's very big problems.

11. So if you walk past E3 this week, try to be understanding. Remember: Gaming is a very young business and, like most small children, it is loud and confused. When games grow up, they just might save the world.

---

[1] **dragon:** a large imaginary animal that has wings, a long tail, and can breathe out fire
[2] **brain:** the part of the body, in the head, which is responsible for thinking
[3] **tic tac toe:** a game that two people play that looks like this
[4] **climate change:** the world is changing because it is getting warmer
[5] **curing:** finding a medicine or treatment that makes an illness disappear

Source: Adapted from "Good Fun is Not Frivolous," by Raph Koster in *LA Times*, May 15, 2005. Reprinted by permission of Los Angeles Times Reprints.

◖ READ FOR MAIN IDEAS

Complete the main idea of Reading One. Circle one clause in column **B** and one clause in column **C**. Then write the complete main idea on the lines.

A	B	C
Everyone should take gaming seriously	because everyone needs to learn about game design, because games are about learning,	and games could one day help save the world. and the game business is earning as much as the film business now. and learning is good for our brains.

Main Idea

_____

_____

_____

_____

◖ READ FOR DETAILS

Complete the sentence in column **A** with the appropriate phrase from column **B**.

A

1. The computer and video gaming business earns as much money as __c__.

2. Our brains are good at combining ____.

3. Finding patterns is fun, and fun is ____.

4. When we play games, we practice seeing ____.

5. A game with very easy patterns is ____.

6. Most games are about ____.

7. Raph Koster thinks game designers will start to design ____.

8. The E3 looks loud and confused because gaming is ____.

B

a. a very young business

b. patterns

c. the film business

d. a boring game

e. subjects like dragons that are not serious or real

f. the reward we get for learning

g. many steps

h. games that help solve big world problems

118 UNIT 6

MAKE INFERENCES

Put a check (✓) next to all of the words that can complete the sentence.

According to Reading One, a well-designed game is _____.

____ 1. colorful   ____ 6. childish   ____ 11. full of patterns

____ 2. complex   ____ 7. entertaining   ____ 12. about dragons

____ 3. loud   ____ 8. serious   ____ 13. about real problems

____ 4. confused   ____ 9. violent

____ 5. fun   ____ 10. rewarding

EXPRESS OPINIONS

Discuss the questions in a small group. Give your opinions. Then share your answers with the class.

1. Raph Koster says that games are good at teaching. Do you agree? What are some things that you have learned from games? (You can talk about computer games as well as games that are not played on computers.)

2. Koster thinks that games will help us solve big world problems. Do you agree?

B READING TWO: Saving the World with Computer Games

Read the article about serious video games.

Saving the World with Computer Games

1 Last week, I was pushing bags of food out of an airplane to starving[1] people on the ground below. The wind suddenly changed direction, and 48 bags of food almost landed on a group of small houses. My heart jumped. Carlos the pilot yelled at me. I was there to save people, not to destroy their houses.

2 I was playing *Food Force*, a video game in which players have to get food to starving people in countries at war.

3 For a long time, video games have put players in worlds full of dragons or spaceships. But *Food Force* is part of a new generation[2]: games that put people in the real world, full of real problems. And the games' designers aren't just selling entertainment. They say that games can be more than just childish fun, they can actually change the world.

---

[1] **starving:** very hungry; near death because of hunger
[2] **generation:** a group of products that are at the same stage of development

(continued on next page)

Serious Fun   119

4. The *McVideogame* is another serious game in which players run a fast-food company. It's about serious topics, but the game makes you laugh. There are farms for the cows and crops, fast-food restaurants to sell burgers, and an office to run the business. The managers in each place tell the player when something goes wrong. When workers are unhappy because of low pay, the player can fire[3] them. When a law makes it difficult to run the business, the player can bribe[4] the people responsible for enforcing the law. When there isn't much food for the cows, the player can feed them garbage to make them fat. It's very difficult to keep the company running. Most players lose all of the money they started with, and the company goes under[5]. People who play the *McVideogame* learn about the big problems that fast food creates. And many of them decide never to eat fast food again!

5. "Games are really good at helping people understand complex situations," says Suzanne Seggerman, an organizer of the 2006 Games for Change meeting. She explained that people—especially young people—don't pay attention to the newspaper or to TV news. And since there are so many world problems to solve, she asks "Why not try something new?"

---

[3] **fire:** to make someone leave his or her job
[4] **bribe:** to illegally pay money or offer gifts to officials in order to persuade them to do something for you
[5] **goes under:** if a business goes under, it has serious problems and fails

Now read each statement. Decide if it is true or false. Write **T** (true) or **F** (false) next to it. Compare your answers with a classmate's.

_____ 1. The writer of the article was on an airplane last week.

_____ 2. *Food Force* is a game about spaceships and dragons.

_____ 3. Some new computer games are teaching about real-world problems.

_____ 4. The *McVideogame* teaches people how to run a fast-food business.

_____ 5. Suzanne Seggerman thinks that games are a good way to learn about complex situations.

C INTEGRATE READINGS ONE AND TWO

STEP 1: Organize

Look at the outline of the main ideas in Readings One and Two. Fill in the details that illustrate these main ideas. Choose from the list of details.

Dragons

~~Brain sees patterns.~~

Living with climate change

Brain chunks information.

Games let us practice seeing patterns.

Brain sends us feeling that we call "fun."

Well-designed games have complex patterns.

Curing cancer

Spaceships

Teaching problems that fast food creates

Feeding starving people (*Food Force*)

120   UNIT 6

OUTLINE

Main Ideas	Details
1. Learning is fun.	a. Brain sees patterns. b. c.
2. Games are about learning.	a. b.
3. Most games teach childish subjects.	a. b.
4. Serious games might help save the world.	a. b. c. d.

STEP 2: Synthesize

You are part of a parent Listserv (an e-mail group). Every week you get e-mails from people asking for advice about many parenting issues. You get this message.

TO: student@Northstar.com
DATE: June 10, 2007
FROM: ParentNetwork@lists.austin.edu
RE: Advice wanted

My children (ages 11, 13, and 14) love to play computer games. I don't think that all computer games are bad for children. But I do think that some are very violent and give children bad ideas. I don't want my children to learn how to steal[1] cars. (I think that is what they learn in *Grand Theft Auto*. My son plays this game with his friends.) The problem is that I don't know very much about computer games. How do I know which games are good? I don't mind buying games for them. I just want to make sure the kids will stay interested in the games for more than one day. I also want the kids to learn something useful. Does anyone have any advice about what I should look for?
Thanks,
Nancy

[1] **steal:** to take something that doesn't belong to you

Write a response to Nancy. Use information from the outline in Step 1.

TO: ParentNetwork@lists.austin.edu
DATE: June 10, 2007
FROM: student@Northstar.com
RE: Advice wanted

Nancy:

You are right, most games teach …

_____
_____
_____
_____ .

You should look for serious games. They teach …

_____
_____
_____
_____ .

Some examples of serious games are …

_____
_____
_____
_____ .

You should also look for games that are well designed. Well-designed games …

_____
_____
_____
_____ .

Good luck.

Sincerely,

_____
(your name)

3 FOCUS ON WRITING

A VOCABULARY

REVIEW

Complete each sentence with the correct word or phrase from the box.

childish	designer	figure them out	~~survival~~
combine	digital	patterns	take him seriously
complex	entertainment	serious	violent

1. *World of Warcraft* is about death, but *Food Force* is about ___survival___.
2. People who make games create complicated problems. Players try to _____.
3. Some people play games to learn things for work, but I only play for _____.
4. A good computer game is quite simple at first, but then it becomes more _____.
5. Many people think computer games are _____. But actually, adults often love playing them.
6. People laugh at Bob all the time because he is a really funny guy. But at work, his co-workers _____.
7. My old camera finally broke, so I bought a new _____ camera. Now I can look at my photos on my computer as soon as I take them.
8. I thought *Dead Poets Society* was going to be a funny movie. But it was actually very _____.
9. The Nelsons have a furniture company together. Paul is the _____, and Dennis is the builder.
10. At first, the painting looked very confusing. But after awhile, I began to see _____ that looked like flowers in it.
11. My brother wants to _____ our money so that we can buy a computer this summer. But I think we should each save and buy separate computers so that we can use them whenever we want.
12. I am looking for a game about peace, not a _____ game about killing dragons or monsters.

Serious Fun **123**

EXPAND

Look at the pictures and study the words.

A computer

- screen
- characters
- mouse

A board game

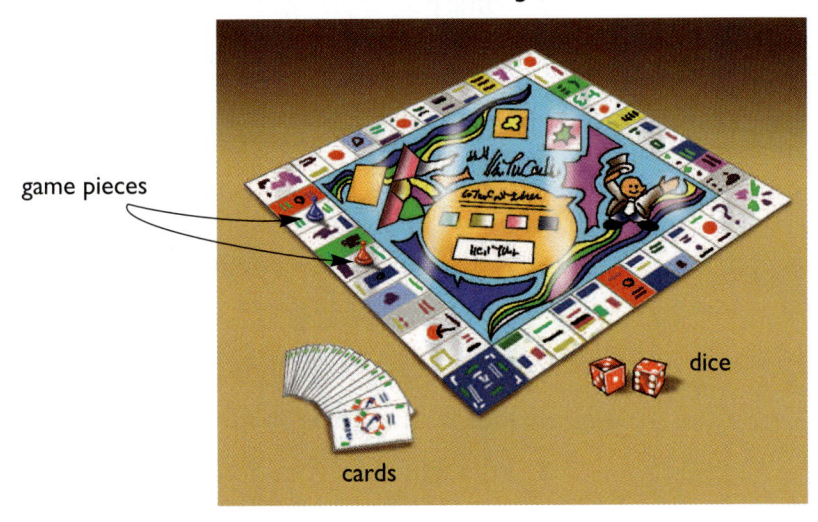

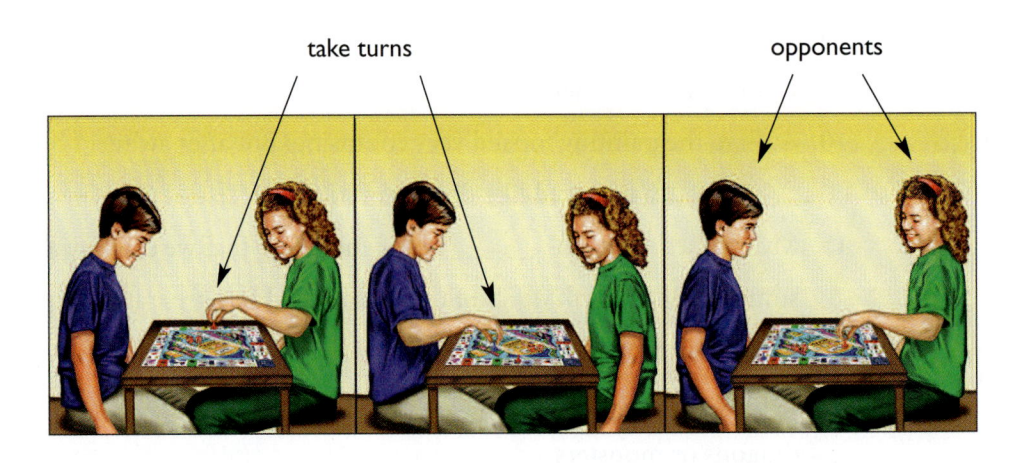

- game pieces
- dice
- cards

- take turns
- opponents

124 UNIT 6

Now complete the text with words from the box.

~~board game~~	character	game piece	opponent	take turns
card	dice	mouse	screen	

Traditional Games vs. Computer Games

Traditional games are still very popular in American households. Usually in a __board game__ (1.), there are several players. Each player chooses a _____ (2.). The first player rolls the _____ (3.) and moves his or her piece the correct number of squares. The player then follows the directions on the square he or she lands on. Sometimes the player has to take a _____ (4.) and follow the directions on it. Players _____ (5.) doing this until someone wins. To win you usually have to finish first.

Computer games are different. Players sometimes choose a _____ (6.) when they play a computer game. This is just a digital person or animal or monster that you want to be in the game. Sometimes in computer games, your _____ (7.) is another player. But sometimes you just play against the computer. To move forward in a computer game, you usually have to click on a digital picture on the computer _____ (8.). You use your _____ (9.) to do this.

Serious Fun **125**

CREATE

Look at the comic strip. Jamal is playing **Adventure Ecology**. Andy is his roommate. Andy doesn't like computer games. Complete the conversation for each picture. Try to use as many words from the box as you can.

board game	childish	entertainment	patterns	take turns
boring	complex	figure out	serious	violent
card	dice	game piece	survival	
characters	digital	opponent	take . . . seriously	

Jamal: Hey Andy. You've got to check out this new game!

Andy: Jamal, you're 22 years old. When are you going to stop playing those _____ games?

Jamal: But this game isn't _____. It's really very _____. It's teaching me about ecology! And it's fun too!

Andy: Well, I don't understand how a computer can teach you much. I think computer games _____ _____

Jamal: You are right—some are like that. But in the good ones you have to _____ _____

Andy: Well, OK. Maybe this one is good, but I can't play it with you since my computer is broken.

Jamal: _____ _____

Andy: _____ _____

Jamal: _____ _____

B GRAMMAR: Expressing Habitual Present with *When-* Clauses

1 Read the paragraph about a game called *Third World Farmer*. Circle the word **when** every time you see it. Underline the verbs in each **when-** sentence.

> When my son comes home from school, he plays *Third World Farmer* every afternoon. *Third World Farmer* is a computer game for learning about farm life in other countries. The goal of the game is to be a successful farmer. When you are successful, you plant more crops and buy animals. When you aren't successful, you don't have enough food to feed your family, and they can die.

EXPRESSING HABITUAL PRESENT WITH *WHEN-* CLAUSES

1. Use **when-** clause + independent clause with the **simple present** in both clauses to show a general rule or something that is always true.	**When** my son **comes** home from school, he **plays** *Third World Farmer* every afternoon. **When** you **are** successful, you **plant** more crops.
2. A **clause** contains a subject and a verb. A **when-** clause contains **when** + subject + verb. It cannot stand alone as a sentence. It needs to be attached to an independent clause. An **independent clause** can stand alone as a sentence.	[s] [v] **When you are successful**, you plant more crops. [s] [v] **You plant more crops.**
3. The **when-** clause can come at the end of the sentence. In this case, you do not need a comma in between the clauses.	You plant more crops **when you are successful**. INCORRECT: You plant more crops, when you are successful.

2 Read the sentences. Complete each one with the correct form of the verb in parentheses.

1. When Joey plays computer games, he _____ anyone talking to
   (not hear)
   him.

2. Carla gets very angry when she _____ a game.
   (lose)

(continued on next page)

Serious Fun   **127**

3. In the game of Monopoly, when you pass Go, you _____ money
   (get)
   from the bank.

4. When the children ask to watch TV, I usually _____ them to play
   (tell)
   a game instead.

5. In chess, when you lose a king, the game _____ over.
   (be)

3 Read each sentence. Add a comma if the sentence needs it.

1. When I have to buy birthday presents for kids _____ I usually buy games.
2. Coleman is a good sport. He says "congratulations" to the winner _____ when he loses a game.
3. Olivia chooses dominoes _____ when it is her turn to pick a game.
4. When we have plenty of time _____ our family loves playing Monopoly.
5. Allen plays *World of Warcraft* _____ when he has free time.

4 Finish the sentences. Make sure you use the correct form of the verb.

1. When I win a game, _____.
2. I am often very happy when _____.
3. When I lose a game, _____.
4. When I have free time, _____.

C WRITING

In this unit, you read about a new kind of game: serious video games that teach about real life. Do you know such a game? What do you think of it?

You are going to **write a review of a game that teaches something**. The game can be a computer game or a board game. You will give a short description of the game. Then you will give your opinion of the game and your reasons for liking or disliking it. Use the vocabulary and grammar from the unit.*

---

*For Alternative Writing Topics, see page 132. These topics can be used in place of the writing topic for this unit or as homework. The alternative topics relate to the theme of the unit, but may not target the same grammar or rhetorical structures taught in the unit.

PREPARE TO WRITE: Brainstorming

1. For 10 minutes, write down as many games as you can remember playing. This is called **brainstorming**. It is important in brainstorming never to call anything a "bad idea." Just **keep writing new ideas** down.

2. When your 10 minutes is up, look at your list. Think about which game teaches something useful. You can begin by crossing out the games that don't teach anything useful.

3. Now you can answer the following questions:

   What is the name of the game you want to write about? _____

   What useful thing does the game teach? _____

WRITE: A Review

The purpose of a **review** is to give people **useful information** about a product as well as a **clear opinion** of the product so that people can decide if they want to buy it. When you write a review, it is important to include the following parts:

> 1. a topic sentence that states your opinion
> 2. a brief description of the thing that you are reviewing
> 3. reasons for your opinion

Note that a review does not have to be as persuasive as the letter to the editor that you wrote in Unit 4. Your goal is to **give people information**, not to sell the game.

1 Read this review of a computer game called Third World Farmer. Label the topic sentence (**TS**), the description (**D**), and the reasons (**R1, R2**, etc.) for the writer's opinion.

> *Third World Farmer* is a good computer game for learning about farm life in poor countries. The goal of the game is simply survival. When you aren't successful, you don't have enough food to feed your family, and they can die. This is a simple but good game for a number of reasons. First of all, it's free! You can find it on the Internet. If you don't like the game, you don't lose any money. Additionally, it teaches about the many things that a farmer cannot control in his life, like the weather, crop diseases, and war. Finally, the game is complex, so it stays fun for awhile. I played it five times and I still don't understand the patterns.

2 Look at this review of Scrabble. It is missing a topic sentence and a description. Choose the best topic sentence and description from the lists below. Write them on the lines.

_____
_____

There are a number of reasons that Scrabble is such a great game. First of all, Scrabble is fun because it lets players play with language. This is especially important for kids. They can learn and play at the same time. Secondly, it is good for many different levels of spellers. You can make two-letter words or seven-letter words. But it is most fun if you play with someone who is at about the same skill level as you. If your opponent is too good or bad, it will not be fun.

Topic Sentences

a. Scrabble was my favorite game when I was a kid.

b. Scrabble can be a good game for learning spelling and math.

c. Scrabble is a wonderful game that has been around for about 60 years.

Descriptions

a. Scrabble letters all have different points on them. When you put "J" (8 points) on a dark blue square, you get triple letter points. Then you have 24 points.

b. Players in Scrabble spell words that connect to each other and get points for each letter they use. The winner is the person with the most points at the end of the game.

c. When you play Scrabble, you always have seven letters. Sometimes it is hard to think of a word when you have, for example, four i's, two e's, and a y.

3 Now write the first draft of your review of a game that teaches something. Use the game you selected on page 129. Include a topic sentence with your opinion, a short description of the game, and reasons for your opinion.

REVISE: Showing Order of Importance

When **giving reasons for an opinion**, it is useful to introduce each one with a word to show order of importance. These order words separate the reasons and make them clearer to the reader. Here are some **words or phrases that show order of importance.**

First of all, …	Additionally, …	Above all, …
Secondly, …	Finally, …	Most importantly, …

130   UNIT 6

1 Look again at the review of Third World Farmer. Circle the words that introduce each reason for the writer's opinion.

> *Third World Farmer* is a good computer game for learning about farm life in poor countries. The goal of the game is simply survival. When you aren't successful, you don't have enough food to feed your family, and they can die. This is a simple but good game for a number of reasons. First of all, it's free! You can find it on the Internet. If you don't like the game, you don't lose any money. Additionally, it teaches about the many things that a farmer cannot control in his life, like the weather, crop diseases, and war. Finally, the game is complex, so it stays fun for awhile. I played it five times and I still don't understand the patterns.

2 Read this review of Food Force. Add words to make the order of importance clearer. Leave the space blank if no order word is needed. Make sure you use proper punctuation and capitalization.

> *Food Force* is a good game for learning about how the United Nations gets food to people in countries at war. _____ The goal is to deliver food to starving people so they can survive. There are a number of things that make this a good game. _____ *Food Force* doesn't feel like an educational game. The art is pretty good, it moves fast, and there are loud noises like "non-serious" computer games. _____ It has six different "missions" or games that you can play, so there is variety. It will take a long time to get bored with this game!
>
> _____ You can learn a lot from this game. I used to think that getting food to starving people was easy. Now I know that it is a very complex project.

3 Now go back to the first draft of your review. Add words to show order of importance in the reasons for your opinion. It will make your review clearer.

Serious Fun **131**

◀ EDIT: Writing the Final Draft

Write the final draft of your review. Carefully edit it for grammatical and mechanical errors, such as spelling, capitalization, and punctuation. Make sure you used some of the vocabulary and grammar from the unit. Use the checklist to help you write your final draft. Then neatly write or type your review.

✓ FINAL DRAFT CHECKLIST

- ◯ Does your review offer useful information for someone who is thinking about buying the game?
- ◯ Does it give a clear opinion of that game?
- ◯ Does it start with a topic sentence that states your opinion?
- ◯ Does it include a brief description of the game?
- ◯ Do you use *when-* clauses to explain the game?
- ◯ Does your review include reasons for your opinion?
- ◯ Do you use order words to show the order of importance of your reasons?
- ◯ Do you use new vocabulary that you learned in this unit?

ALTERNATIVE WRITING TOPICS

Write about one of the topics. Use the vocabulary and grammar from the unit.

1. Find a serious game to play online. There are many that you can play for free. Play it and write a review of the game. Do you think the game is well designed? What does it teach?

2. Many parents and teachers think that it is bad for kids to play computer games. Raph Koster (and many others) think that everyone learns a lot from computer games (though some things may not be useful). What is your opinion? Write a letter to a newspaper on this topic.

3. Choose a world problem and think about how you might design a game to help people learn about this problem. Write a plan for a game. What would you like the game to teach? Would it be a computer game or a board game? Give your reasons for choosing one type of game over the other.

RESEARCH TOPICS, see page 228.

UNIT 7
The Best Produce There Is

1 FOCUS ON THE TOPIC

A PREDICT

Look at the picture and discuss the questions with the class.

1. Where do you buy fruits and vegetables?
2. How do you choose the fruits and vegetables you buy? What do you look for?
3. Do you know where your fruits and vegetables come from?
4. Read the title of the unit. What does "produce" mean? Where might you see the word?

B SHARE INFORMATION

When you shop, how do you choose your fruit? Do you choose it by its color? Do you choose it by its size? For each kind of fruit, check (✓) each box that shows how you choose that fruit. Add a fruit of your choice to the list.

FRUIT	COLOR	SIZE	SOFTNESS/ HARDNESS	SMELL	PRICE	WHERE IT COMES FROM
Apples						
Bananas						
Pears						
Strawberries						
_____						

In a small group, share and discuss your answers. For example, if you checked "size" for apples, what size do you look for? Why?

134   UNIT 7

C BACKGROUND AND VOCABULARY

Read the gardening chart for San Francisco. Try to understand the boldfaced words without looking them up in a dictionary.

VEGETABLE GARDENING YEAR-ROUND IN SAN FRANCISCO

Season	Crops	Advice
Spring	Peas	Peas grow very well when it seems too cold for many other vegetables. **Insects** love little pea plants, so be careful. You can use **chemicals** to keep them away. Or if you are **concerned about** using dangerous chemicals, try the **old-fashioned** way to keep insects away: put a little bit of soapy water on the plants. Make sure that you don't let the **weeds** get too big in the spring. Get them out of your garden so that your vegetables can have more space to grow!
Summer	Tomatoes Squash	One of the best things to do in summer is to **pick** a nice red **ripe** tomato and eat it right away. Sometimes tomatoes seem like a lot of work. They need a great deal of sun, and you have to water them often. But **it's worth it** every time. Scientists now say that tomatoes are really good at fighting some illnesses like **cancer**. So plant lots of them! And don't forget to plant some squash. Squash is good for you too.
Fall	Radishes Cauliflower	There is a lot of **produce** to pick in the fall. You should make sauce from tomatoes and freeze[1] squash to eat during the winter. Then, if you have time, you can plant some radishes and cauliflower.
Winter	Lettuce Spinach Onions	While it is snowing in the rest of the United States, you should plant some lettuce, spinach, and onions. You can have **fresh** vegetables from your garden even in winter.

---

[1] **freeze**: preserve food for a long time by keeping it very cold in a freezer

The Best Produce There Is

Now match the words with their definitions.

_f_	1. insects	a.	not modern or new
____	2. chemicals	b.	it will be useful—you will benefit from it
____	3. concerned about	c.	ready to eat
____	4. old-fashioned	d.	substances made by or used in chemistry
____	5. weeds	e.	not canned or frozen
____	6. pick	f.	tiny animals that eat plants
____	7. ripe	g.	to pull off a fruit or vegetable from a plant or tree
____	8. it's worth it	h.	fruits and vegetables
____	9. cancer	i.	worried about
____	10. produce	j.	an illness that can grow anywhere in your body and is very dangerous
____	11. fresh	k.	plants that grow naturally and that you don't want in your garden

2 FOCUS ON READING

A READING ONE: Organic Produce vs. Regular Produce

Mr. Green has a newspaper advice column called "Ask Mr. Green." People with questions about produce and other food write to him. Read the letter to Mr. Green. The writer asks two questions. How will Mr. Green answer the questions? Write your ideas for each answer on the lines.

Dear Mr. Green:

Lately I see more and more "organic" fruits and vegetables in the supermarkets. I'm confused. Often the organic apples or strawberries aren't as shiny or as large as the regular ones, but they can cost a lot more! So tell me, what exactly are organic fruits and vegetables? And why are they so expensive?

Confused Shopper
Bakersfield, CA

---

1. _____
2. _____
   _____

136   UNIT 7

Now read Mr. Green's answer. Were your ideas correct?

ASK MR. GREEN:
Organic Produce vs. Regular Produce

Dear Confused Shopper:

1 You're right. Sometimes organic **produce** doesn't look as nice as regular produce, and it often costs twice as much. Let me explain why.

2 Since about 1950, farmers in the United States have used **chemicals** to grow their fruits and vegetables. They use pesticides[1] to kill **insects** that eat their plants. They use herbicides[2] to kill the **weeds** that kill their plants. These chemicals are a great help to farmers. By using them, farmers can grow more produce on the same amount of land. This means that shoppers can find more produce in the stores.

3 Farmers also use chemicals to make fruits and vegetables **ripe**. For example, they often **pick** tomatoes while they are still green, and then put them in a box to go to a supermarket. The green tomatoes turn red and get ripe because of a chemical that is in the box with them. Because some produce can be picked early, it can travel long distances to stores. As a result, we can find most kinds of regular fruits and vegetables all year long.

4 Some people argue[3], however, that there are problems with using all these chemicals. When we eat produce, we're also eating a little bit of the chemicals. Small amounts of these are safe to eat. But larger amounts—a little bit every day—can cause illnesses. Many scientists believe that these farming chemicals cause **cancer**.

5 Herbicides and pesticides can also be very bad for nature. They sometimes kill animals such as fish and birds, and they can poison[4] rivers that are near farms. Farm workers who pick the crops often get very sick from the chemicals. Because of problems like these, some farmers are going back to growing produce the **old-fashioned** way—without chemicals. We call this kind of produce *organic*.

6 Organic produce is more expensive than other produce for several reasons. For instance, many organic farmers can't grow as much produce as other farmers. Their farms are usually smaller, and, of course, they don't use herbicides and pesticides. Also, because they don't use ripening chemicals, their produce has to arrive at the stores very soon after it's picked. So it is usually **fresh**, but this too costs money.

7 **Is it worth it**? That's up to you to decide. But if you're not familiar with organic produce, you might want to try it. More and more shoppers are buying organic produce. Many of these shoppers say that they're not just **concerned about** their own health. They are concerned about the health of our whole world.

Mr. Green

---

[1] **pesticides:** chemicals that kill insects and other small animals that eat crops
[2] **herbicides:** chemicals that kill weeds
[3] **argue:** clearly explain that something is true
[4] **poison:** make land, lakes, rivers, air, etc., dirty and dangerous

◀ **READ FOR MAIN IDEAS**

Check (✓) the ideas that Mr. Green discussed in his answer.

_____ 1. He explained how much organic fruits and vegetables cost.

_____ 2. He discussed the kinds of insects that can destroy crops.

_____ 3. He discussed the use of chemicals in growing regular produce.

_____ 4. He explained why regular produce may be bad for your health.

_____ 5. He explained what organic produce is.

_____ 6. He explained why organic fruits and vegetables are expensive.

_____ 7. He explained where people can buy organic produce.

◀ **READ FOR DETAILS**

*Read each statement. Decide if it is true or false. Write **T** (true) or **F** (false) next to it. If the statement is false, write a true statement after it.*

__F__ 1. Organic produce looks the same as regular produce.
   Organic produce doesn't look as nice as regular produce.

_____ 2. Organic produce can cost twice as much as regular produce.

_____ 3. Farming chemicals kill insects, but they don't kill fish and birds.

138   UNIT 7

_____ 4. Some scientists believe that farming chemicals cause cancer.
_____

_____ 5. Organic farmers rely on chemicals to make fruit ripe.
_____

_____ 6. With chemicals, farmers can grow more produce on the same amount of land.
_____

_____ 7. Regular produce often has to arrive at stores quickly.
_____

◀ MAKE INFERENCES

Read the statements and check (✓) the ones that Mr. Green probably agrees with. Then discuss your answers with a partner.

_____ 1. Organic produce is a waste of money.

_____ 2. Most farmers use chemicals because they help the fields give more produce.

_____ 3. One problem with farming chemicals is that they sometimes kill the crops.

_____ 4. Shoppers like being able to buy tomatoes while there is snow outside.

_____ 5. Chemicals in herbicides and pesticides are dangerous for people.

_____ 6. One reason organic produce is more expensive is because birds sometimes eat the fruit in the fields.

_____ 7. Organic produce needs to travel from the field to the stores quickly.

_____ 8. Organic produce is becoming more popular because people are concerned about the problems with farming chemicals.

◀ EXPRESS OPINIONS

What about you? Do you buy organic or regular produce? Why? Discuss the questions with a partner. Give your opinions. Write them below.

Your Opinion

_____

_____

_____

_____

_____

Your Partner's Opinion

_____

_____

_____

_____

_____

B READING TWO: Miles to Go Before You Eat

The following article is from *Sierra Magazine*. The writer tells about another way to look at produce in the United States.

Read the article and think about this question: "Is organic produce always best for the world?"

Miles to Go Before You Eat

By Paul Rauber

1 Your refrigerator is empty. You get on your bike to go grocery shopping. You bring your own bags so that you don't have to use plastic bags from the store. You buy organic bananas, a beautiful pineapple, and organic grapes, strawberries, and spinach. You are feeling good about feeding your family healthy food. You think about how lucky you are. You can buy all of these fruits and vegetables in November in Des Moines, Iowa!

2 You are doing good things for your family and for the environment, but you could do better.

3 Riding your bike saves gasoline. But the pineapple you just bought traveled to your town on an airplane from Hawaii. Your grapes traveled about 7,000 miles by boat and truck from Costa Rica. As a matter of fact, food in the United States travels an average of 1,500 miles from the farm to the dinner plate.

4 Buying organic food, riding a bike, and avoiding plastic bags are all good things to do for the environment. But if you are buying organic pineapples from Hawaii, you may not be seeing the whole picture. Maybe one of the best things we can do for the environment is to eat local produce. It uses less gasoline. It pollutes less. And it probably tastes better, too, since it is fresher.

5 Buying only local produce won't be easy at first. You will have to stop eating produce that doesn't grow nearby, like bananas. And you will be spending a little more on your food. But the world will be healthier, and so will you.

6 Take a look at how much gasoline each of these fruits uses to get to Des Moines, Iowa:

Pineapple (Costa Rica) 0.03 gallon of gasoline

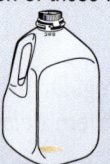

Pineapple (Hawaii) 0.53 gallon of gasoline

7 Pineapples use a lot of gasoline. But if you must buy one, notice that the Costa Rican pineapple makes more than half of its trip by boat. Boats don't use very much gasoline. Pineapples from Hawaii, however, travel by air.

Apple (Iowa) 0.10 tablespoon of gasoline

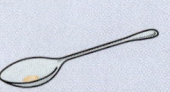

Apple (Washington) 1.92 tablespoon of gasoline

8 Apples from Iowa travel only 60 miles in small trucks to Des Moines. The ones from Washington must travel 1,722 miles in large trucks.

Grapes (California)
3.5 tablespoons of gasoline

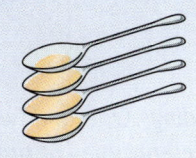

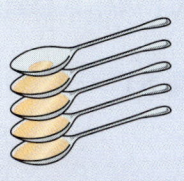

Grapes (Chile)
4.2 tablespoons of gasoline

9 About the same amount of gasoline is used to bring grapes from Chile or California. This might be surprising. The reason is that the grapes from Chile made most of their journey by boat. Then both kinds of grapes came to Des Moines in big trucks.

Source: Adapted from "Miles to Go Before You Eat, Why it Pays to Buy Locally Grown Food" by Paul Rauber in *Sierra Magazine*, May/June 2006. Reprinted with permission of *Sierra*, the magazine of the Sierra Club.

Now circle the best ending for each statement.

1. Riding a bike, using your own shopping bags, and buying healthy food are _____.
   a. good things to do for the environment
   b. good to do, but not enough
   c. not important

2. Most food that we eat in the United States travels _____.
   a. 7,000 miles by airplane and truck
   b. about 1,500 miles from the place it is grown to the place it is eaten
   c. by boat from Chile or Costa Rica

3. The author says that local produce is best because _____.
   a. it uses less gas and it pollutes less
   b. it is organic and uses no chemicals
   c. it is cheaper than produce that comes from far away

4. "If you are buying organic pineapples from Hawaii, you may not be seeing the whole picture" means that _____.
   a. Hawaiian pineapple farmers all use chemicals on their fruit
   b. if you think buying organic pineapples from Hawaii is a good thing to do, you need to learn more about how they travel
   c. regular produce is better than organic produce because it travels less

5. If you eat only local produce, you will have to _____.
   a. only eat what is in season, and spend a little more money
   b. stop eating bananas
   c. ride your bike more and buy more apples

6. Produce uses the most gas when it travels _____.
   a. by boat
   b. by truck
   c. by airplane

C INTEGRATE READINGS ONE AND TWO

STEP 1: Organize

Read the statements based on Readings One and Two. Then complete the chart with the advantages or disadvantages of different types of produce. Write the underlined words in each statement in the appropriate box in the chart.

Reading One

1. Sometimes organic produce ~~doesn't look as nice~~ as regular produce.
2. We can find most kinds of regular fruits and vegetables <u>all year long</u>.
3. Farming <u>chemicals cause cancer</u>.
4. Some farmers have gone back to growing produce the old-fashioned way— <u>without chemicals</u>.
5. Organic produce is <u>more expensive than regular produce</u>.
6. It is <u>usually fresh</u>.

Reading Two

7. It <u>uses less gasoline</u>.
8. It <u>pollutes less</u>.
9. It probably <u>tastes better</u> too, since it is <u>always fresh</u>.
10. You will have to <u>stop eating produce that doesn't grow nearby</u>, like bananas.
11. And you will be <u>spending a little more</u> on your food.
12. But the <u>world will be healthier</u>, and so will you.

	ADVANTAGES	DISADVANTAGES
Regular produce		
Organic produce		doesn't look as nice
Local produce		

142 UNIT 7

STEP 2: Synthesize

Mr. Green has received another letter from a reader. Read the letter. Then complete Mr. Green's reply. Use information from the chart in Step 1.

Dear Mr. Green:
My daughter is coming home from college for the summer to work here in Des Moines. She does not eat meat. She eats mostly vegetables. She has told me that she doesn't eat "regular" produce anymore. She prefers organic produce now. And she has also told me that she is a "locavore"—she only eats food that comes from less than 100 miles away. Are they good ideas, or is she just crazy?

Worried in Des Moines

Dear Worried:
There are actually more and more people like your daughter these days. I can tell you some of the most common reasons for eating local organic food.

Of course regular produce has some advantages. For example, . . .

_____

_____

But many people do not eat regular produce as much because . . .

_____

_____

People choose organic produce because . . .

_____

_____

And "locavores" think that local produce is the best choice because . . .

_____

_____

Maybe you can put your daughter in charge of cooking for your family this summer! Good luck!

Mr. Green

The Best Produce There Is **143**

3 FOCUS ON WRITING

A VOCABULARY

◀ REVIEW

Cross out the word or phrase that is not related to the boldfaced word.

1. **chemicals:** herbicides, ~~orange juice,~~ fake sugar
2. **ripe:** yellow banana, green strawberry, red apple
3. **pick:** crops, fruit, airplanes
4. **cancer:** illness, death, health
5. **produce:** potato, apple, soup
6. **it's worth it:** it will be a problem, it will be useful, you'll benefit by it
7. **concerned about:** worried, thinking, angry
8. **old-fashioned:** milking cows by hand, separating eggs with an electric machine, planting corn with a stick
9. **fresh:** tomatoes from the can, grapes off the vine, apples from the tree
10. **insect:** bee, bird, fly
11. **weeds:** delicious, unwanted, plants
12. **local:** nearby, neighbors, airplane trips
13. **environment:** nature, rivers and mountains, meat and milk
14. **pollute:** dirty air, driving cars, carrots from your garden

◀ EXPAND

1 Read the excerpt from a journal. Pay attention to the boldfaced words.

> It's June in California. The market is full of wonderful produce. The potatoes always look good. They grow **year round**. The peaches and strawberries are **in season** now. I see lots of them. They taste really **sweet** this year—I won't need to use much sugar when I make pies and jam. But there are no fresh peas. Peas must be **out of season**.
>
> Produce from the supermarket usually tastes **bland**, which is why I prefer produce from the farmers' market. Shopping at the farmers' market **saves gas**, too, because I can ride my bike there. Getting exercise and eating plenty of local fruits and vegetables are both really **healthy** things to do.

144 UNIT 7

Now circle the best definition (**a** or **b**) for each new word or phrase.

1. **year round**   a. growing all year   b. growing in the ground
2. **in season**   a. ripe at this time   b. still growing in the summer
3. **sweet**   a. tasting like sugar   b. tasting fresh
4. **out of season** a. growing in the winter   b. not ripe at this time
5. **bland**   a. delicious   b. without much taste
6. **saves gas**   a. uses gas later   b. uses less gas
7. **healthy**   a. good for your whole body b. helping you to lose weight

2 Complete the journal entry with the appropriate words or phrases from the box.

bland	~~fresh~~	it was worth it	picked	save gas
concerned about	healthy	local	pollute	sweet
environment	in season	out of season	ripe	year round

Saturday . . .

I tasted lots of fruit while I was at the market today. The blueberries were so ____fresh____ (1)! The farmer probably _____ (2) them this morning. And apricots are finally _____ (3). The apricot I tasted seemed to have sugar on it. It was so _____ (4)! One guy was selling oranges, but they tasted a little _____ (5). I think that these oranges stayed in a refrigerator for at least a couple of weeks. We can buy oranges _____ (6), but they often don't taste so good. I wanted to buy some sweet potatoes, but there were none. I guess they are _____ (7). I asked my favorite farmer about blackberries, but he said that they are not _____ (8) yet. He might have some in a couple of weeks. I bought

(continued on next page)

The Best Produce There Is **145**

bland	~~fresh~~	it was worth it	picked	save gas
concerned about	healthy	local	pollute	sweet
environment	in season	out of season	ripe	year round

some _____ honey. The honey came from bees only three miles
        9.
from my house. As I was leaving, I had to buy a cookie. I know cookies aren't

_____, but they sure taste good!
    10.

After I went to the market, I picked up my new car! I bought a hybrid

electric car because I want to _____. These hybrid electric cars
                                      11.

_____ less than regular cars, so they are better for the
   12.

_____. It was a little expensive, but I think _____.
      13.   14.

I am _____ the environment. Buying local produce and driving
       15.

a hybrid electric car are two small things that I can do to make it better.

CREATE

In many cities in the United States, people pay a local organic farmer to deliver a box of fresh vegetables to their houses every week. Often, there is a letter from the farmer in the box. The letter usually tells a little bit about what is in the box and what is happening on the farm.

Study the list on the left side of the letter. Then complete the letter, using information from the list and some of the words from the box.

bland	fresh	it's worth it	pick	save gas
concerned about	healthy	local	pollute	sweet
environment	in season	out of season	ripe	year round

146   UNIT 7

Tuttle Family Farms
Modesto, California
May 5, 2007

In this week's box:

*Strawberries
(eat these right away)*

Potatoes

Lettuce

Spinach

*Apricots
(new this week)*

*Peas
(These are the last peas for this year . . . enjoy them!)*

Greetings and Happy Spring!

The weather is becoming very warm, and we are very busy on our farm. Rick is planting a new kind of squash that you will all be eating in July. The peaches are starting to look good. If the weather stays warm, you might get some peaches in your box next week.

The tomatoes are also looking good. Those are my favorites. They will be ready in about three weeks. If you have never had one of our organic tomatoes, get ready for a delicious surprise! Regular tomatoes from the store . . .

_____
_____
_____

The strawberries . . .

_____
_____
_____

We are excited to send you apricots this week . . .

_____
_____
_____

And finally, . . .

_____
_____

Enjoy your box this week!

Sincerely,
Emily

B GRAMMAR: *Wh-* Questions in the Simple Present Tense

1 Read the questions about produce. Look at the verbs in the questions. What is the difference between the verbs in column A and those in column B?

A	B
What **do** people **look for**?	Who **grows** apples near Des Moines?
Who **should** I **ask** about local produce?	What **grows** in Alaska?
Where **can** we **buy** fruits and vegetables?	
How **do** you **choose** fruits and vegetables?	
How **does** a fresh tomato **taste**?	

WH- QUESTIONS IN THE SIMPLE PRESENT TENSE AND WITH *CAN* AND *SHOULD*

1. ***Wh-* questions** ask for **information**. They cannot be answered by *yes* or *no*.
   A: What do people look for?
   B: They look for ripe, sweet fruit.
   Wh- questions start with a ***wh-* word** like *what, where, when, who, why,* and *how.*

2. To form **most *wh-* questions** in the simple present tense, use ***do*** or ***does*** and the **base form** of the verb.

Wh- Word	Do/Does	Subject	Base Form	
Where	**do**	you	**buy**	fruits and vegetables?
How	**does**	the spinach	**taste**?	
Who	**do**	I	**ask**	about local produce?

   EXCEPTION: With the verb **be,** do not use *do* or *does*.

Where	**is**	the farmers' market?
Who	**are**	the organic farmers around here?

3. Some ***wh-* questions** use ***can*** or ***should*** instead of *do* or *does*.

Where	**can**	we	**buy**	fruits and vegetables?
Who	**should**	I	**ask**	about local produce?

4. To form ***wh-* questions about the subject** of a sentence, do not use *do* and *does*. Use the third-person singular form of the verb.

Subject	Third-Person Singular	
Who	**grows**	apples near Des Moines?
What	**grows**	in Alaska?

---

2 Read the answer. Then complete the question.

1. Q: Why <u>do you buy local food</u>   ?

   A: I buy local food because I want to help local farmers.

2. **Q:** Where _____ ?

   A: I live in Portland, Oregon.

3. **Q:** What _____ ?

   A: Apples, grapes, carrots, and potatoes grow nearby.

4. **Q:** When _____ ?

   A: Grapes are in season in September.

5. **Q:** How _____ ?

   A: Oregon grapes taste fresh and delicious.

3 Read each sentence. Write a question that the underlined words can answer.

1. <u>Strawberries</u> grow in Watsonville, California.

   What grows in Watsonville, California ?

2. Apples can grow <u>in most of the United States</u>.

   _____ ?

3. <u>Picking berries</u> is my favorite thing to do in summer.

   _____ ?

4. Pineapples travel to New York <u>by airplane</u>.

   _____ ?

5. <u>Organic farmers</u> know how to farm without dangerous chemicals.

   _____ ?

4 Vincent lives in Anchorage, Alaska. He is listening to a radio show about local produce. The speaker is talking about how important it is to eat local food. Vincent didn't know that people could grow produce around Anchorage because there is snow in Anchorage for many months of the year. The radio show takes questions by e-mail, so Vincent sends a few questions.

Write some questions that Vincent might have for the speaker.

1. What _grows near Anchorage_ ?
2. How _____ ?
3. Why _____ ?
4. Who _____ ?
5. When _____ ?
6. Where _____ ?
7. _____ ?

The Best Produce There Is **149**

C WRITING

A brochure

In this unit, you read about different types of produce (regular, organic, and local). Which type do you think is best? Why do you think so?

You are going to **write a brochure about the type of produce you think is best.** Your goal will be to convince certain people to buy the produce. Using a question-answer format, you will list its advantages for these people. Then you will add one or two disadvantages, making sure you suggest solutions. And don't forget to give an interesting title to your brochure. Use the vocabulary and grammar from the unit.*

◀ PREPARE TO WRITE: Asking Yourself Questions

One way to **get ideas** before you start to write is to think about all of the **questions** that a person might have about your topic.

1 Someone wants to write a brochure about the advantages of drinking water. Read that person's list of questions. Notice the kind of questions and how they are organized.

> BROCHURE: Water is the healthiest drink
> - Why should people drink water?
> - Why is water good for you?
> - What kind of water is good for you?
> - Is all water good for you?
> - Where should I get my water from?
> - What are some benefits of water?
> - How can I convince my children to drink water?
> - Is it OK to drink water from my kitchen tap, or should I buy bottled water?

2 Review this unit carefully for information about the produce you want to write about. Write as many questions as you can think of about this topic. Think about questions that you have, as well as questions that other people might have.

3 Share your list with a partner. Ask your partner to think of more questions. Add them to your list.

---

*For Alternative Writing Topics, see page 154. These topics can be used in place of the writing topic for this unit or as homework. The alternative topics relate to the theme of the unit, but may not target the same grammar or rhetorical structures taught in the unit.

WRITE: A Brochure

The purpose of a **brochure** is to **convince a certain group of people** to do or buy something. When a brochure uses a **question-answer format**, the questions should be questions that these people might have. So before you write your brochure, **think about your audience** (the people you are writing for) and what questions *they* might have. Which information is most important for *that* audience?

1 *Read each advantage of drinking water. Is this information most important for parents or for single people with no children? Check (✓) the appropriate column. Discuss your answers with a partner.*

ADVANTAGE	Parents who don't have much money	Singles who exercise a great deal	Both
1. Children who drink water have better teeth.			
2. Water gives people energy.			
3. Water is cheap.			
4. Water helps muscles feel better after exercise.			
5. Water helps brains work better.			
6. Water can help you not get fat.			
7. Colds and flu go away faster if you drink water.			
8. Children who drink water instead of soda and juice become healthier adults.			

The Best Produce There Is

2 These excerpts come from two different brochures about drinking water. One brochure is for parents, the other one is for single people. Read each excerpt and decide which brochure it belongs to. Write **P** (parents) or **S** (singles) next to the excerpt.

_____ 1. It is important to develop good habits when we are young. Children who drink water are healthier when they are young. But they also become healthier adults. They have fewer problems with their teeth, and they aren't overweight.

_____ 2. Our bodies lose lots of water every day. We lose water when we breathe and when we exercise. Often, when we are thirsty, we drink coffee, tea, and soda. But drinking these things actually makes our bodies lose more water. The best thing to drink is water.

_____ 3. No other drink is as cheap as tap water. A glass of water from your kitchen costs less than one penny. Add up all of the money that you spend on soda, juice, coffee, and tea for just one week. Think about how much money you can save in one year if you and your family drink water instead. And think about the money you will save at the dentist.

_____ 4. Drinking water can help you lose weight. Often, when we think we are hungry, we are actually thirsty for water. If you get in the habit of drinking water, especially before every meal, you will eat less. Try drinking water next time you feel like a snack and see what happens.

3 Choose an audience for your brochure. You might consider parents, teenagers, people who have health problems, or another group. Describe your audience below. Review the advantages of your kind of produce and list the most important ones for your audience.

Audience: _____

Advantages of _____ that are important for this audience:

- _____
- _____
- _____
- _____
- _____

4 Look at the advantages you listed above and think how you will organize them. You need to have two or three short paragraphs in your brochure. Write a question to lead your readers into each paragraph. Refer to the list of questions you wrote in Prepare to Write for question ideas (page 150).

5 Now write the first draft of your brochure. First, write a title that will make your audience want to read the brochure. Then write your questions and develop an answer to each question. As you write, be sure to remember who you are writing for.

◀ REVISE: Acknowledging Disadvantages

1 Read the two paragraphs. Decide which one (**A** or **B**) does a better job of convincing readers that it is important for children to drink water. Put a checkmark (✓) next to it. Discuss your answer with a partner.

A. ○

> It is important for people to develop good habits when they are young. Children who drink water are healthier. They have more energy and they get sick less. But they also become healthier adults. They have fewer problems with their teeth, and they aren't overweight. If people develop good habits when they are young, they will not need to change bad habits later.

B. ○

> It is important for people to develop good habits when they are young. Children who drink water are healthier. But they also become healthier adults. They have fewer problems with their teeth, and they aren't overweight. Many parents say that it is difficult to convince children to drink water. One thing parents can do is tell children that they have to drink a glass of water before they have a glass of juice. Soon, they will get used to the taste of water, and they will thank their parents later!

You probably noticed that Paragraph B includes a **disadvantage**. It often helps to include a disadvantage in your brochure to show readers that you know there can be some problems. If readers think that you don't know the disadvantages of something, they might not believe you. Note that it also helps to suggest a **solution** to the disadvantage that you mentioned.

2 Now go back to the first draft of your brochure. Did you include a disadvantage? If you didn't, add one or two. You should also suggest a solution to each disadvantage as Paragraph B does.

Examples of brochures

The Best Produce There Is

◀ EDIT: Writing the Final Draft

Write the final draft of your brochure. Carefully edit it for grammatical and mechanical errors, such as spelling, capitalization, and punctuation. Make sure you used some of the vocabulary and grammar from the unit. Use the checklist to help you write your final draft. Then neatly write or type your brochure.

✓ FINAL DRAFT CHECKLIST

- ○ Does your brochure tell about the advantages of a type of produce?
- ○ Does it include the most important advantages for the audience you chose?
- ○ Does it use questions and answers to present each main point?
- ○ Will the title look interesting to the audience you are writing for?
- ○ Are the questions and answers written with the audience in mind?
- ○ Do you include one or two disadvantages in your brochure?
- ○ Do you suggest solutions to these disadvantages?
- ○ Are your questions grammatically correct?
- ○ Do you use new vocabulary that you learned in this unit?

ALTERNATIVE WRITING TOPICS

Write about one of the topics. Use the vocabulary and grammar from the unit.

1. Write a letter to Mr. Green. In your letter, first tell about something you see in stores and don't understand. Then ask one or two questions about it. For example, you might see tomatoes that say "vine-ripened." But you thought all tomatoes grew on vines. So what does "vine-ripened" mean?

2. Write a short explanation of organic food for an article in a children's magazine. The children who read the magazine are 8 to 12 years old. Most of them live in big cities, and most are not familiar with organic food. Before you write the explanation, think of your audience and of the content and tone that is best. What will interest your readers? What will they need to know?

3. Is it possible to be a "locavore" (a person who eats only local food) in your town? Write a letter to the editor of your town's newspaper. Describe what a locavore in your town can and can't eat. Then say if you think it is a good idea for people in your town to try being locavores.

RESEARCH TOPICS, see page 228.

UNIT 8
"I'll take the train, thanks."

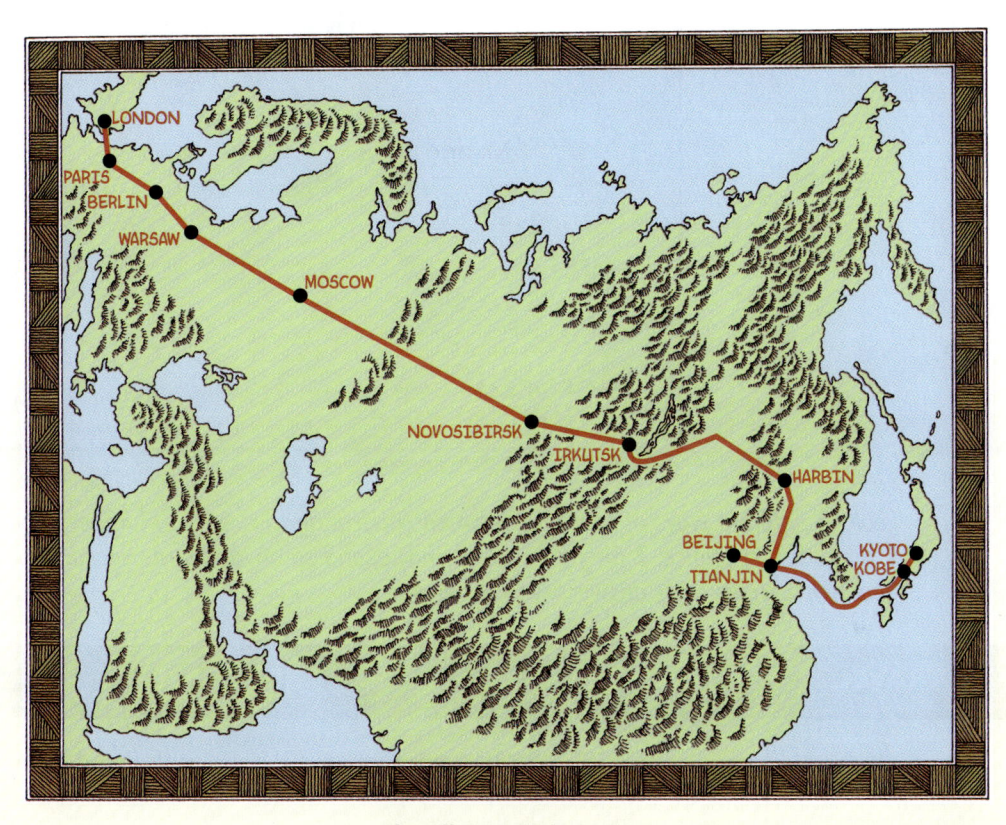

The Climate Train Route

1 FOCUS ON THE TOPIC

A PREDICT

Look at the map. It shows the route that a group of travelers (called the "Climate Train") took in 1997 to go from London, England, to Kyoto, Japan. Discuss the questions with the class.

1. How do you think these people traveled?
2. Why do you think they traveled this way?
3. Why do you think they were going to Kyoto?

B SHARE INFORMATION

Imagine that you live in Madrid, Spain, and you have a two-week vacation. You want to go to Florence, Italy. Florence is about 1,000 miles from Madrid. How will you travel?

Look at different ways of traveling between Madrid and Florence. Number your choices *1* for your first choice, *2* for your second choice, and so on, and write reasons for your decision. Discuss your answers with a partner.

WAY TO TRAVEL	NUMBER	REASON(S)
Plane	5	It's very fast, but it's expensive, and it makes a lot of pollution[1].
Train		
Car		
Bicycle		
Train + Boat		

[1] **pollution:** the process of making air, water, soil, etc., dangerously dirty

156   UNIT 8

C   BACKGROUND AND VOCABULARY

Most scientists all over the world agree that one of the biggest problems in the world right now is climate (weather) change. All of the pollution is making the world's climate warmer. This is called *global warming.* The only way to stop or slow down[1] global warming is to make less pollution. People all over the world are changing their lives to make less pollution.

A reporter asked people from all over the world the following question. Read their answers. Pay attention to the boldfaced words.

> Lots of people are changing their lives to slow down global warming. What's your reaction to that?

1. "I'm one of those people. And I really **appreciate** how the changes we made to slow down global warming have other effects on my life. For example, my wife and I started hanging up the laundry every Saturday morning. This is our time to tell each other about the week. We are working, yes, but we are doing it together."

   Wendell Knox
   London, England

2. "In the city, I walk or ride a bike. When I have to travel to the suburbs, it gets difficult. I have to **arrange** things carefully. I have to make sure I get to the train station to take an 8:10 train. When I arrive at my stop, I have to walk nine blocks to meet my bus. This takes exactly 17 minutes. If I miss that 8:50 bus, I have to wait an hour for the next bus."

   Sophia Chabot
   New York City, USA

---

[1] **slow down:** to make something slower

"I'll take the train, thanks."   **157**

3. "It's stupid. All these people trying not to use gas or oil. If you live on an island, what are you going to do? Swim to work? No, you're going to take a **ferry**. People are crazy."

Timothy Miles
Vancouver, Canada

4. "I don't understand why countries have different laws about pollution. Pollution doesn't stop at the **border**. It goes right over from one country to the next."

Dorte Manheim
Hamburg, Germany

5. "We know how pollution is made. But stopping it? Slowing down global warming? That's **complicated**. How do we ask people to stop driving? Stop flying? Stop using plastic?"

Tina Bahovec
Luxembourg City, Luxembourg

6. "I live in a small town on the **coast** of Newfoundland. Everyone in my town works hard to make as little pollution as possible. But every day we see more and more pollution coming from the ocean onto our beaches. When you see this every day, you want to do something about it."

Michael Morse
Port Aux Basques, Canada

7. "South Africa made it illegal in 2003 to use or sell plastic bags. People said, 'No, don't take them away. They're so **convenient**. We use them all the time. We need them for shopping.' But now people use cloth or paper bags, and there is less pollution."

Claire Heese
Franschhoek, South Africa

8. "I don't think about global warming at all. If I want to go somewhere, I just get in the car and drive. If I need to take a train or a plane, I check the **schedules** and go. Let someone else bike, walk, or ride a horse."

Jeanne Demarais
Paris, France

9. "Every year I visit my parents in Florida. This flight from London makes as much pollution as six months of driving. So with a **round-trip** ticket, it's double that. But what can I do? I have to visit my parents."

Milo Slater
London, England

10. "I'd like to see our president drive an electric car. He should **set an example** by making less pollution. A lot of people would do the same thing. I'm sure of it."

Thad Davidson
Washington, D.C., USA

Now write the words next to their definitions.

| appreciate | ~~border~~ | complicated | ferry | schedule |
| arrange | coast | convenient | round-trip | set an example |

1. ____border____ : the official line that separates two countries
2. _____ : useful to you because it makes something easier
3. _____ : to do something that you hope other people will copy
4. _____ : list of times that ferries, trains, buses, etc., leave or arrive at a particular place
5. _____ : to organize and plan
6. _____ : boat that takes people, and sometimes cars, back and forth between two places
7. _____ : not simple; with lots of details
8. _____ : when a ticket takes you from one place to another and back again
9. _____ : where the land meets the sea
10. _____ : to understand or enjoy the good qualities of something

2 FOCUS ON READING

A READING ONE: The Climate Train

Every year since 1996, scientists and governments from all over the world go to a conference (a large meeting) to talk about pollution—how it's made, why it's bad, how to make less of it. At the Kyoto conference in 1997, they wrote a plan for lowering[1] the amount of pollution around the world. This plan is called the Kyoto Protocol. This important plan is still used today for helping countries around the world slow down global warming.

The following article is about a group of scientists who went to this important conference in Kyoto, Japan.

---

[1] **lowering:** reducing something in amount, making it less

What do you expect to find in this article? Check (✓) the things you think you will find.

_____ 1. A description of the pollution made by different kinds of transportation

_____ 2. The cost of different kinds of transportation

_____ 3. A description of the journey taken by the Climate Train

_____ 4. The number of scientists who joined the Climate Train

_____ 5. The different ways people can make less pollution

_____ 6. The date of the next conference

Now read the whole article. Were your guesses correct?

THE CLIMATE TRAIN

By Jackson Karl

1   In December 1997, thousands of scientists traveled to Kyoto, Japan, for an international conference on global warming. Months before the conference, most of these people began buying airplane tickets. But one English scientist named Ben Matthews thought that flying to Kyoto didn't seem right. He thought, "Flying is the most **convenient** way to travel from London to Kyoto, but airplanes make more pollution per person than cars, buses, or trains. Is it right to travel on airplanes so that we can talk about ways to make less pollution?" Ben believes that in order to make less pollution, all people—even scientists—need to change the way they live. He decided to **set an example**.

2   He began to plan a trip to Kyoto that created less pollution than an airplane trip. Other people soon joined him. In the end 36 people from 14 countries agreed to travel by land and sea to Kyoto. The group called itself the "Climate Train."

3   Planning the Climate Train trip was **complicated**. Ben and his fellow travelers had to carefully choose a route, check **schedules**, buy tickets, and **arrange** hotels—all in different languages.

4   The Climate Train group left London on November 7. They had to be at the Kyoto conference by December 1. They took different trains through Paris, Berlin, Moscow, Beijing and finally to Tianjin, on the **coast** of China.

5   While they were traveling, the Climate Train group worked a lot, but they also had fun. They especially liked talking to other travelers and listening to Russian pop music. One evening, some of the other travelers even started dancing on the tables of the restaurant car!

6   Everyone had a good time at the Chinese **border**. The border police took away the group's fresh fruit and vegetables. They didn't mind because they saw the colorful packages of Chinese food for sale. They didn't know what was inside, but they had fun tasting each of them.

7   From Tianjin, they traveled for two nights on a **ferry** to Kobe, Japan. Most of the group got seasick[1], so they couldn't work or have fun. But they all felt better when they saw the large group of journalists waiting for them in Kobe.

8   After talking with the journalists, a few Climate Train travelers took the train to Kyoto. The rest of the group

---

[1] **seasick:** feeling very sick because of the movement of a boat or ship

160   UNIT 8

rode their bicycles. The bicyclists took three days to ride the 80 kilometers from Kobe to Kyoto.

9   At the conference, the Climate Train travelers talked with many people about their journey[2]. They were glad to show the world that people can travel long distances in ways that make much less pollution than flying.

10 The long journey helped the travelers understand the reasons for the Kyoto conference. They realized that all the land they crossed in their journey is connected. The borders can't stop the pollution. The beautiful countryside they saw out the windows of their train will change if the climate continues to change. This made them all very sad and ready to work harder to stop global warming.

11 Because of the Kyoto conference, people around the world agreed to change their lives to help slow down global warming. The people on the Climate Train hope that their trip set a good example. It showed the kinds of changes people can make in how they travel. The five-week **round-trip** journey was difficult, but only because so few people travel this way. Says Ben, "If more people travel this way, it will become easier." Perhaps there will come a day when buying a round-trip train/ferry ticket from London to Kyoto will be as easy as buying a plane ticket. If more travelers take trains and ferries, the world's climate will be healthier, and travelers will **appreciate** the world's different countries and cultures more.

[2] **journey:** a long-distance trip

Source: Based on information on http://www.chooseclimate.org/climatetrain/.

◖ READ FOR MAIN IDEAS

Read the questions. Circle the best answer for each question.

1. What is the main reason that the Climate Train group traveled by land?
   a. To make less pollution
   b. To save money
   c. To learn about other cultures

2. Was the Climate Train group happy that they chose to travel by land?
   a. No. They will take a plane next time.
   b. Yes. They were happy, though it was sometimes difficult.
   c. Yes. They were happy because it was an easy way to travel.

3. What is the most important thing the Climate Train group came to understand on their journey?
   a. Pollution doesn't stop at borders. An international conference is necessary to solve the problem.
   b. Russian trains have fun restaurant cars.
   c. It's important to speak many languages so that you can talk with lots of people.

4. What do the Climate Train travelers hope that other people will do?
   a. Spend more time at borders
   b. Travel by land and sea instead of by air
   c. Go to more international climate conferences

◀ READ FOR DETAILS

These statements are false. Correct them. Change a word or phrase in each statement to make it true.

1. The Climate Train was a ~~train in Russia~~. *group of people*
2. The people on the Climate Train were from England.
3. Ben Mathews found it very easy to make the plans for the trip.
4. The group took six weeks to travel from London to Kyoto and back again.
5. The Climate Train travelers liked working with the other people on the train.
6. The Chinese border police gave them fruit and vegetables.
7. Several of the travelers got sick in Japan.
8. All of the travelers rode bicycles from Kobe to Kyoto.
9. The travelers understood that climate does not stop at borders.
10. They think that if more people travel by train and ferry, it will become faster.

◀ MAKE INFERENCES

Read each statement. Check (✓) True or False. Look at the paragraphs indicated in parentheses to help you.

	True	False
1. Most people going to Kyoto didn't think going to a climate conference by plane was a problem. (*paragraph 1*)	○	○
2. Ben Matthews usually travels long distances by airplane. (*paragraph 1*)	○	○
3. The Climate Train travelers found it difficult to communicate with other travelers. (*paragraph 5*)	○	○
4. The Climate Train travelers looked forward to talking to journalists about their trip. (*paragraph 7*)	○	○
5. Most Climate Train travelers came on the trip with a bicycle. (*paragraph 8*)	○	○
6. The Climate Train travelers told others at the conference to travel without flying. (*paragraph 9*)	○	○
7. If more people travel without flying, it will be easier because there will be more trains and ferries to choose from. (*paragraph 11*)	○	○

EXPRESS OPINIONS

Read the quote and answer the questions. Then discuss your answers in a small group.

> Some people who don't agree with Ben Matthews say, "You aren't making less pollution. The plane still goes and makes the same amount of pollution with or without you. One person doesn't make a difference."

1. What do you think Ben says to these people who do not agree with him?
   _____
   _____

2. Do you agree with the quote above, or with Ben? Explain your answer.
   _____
   _____

B READING TWO: On the Road with John Madden

Read the magazine article about a well-known figure in the world of American football who travels a lot.

ON THE ROAD WITH JOHN MADDEN

By Steve Mac

1 John Madden is famous for a lot of things. Some people remember him as the coach[1] for the Oakland Raiders football team—a job he held for 10 years. Some people know that in 2006 he was voted into the Football Hall of Fame[2]. But most people know him as a football commentator[3] on TV, something he's done every Sunday night of football season for over 25 years. And because he's so famous, Madden is also in many TV commercials.

John Madden commentating a football game

[1] **coach:** someone who trains a person or team in a sport
[2] **Football Hall of Fame:** a museum about special and important people in football
[3] **commentator:** someone on television or radio who describes an event as it is happening

(continued on next page)

2. As a football commentator, John Madden travels about 80,000 miles (130,000 km) during each football season—a football game in Philadelphia on Sunday, a party in Detroit on Tuesday, filming a TV commercial in Los Angeles on Saturday. He might be the perfect example of a jet-setter[4], except for one thing: He never travels by plane.

3. John Madden is one of 25 million people in the United States who are afraid of flying. These people spend millions of dollars every year trying to cure[5] their fear of flying. They go to classes, they see psychologists, and they take medications to help them with their fear. They think that they can't live normal lives if they can't fly.

4. John Madden decided not to try to cure his fear of flying; he decided to work with it. While he was coaching the Oakland Raiders, he traveled by train. Then he bought a motor home and decided that was the best way to travel. "It's not the fastest way to travel," says Madden, "but it's definitely the most comfortable." He has owned several motor homes over the last few years. The last one he bought is 45 feet long with a living room, office, small kitchen, and 1-1/2 bathrooms. He has three TVs and a full-size refrigerator.

5. Madden travels with several people who drive for him. This way he can be on the road 24 hours a day. He says that he is as comfortable in his motor home as a first-class airplane passenger. His fear of flying doesn't seem to get in his way[6] at all. He is a great example for people who are afraid of flying.

---

[4] **jet-setter:** a person who travels all over the world a lot, usually by plane (jet)
[5] **cure:** to make an illness or problem disappear
[6] **get in his way:** to prevent him from doing something

Now answer the questions.

1. How does John Madden travel?
   _____

2. Why does he choose to travel this way?
   _____

3. How did he travel before?
   _____

C INTEGRATE READINGS ONE AND TWO

STEP 1: Organize

The Climate Train travelers and John Madden both prefer not to travel by plane. When they choose a different way to travel, what is the most important thing to them?

Fill in the lists. You can use some items from the box (you don't need to include all of them). Then compare your lists with a partner's.

being able to work while traveling	not feeling afraid
comfort	scenery
cost	setting an example
learning about other places	speed
low pollution	traveling with others

Climate Train Travelers

Very important things while traveling:

_____
_____
_____

Somewhat important:

_____
_____
_____

Not so important:

_____
_____
_____

John Madden

Very important things while traveling:

_____
_____
_____

Somewhat important:

_____
_____
_____

Not so important:

_____
_____
_____

STEP 2: Synthesize

Imagine you are a journalist. Your boss asks you to write a story about alternatives[1] to flying. To help you write this article, he or she suggests you join one of the following:

1. The Climate Train group as they travel to the next climate conference
2. John Madden as he travels around the country during football season

Complete the following e-mail to your boss, explaining who you would like to go with and why. Explain also why you don't want to join the other trip. Use information from the lists in Step 1 to provide your reasons.

---

[1] **alternatives:** things you can choose to do or use instead of something else

Dear _____ ,
         (your boss's name)

I would like to travel with _____.
Most of our readers fly for long trips. But from this article they could learn that other ways of traveling are better than flying because …

_____

_____

Of course, I'll have to explain some of the disadvantages. For example, …

_____

_____

I don't think joining _____ makes a good story.
Our readers don't really want to learn about …

_____

_____

Thanks a lot for giving me this choice. I'm really excited about my trip and look forward to writing this article.

Sincerely,

_____
         (your name)

3 FOCUS ON WRITING

A VOCABULARY

REVIEW

1 *Read the statements. Each statement could be said by one of the travelers in the chart. Who is most likely to say what? Write the number of each statement under the correct traveler. Some statements could be said by more than one traveler.*

166   UNIT 8

TRAIN PASSENGER	AIRPLANE PASSENGER	FERRY PASSENGER	BICYCLE RIDER	MOTOR HOME OWNER
	1			

1. "I'm going from Chicago to Frankfurt. This is the least **complicated** way to go."
2. "When I travel this way, I don't have to deal with tickets and **schedules**. I can leave when I want, and I can stop when I want. It's not free—I do have to pay for gas. But for me, it's the best way to go. Besides, I LOVE to drive."
3. "I usually **arrange** my plans myself. It's easy on the Internet, and I don't have to pay a travel agent."
4. "I'm trying to **set an example** for my children. I'm getting lots of exercise and I don't make any pollution."
5. "I think I can finally see the **coast**. It will be good to get on land again."
6. "All of the passengers had to get off at the **border**; then we all got back on and continued our trip."
7. "I love traveling this way. It's so **comfortable**. There is lots of room. I can stand up and take a walk. I can sit down at a table and eat a hot dinner."
8. "I know. I know. It eats a lot of gas. But there is nothing more **convenient**. I've got everything I need wherever I go in the country."
9. "I **appreciate** the older, slower, relaxed ways of traveling overland."

2 Complete the sentences with the correct words from the box.

appreciates	border	complicated	~~ferry~~	schedule
arrange	coast	convenient	round-trip	sets an example

1. Linette lives on Bainbridge Island. To get to work in Seattle, she drives over to Winslow and takes the _____ferry_____ into the city every day.
2. Traveling to the small town in the Sahara Desert to visit my sister was very _____ and uncomfortable.
3. I need to check the bus _____. Then we can _____ the trip to New Orleans.
4. Make sure that you have your passport. They always check it at the _____.

"I'll take the train, thanks." **167**

5. Nicole _____ the beach and warm weather. That's why she lives on the _____.

6. Remember not to buy _____ tickets! We're moving to Greece for two years. We don't know when we'll return.

7. My son's teacher _____ for the children in her class. She always reuses plastic bags instead of throwing them in the trash.

8. I prefer to take my car instead of the bus. It's more _____. I can go where I want, leave when I want, and stop to sightsee when I want.

EXPAND

Read each one of the statements made by travelers. Then copy the boldfaced word(s) in the appropriate column in the chart.

RESEARCHING A TRIP	THE COST OF A TRIP	ARRANGING A TRIP	PART OF A TRIP

1. "I got my tickets to London about five months ago. If you buy them now, I don't think they'll be as **cheap**. But who knows. Maybe you'll get lucky."

2. "I can't believe this! My boss is making me go to this conference in Madrid next week. I was planning to go on vacation to Paris then. I **booked tickets** three months ago. I don't think I will get my money back. Ay!"

3. "When you fly to Europe, look at **fares** to London, Paris, or Frankfurt. Tickets are cheaper to these cities because more planes fly there."

4. "I heard you want to visit Bali this summer. Did you **look into** how to get tickets yet? Try the Hotwire website. They have lots of choices of flights. You might also try a travel agent. When I was young, I took subways and city buses around new cities. Now, when I travel with my husband and children, it's just easier and cheaper to **rent a car**."

5. "Our final **destination** is Los Angeles. But I think we'll visit Santa Cruz, the Hearst Mansion, and Santa Barbara on our way down there."

6. "I got **a great deal** on a bus ticket from Sydney to Adelaide, Australia. It costs only $125—less than half the price of the plane trip. The only problem is it'll take almost 48 hours to make the trip."

CREATE

Read the information.

Ben is talking to his co-worker, Alice. They are making their plans. They want to travel from London to Warsaw for another important conference. Ben does not want to take a plane for the same reasons he didn't take a plane to Kyoto in 1997. Alice wants to fly because she doesn't have a lot of time.

Now complete the conversation between Ben and Alice. Use at least eight of the words from the box.

a great deal	cheap	destination	rent a car
appreciate	coast	fares	round-trip
arrange journey	comfortable	ferry	schedule
book tickets	complicated	look into	set an example
border	convenient	pollution	

ALICE: Ben, we need to **arrange** our trip to Warsaw. I saw some **great deals** on the LOT Polish Airline website. Do you want me to buy the tickets?

BEN: _____

ALICE: _____

BEN: _____

ALICE: _____

BEN: _____

"I'll take the train, thanks."   **169**

B GRAMMAR: Superlative Form of Adjectives

1 Read the excerpt from Reading Two. Notice the boldfaced words. Then answer the questions.

> While he was coaching the Oakland Raiders, he traveled by train. Then he bought a motor home and decided that was **the best** way to travel. "It's not **the fastest** way to travel," says Madden, "but it's definitely **the most comfortable**."

1. Which way of traveling around the country does John Madden think is better—by train or by motor home?
2. How do you know?

SUPERLATIVE FORM OF ADJECTIVES

1. Use the **superlative** form of adjectives to compare three or more people, places, or things.	Flying is **the fastest** way of traveling. Ben is **the smartest** person I know.
2. If the adjective has **one syllable**, use **the** before the adjective and add **-est** at the end of the adjective. Add only **-st** if the word ends in **-e**.	fast the fast**est** old the old**est** large the larg**est**
3. When a one-syllable adjective ends in a consonant + vowel + consonant, **double the last consonant** and add **-est**.	big the big**gest** hot the hot**test**
4. If a **two-syllable** adjective ends in **-y**, change y to i and add **-est**.	easy the eas**iest** busy the bus**iest**
5. Some adjectives have **irregular** superlative forms.	good the best bad the worst
6. For most adjectives that have **two or more syllables**, add **the most** before the adjective. Add **the least** for the negative form.	Flying is **the most expensive** way of traveling. Biking is **the least expensive** way of traveling.

7. After a superlative adjective, we often use a **prepositional phrase** starting with *in* or *of*.	Ben is the most famous scientist **in the group**. Flying is the most expensive **of all the ways to go to Los Angeles**.

2 Read the chart comparing ways to travel between London and Bristol, England. Then complete each sentence with the superlative form of the adjective in parentheses.

LONDON TO BRISTOL, ENGLAND			
	Car	**Plane**	**Train**
Price	£65 (for gas)	£185	£104
Time	two hours	35 minutes	three hours
Comfort	Small seats Can't stand up	Small seats Can stand up	Large seats Can stand up
Convenience	Can leave when you want Takes you directly to where you will stay	Have to leave when plane is scheduled Have to get from airport to where you will stay	Have to leave when train is scheduled Train has many stops and arrives in the city center

1. Traveling by car is _____the cheapest_____ way to go.
   (cheap)
2. Traveling by plane is _____ way to go.
   (expensive)
3. Traveling by plane is _____ way to go.
   (fast)
4. Traveling by train is _____ way to go.
   (slow)
5. Traveling by car is _____ way to go.
   (comfortable)
6. Traveling by train is _____ way to go.
   (comfortable)
7. Traveling by car is _____ way to go.
   (convenient)

"I'll take the train, thanks."

3 Read the paragraph and correct the five errors in the superlative form.

> Tomi lives about 10 kilometers outside of Dublin. She works in the city every day. It was complicated trying to decide how to get to work every morning. Driving her car was the most fastest way to go. But she didn't like making all that pollution, and gas is expensive. So she thought about the train. But the train was expensive too, and the train schedule didn't work with her schedule. A friend suggested she bike to work. This sounded like a worst idea of all. Riding a bike isn't comfortable and it is hard work. But after she thought about it, she realized it was the intelligentest choice. Biking was the most cheap way to get to the city. It made the leastest amount of pollution. And she could get her exercise while she went to work. Now that's convenient!

C WRITING

In this unit, you read about a scientist who convinced 35 other scientists to travel to Kyoto with him by train, ferry, and bicycle. Now imagine that you and some co-workers are planning a trip to go to a two-day conference together.

You are going to **write an e-mail to your co-workers explaining the best way to travel to that conference and why**. To convince your co-workers, you will list the advantages of your choice and the disadvantages of the other choices. Then you will add one or two disadvantages of your choice, explaining that they are not big problems. Use the vocabulary and grammar from the unit.*

---

*For Alternative Writing Topics, see page 178. These topics can be used in place of the writing topic for this unit or as homework. The alternative topics relate to the theme of the unit, but may not target the same grammar or rhetorical structures taught in the unit.

◀ PREPARE TO WRITE: Charting

Making a chart of your ideas can be helpful when you have to write about a lot of information.

1 *Read the chart comparing ways to travel from San Francisco to Los Angeles (about 400 miles or 650 kilometers). Notice how the information is organized.*

SAN FRANCISCO TO LOS ANGELES		
Way to Travel	**Advantages**	**Disadvantages**
Plane	Fast	Getting to/from the airport can take a long time
		Expensive
		Makes a lot of pollution
Train	Comfortable	Slow
	Low pollution	Expensive
	Nice scenery	
Car	Can leave when you want	Traffic
	Convenient	Tiring
	Cheap	Makes pollution
Bus	Cheap	Slow, many stops
	Can get off to see things	Uncomfortable, crowded
		Makes pollution

2 *Imagine your conference is in a city 200–600 miles (300–900 kilometers) away from where you live. Choose the city where you will go and think of two or three ways to make the trip. Make a chart showing the advantages and disadvantages of these ways to travel. You might want to think about the following:*

- cost
- comfort
- pollution
- time
- convenience

3 *Look at your chart. Choose the best way to go on the trip.*

"I'll take the train, thanks." **173**

WRITE: A Persuasive E-mail

To **persuade or convince** people that your choice is the best choice, you have to explain the **advantages of your choice** and the **disadvantages of the other choices**. It's also important to talk about **one or two disadvantages of *your* choice**. This helps to convince your reader that you did your research and made a good decision.

1 *Read the e-mail and follow the instructions below.*

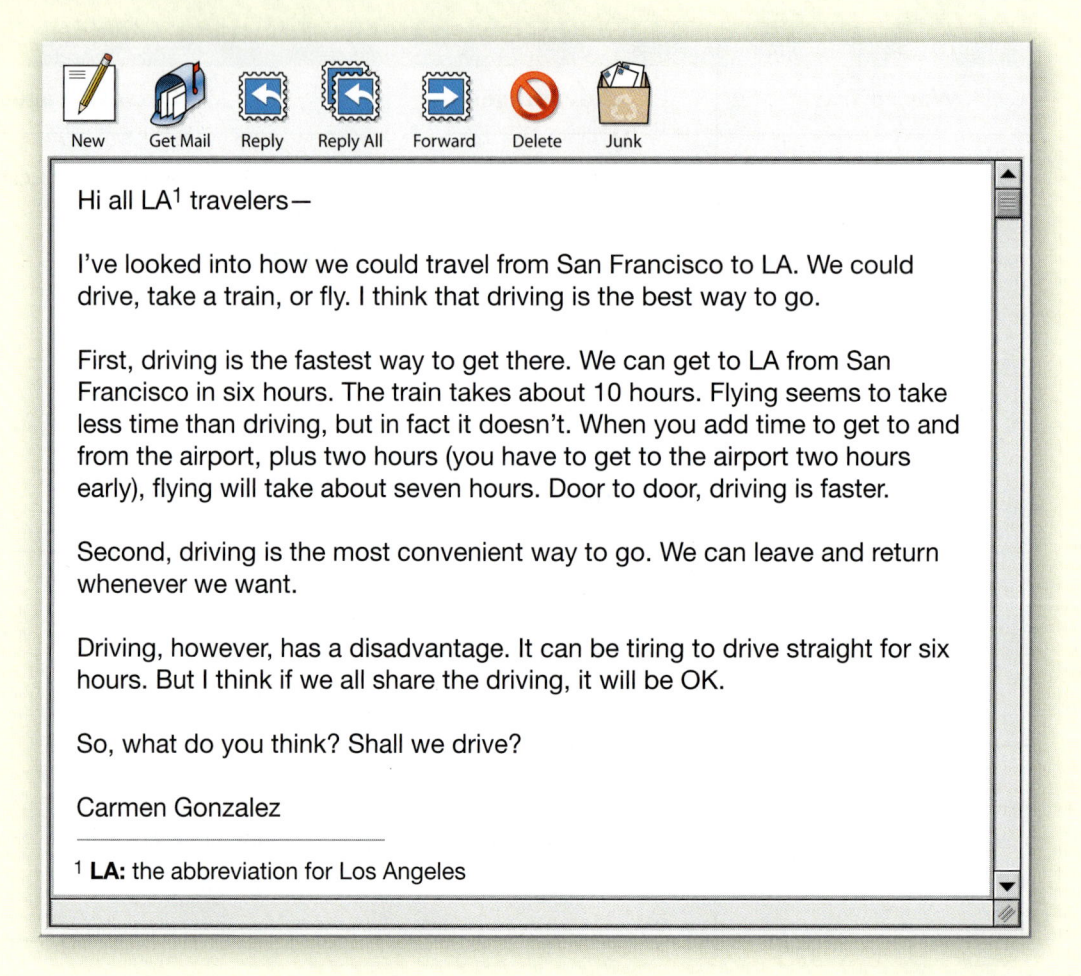

Hi all LA[1] travelers—

I've looked into how we could travel from San Francisco to LA. We could drive, take a train, or fly. I think that driving is the best way to go.

First, driving is the fastest way to get there. We can get to LA from San Francisco in six hours. The train takes about 10 hours. Flying seems to take less time than driving, but in fact it doesn't. When you add time to get to and from the airport, plus two hours (you have to get to the airport two hours early), flying will take about seven hours. Door to door, driving is faster.

Second, driving is the most convenient way to go. We can leave and return whenever we want.

Driving, however, has a disadvantage. It can be tiring to drive straight for six hours. But I think if we all share the driving, it will be OK.

So, what do you think? Shall we drive?

Carmen Gonzalez

[1] **LA:** the abbreviation for Los Angeles

1. **Paragraph 1:** Circle the writer's choice.
2. **Paragraphs 2, 3:** Circle the two sentences that state the advantages of this choice.
3. **Paragraph 2:** Underline the sentences that state the disadvantages of the other ways of traveling.
4. **Paragraph 4:** Underline twice the sentence that states the disadvantage of the writer's choice.

174 UNIT 8

2 A manager in London is working on an e-mail to his co-workers about the travel choices to a conference in Bristol. Use the information in the London to Bristol chart (see page 171) to help him complete the e-mail.

Dear James, Melissa, and Deirdre,

I've looked into how to get to our conference in Bristol. We can drive a rental car, take a train, or fly. I think a plane is the best way to go.

(1)_____. It takes only 35 minutes.

The train (2)_____ and a car

(3)_____.

We have a lot of work to do before and after the conference. We can't waste time traveling. So I think we should fly.

There are some disadvantages to flying.

(4)_____. However, our company

will pay the fare. Also (5)_____.
But it's such a short flight, comfort doesn't matter that much.

Time is the most important thing to me right now, so I think we should fly. Please let me know if you agree with this plan. Then I'll book our tickets.

Thanks,
Ian Mulligan

Notice how both Carmen (*see page 174*) and Ian explain the **disadvantages** of their choice. They follow the explanation with a description of how this disadvantage does not really cause much of a problem.

"I'll take the train, thanks." **175**

3 Look at the chart you made in Prepare to Write (page 173). Think about what is important to you when you travel.

1. Circle the information you think will help show the advantages of your choice of transportation. Give no more than two reasons for making your choice.

2. Underline the information that shows the disadvantages of the other ways of traveling compared with your choice.

3. Underline twice some disadvantages of your choice. Remember, when we explain the disadvantages of our choice, we try to show that in the end, it is not a big problem.

4 Now write the first draft of your e-mail to your co-workers. Use the information from your chart.

REVISE: Connecting Ideas with *And* and *But*

Good writers use different kinds of sentences. One way to make your sentences different is to use the sentence connectors *and* and *but*.

> **SENTENCE CONNECTORS *AND* AND *BUT***
>
> *And* connects **similar** ideas in the same sentence. *But* connects **contrasting** ideas in the same sentence.
> - A few Climate Train travelers took the train, **and** the rest rode their bicycles.
> - The Climate Train group worked a lot, **but** they also found time to have fun.
>
> Notice that when you connect two sentences with *and* or *but*, you use a **comma (,)** between the ideas.
>
> When the **subject of both sentences is the same**, use a **pronoun** as the subject in the second sentence.
>
>   he
> - John Madden is afraid of flying, **but** ~~John Madden~~ doesn't let it stop him from traveling.
>
> Sometimes **two sentences are too long** to connect in the same sentence. In some cases, people use *and* and *but* at the **beginning of the second sentence** to connect the ideas.
> - John meets lots of different people who take the train because they are afraid of flying. **But** he's never met a single person who flies because they are afraid of trains.

1 Combine the sentences with the correct connector word (*and* or *but*). Add the correct punctuation.

1. The drive to Chicago is very long. In some places there is a lot of traffic.

   _____

2. Gas for a long drive is very expensive. Airline tickets are more expensive.

   _____

3. Taking the train to Chicago is relaxing and enjoyable. It is slow.

4. You can buy snacks on the train. You don't have to worry about traffic.

5. You can sleep or read a book on the train. You can't choose who you sit next to.

6. The train ride through the Rocky Mountains of Colorado in the middle of spring is one of the most beautiful journeys in the United States. The rest of the ride across eastern Colorado is really boring.

2 Read the excerpt from a letter. This writer could use more of the connectors **and** and **but**. Insert **and** or **but**, and the correct punctuation and capitalization. Not all sentences need to be connected.

> Last year, I traveled around New Zealand. _____ New Zealand has a wonderful bus and train system, and it's ~~It's~~ a safe place to hitchhike[1]. _____ I didn't take buses or trains. _____ I didn't hitchhike. _____ I rode my bicycle. _____ New Zealand is a beautiful country to see from a bike. _____ It's a safe country to bike through. _____ There are very few cars on the roads. _____ All the drivers are very careful and polite to bikers.
>
> New Zealand is beautiful. _____ It rains a lot there. _____ Riding on a bike was a lot of fun. _____ I got really wet. _____ Even with the rain, I'm still really glad I chose to bike instead of riding in a car, bus, or train.
>
> ---
> [1] **hitchhike:** to travel by asking for free rides in other people's cars

3 Now go back to the first draft of your e-mail. Identify places where you can connect sentences with **and** and **but**. Rewrite your e-mail with these additions. Make sure you are using the correct punctuation and capitalization.

"I'll take the train, thanks."

EDIT: Writing the Final Draft

Write the final draft of your e-mail. Carefully edit it for grammatical and mechanical errors such as spelling, capitalization, and punctuation. Make sure you used some of the vocabulary and grammar from the unit. Use the checklist to help you write your final draft. Then neatly write or type your e-mail.

> **✓ FINAL DRAFT CHECKLIST**
>
> ○ Does your e-mail explain the advantages of your choice of transportation to a specific place?
> ○ Does it state the disadvantages of the other ways of traveling?
> ○ Does it describe one or two disadvantages of your choice and then explain how they really are not problems?
> ○ Do you use the superlative in your e-mail?
> ○ Do you use the superlative correctly?
> ○ Do you use *and* and *but* to connect sentences?
> ○ Do the sentences connected with *and* and *but* have the correct punctuation and capitalization?
> ○ Do you use new vocabulary that you learned in this unit?

ALTERNATIVE WRITING TOPICS

Write about one of the topics. Use the vocabulary and grammar from the unit.

1. Write a paragraph describing ways that you can make less pollution when you travel. Think about the traveling that you do in your daily life (to school, work, or the store, for example) as well as the traveling that you do for vacations.

2. Write a paragraph about someone you know who does not like to fly. Why doesn't that person like to fly? How does he or she travel?

3. Today, airplanes can take us almost anywhere in the world in less than 24 hours. Before airplanes, people couldn't travel to a lot of places so easily. In a paragraph, compare traveling before airplanes and travel today.

RESEARCH TOPICS, see page 229.

UNIT 9
What's Your Medicine?

Modern medicine   Traditional medicine   Home remedies

1 FOCUS ON THE TOPIC

A PREDICT

Look at the pictures and discuss the questions with the class.

1. These three kinds of medicine are practiced today all over the world. Which kind do people in your community use most?

2. Why do you think people choose to use traditional medicine? Why do they choose to use a home remedy?

B SHARE INFORMATION

In this unit you will be reading about some health problems. Read the questions and discuss the answers in a small group. Share your answers with the class.

1. When is the last time you were sick?
2. What was wrong?
3. Did you go to a doctor?
4. If so, what did the doctor do for you?
5. If you didn't go to the doctor, what did you do to get better?
6. How did you know what to do?

C BACKGROUND AND VOCABULARY

Today people have a lot of choice about who can help them when they are sick. They can see modern doctors or traditional healers. But many people choose to treat themselves at home when they have a common health problem.

1 Look at the pictures of several common health problems. Write the letter of the appropriate picture next to the name of the health problem.

180 UNIT 9

____c____ 1. headache

_____ 2. stomachache

_____ 3. earache

_____ 4. toothache

_____ 5. backache

_____ 6. sore throat

_____ 7. fever

_____ 8. sprained ankle[1]

_____ 9. a cold / the flu

2 *Read the list of words and their definitions.*

> **blood:** the red liquid that your heart pumps through your body
>
> **cure:** to make a sick person well again
>
> **fever:** when the body is sick and is hotter than normal
>
> **flow:** when a liquid (water, for example) moves slowly from one place to another
>
> **patients:** people who are getting medical treatment
>
> **popular:** liked by many people
>
> **saliva:** the liquid produced naturally in your mouth
>
> **sore throat:** when the throat is red and painful
>
> **swelling:** an area on your body that becomes larger than usual because of injury or sickness
>
> **swollen:** bigger than usual because of injury or sickness
>
> **treat:** to do something to a sick person to try to make him or her well again
>
> **veins:** the tubes that bring blood back to the heart from the rest of the body

Now use words from the list to complete the short descriptions of home remedies.

1. ____Fever____: The most common remedy for this problem is cool water. Put the sick person in a cool bath or wash the person gently with a cool cloth. Don't put the person in ice water. It could be bad for him or her.

2. **Headache:** In China, some people _____ a headache with a coin (metal money). Hold the coin in your fingers and rub it back and forth across the forehead very hard. It will leave a red mark.

---

[1] **sprained ankle:** something you get when you fall and hurt your ankle but it's not broken

3. **Cold:** Some people believe you can _____ a cold by drinking a lot of orange juice. Orange juice has a lot of vitamin C. This helps the body fight illness.

4. _____: One remedy for this problem is honey. Eat one big spoonful three times a day. Most children love this remedy. The honey is sweet and it feels nice on the throat. In fact, older _____ like it, too!

5. **Stomachache:** A _____ remedy is ginger (a spice from a light brown root). Cook 4 ounces of ginger in 1 quart of water for 1 hour. Drink a glass three times a day.

6. **Toothache:** When you have a toothache, everything that goes in your mouth hurts. Even the _____ in your mouth seems to hurt. For hundreds of years the most common remedy for a toothache was to drink a glass of whiskey and have your neighbor pull out the tooth. These days, people just go to the dentist.

7. **Sprained ankle:** A sprained ankle often gets _____. To bring down the _____, do two things. First, put a bag of ice on the ankle. The cold makes the _____ in the ankle get smaller. Put the ice on the ankle for no longer than 10 minutes every couple of hours. Second, put your foot up high. This helps the _____ _____ back to the heart and makes the ankle go back to its normal size.

2 FOCUS ON READING

A READING ONE: Leech

The following article is an excerpt from an encyclopedia entry. Read the title and the section headings. What kind of information do you think you will find in this article? Check (✓) the things you think you will find.

_____ 1. how many kinds of leeches are in the world

_____ 2. definition of leech

_____ 3. how to catch leeches

_____ 4. description of what leeches eat

_____ 5. stories about people being leeched

_____ 6. how leeches have been used in medicine in the past

_____ 7. how leeches are used in medicine today

_____ 8. how leeches will be used in medicine in the future

_____ 9. why leeches are dangerous to use

Now read the article. Were your guesses correct?

LEECH

1 Biology Leeches are a kind of worm[1] from one millimeter to five centimeters long. They live all over the world. In general, leeches live in lakes and rivers. There are 650 kinds of leeches in the world. Only one kind is used in medicine. They are called medicinal leeches.

2 Medicinal leeches live on the **blood** of other animals. They have suckers[2] at both ends—one for feeding and one for holding on. Their **saliva** has three special chemicals that help them drink the blood. One is an anesthetic[3], which allows the leech to feed without hurting the animal. The second chemical makes the **veins** open wide, and the third makes the blood **flow** from the veins for a long time.

3 A medicinal leech will drink 10 to 15 milliliters of blood at one time. This takes about 45 minutes. After the leech is full, it falls off. The bite will still bleed for another 24 hours because of the chemicals from its saliva.

4 History Leeches have been used in medicine for over 3,000 years. Leeches were most **popular** in Europe in the early 1800s. At this time, people thought that too much blood in a person's body made the person sick. Doctors put three or four leeches (or sometimes up to 50 or 60 leeches!) on a **patient**'s body. The leeches took out the extra blood. Leeches were used to **cure** many illnesses, from **fevers** to broken legs.

5 Unfortunately, leeches often hurt more than they healed. For example, the Russian writer Nikolai Gogol was leeched because he had anemia, an illness caused by too *little* blood. He died a few days later. George Washington had a **sore throat**. He was leeched four times in two days. He too died a few days later. By the mid-1850s, people began to understand some of the problems with leeching, and it became unpopular.

6 In Medicine Today Today, doctors know more about leeches. They know when to use them and why. They understand that the chemicals in the leech saliva make leeches very useful in medicine. For this reason, the United States made it legal in 2004 to use leeches in reattachment surgeries[4].

---

[1] **worm:** a small snake-like animal that lives in the ground
[2] **suckers:** small round parts that connect the leech to the animal it feeds on
[3] **anesthetic:** a chemical that stops you from feeling pain
[4] **reattachment surgeries:** procedures performed when someone's finger or toe is cut off and the doctor puts it back on the hand or foot

(continued on next page)

7   Until now, reattachment surgeries often failed. Take the example of a reattached finger. After surgery, the finger often becomes **swollen** with blood and the veins can't grow back together. The finger soon dies. Leeches take away this extra blood in two ways. One, they drink some of the blood from the finger. This only removes a spoonful of blood, however. The second way leeches remove this blood is the most important. Because of the chemicals in the leech saliva, the bite continues to bleed for hours and hours after the leech falls off. With one or two leeches put on the finger twice a day for 4–5 days, the **swelling** will go away completely. With the swelling gone, the veins can grow back together and the finger lives. Doctors agree that leeches work better than anything else for this problem with reattachment surgeries.

8   There might be other medical uses for leeches too. For instance, some doctors use leeches to **treat** patients with heart disease or knee and elbow pain.

◀ READ FOR MAIN IDEAS

Circle the statement that best summarizes the main idea of each section.

Biology

a. Leeches are worms that suck blood from other animals.

b. Leeches have suckers at both ends.

c. Leeches have both male and female parts.

History

a. People thought that too much blood caused illness. That's why leeches were popular.

b. Leeches killed George Washington and the Russian writer Nikolai Gogol.

c. Doctors treated every kind of illness with leeches. Often this caused a lot of problems.

In Medicine Today

a. Many modern doctors use leeches to treat heart disease or knee and elbow pain.

b. Modern doctors are afraid that leeching will become popular again.

c. Modern medicine is finding that leeches are useful in reattachment surgeries.

◀ READ FOR DETAILS

These statements are false. Cross out the incorrect word and replace it with the correct word to make true statements.

1. Leeches live in ~~oceans~~ lakes and rivers all over the world.

2. A leech bite will still bleed for 12 hours after the leech falls off.

3. Leeches were most popular in Europe in the late 1800s.

4. The United States made it legal to use leeches for reattachment surgeries in 2001.

5. Today, people think sickness comes from too much blood.

6. Leeches help with swelling because they suck out some of the blood and because of the bacteria in their saliva.

7. Doctors disagree that leeches are the best thing to stop swelling after reattachment surgeries.

8. It takes a leech 24 minutes to feed and fall off.

MAKE INFERENCES

Read each statement and decide if you think it is **likely** or **unlikely**. Check the appropriate box.

	Likely	Unlikely
1. All leeches need water to live.	○	○
2. All leeches need blood to live.	○	○
3. Too much blood in the person's body can make a person sick.	○	○
4. Leeches helped to cure people of illnesses in the early 1800s.	○	○
5. Leeching became unpopular in the mid-1850s because George Washington had died after heavy leeching.	○	○
6. Today leeches help veins grow back together.	○	○

EXPRESS OPINIONS

Discuss the questions with a partner. Give your opinions. Then share your answers with the class.

1. Does your country allow doctors to use leeches to treat their patients? Do you think this is a good thing? Why or why not?

2. Imagine your doctor explained that the only way to save your toe after reattachment surgery was to have leeches on it for three days. Would you agree or not? Explain.

B READING TWO: Gross Medicine

Read the story. It describes one man's experience with a traditional African doctor.

GROSS[1] MEDICINE
By Shetal Shah

1. I was trying to lie still and close my eyes. But I had to look.

2. They looked brown like chocolates. In fact, they were dark-green. But these "chocolates" were leeches. They were sucking out the pus[2] from my ankle. They were looking for blood.

3. This happened to me last summer when I rode my bicycle across Botswana, Africa. One day, I fell off my bike and got a small cut on my ankle. I forgot to wash the cut or put a bandage on it.

4. Three days later, I couldn't put on my shoe because my foot was so swollen. The pain in my ankle was terrible. And it was moving up my leg. I needed to find a doctor fast. But in Botswana, near the Kalahari Desert, a trip to the hospital looked like this: one day by car, three days by bicycle, or six days by donkey. This is when I met Ntemidisang and the leeches.

5. Ntemidisang was a traditional doctor from a village four kilometers away. He looked at the cut. He pushed on it carefully. Then he put his hand on my forehead and nodded[3] his head. Yes, I had a fever. He said he had to take the pus out of the ankle before I could bicycle to the city the next day to get some antibiotics.

6. Ntemidisang smiled to help me relax. He put a wet cloth on my forehead and opened a small metal box. Inside this dirty little box were the leeches.

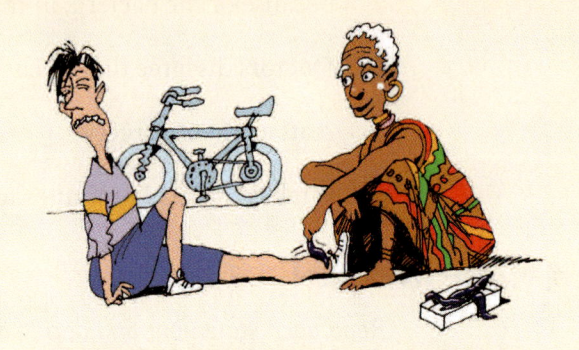

7. I put my head back and watched the stars. I tried to think of other things. But I felt something cool on my skin. Ntemidisang put the leeches gently around the cut on my ankle. Suddenly, I felt them bite, and then I didn't feel anything.

8. Ntemidisang tried to make me laugh and forget about what was happening on my ankle. He wasn't funny, but I laughed.

9. An hour later, my ankle was bandaged and Ntemidisang was smiling. I was smiling too. I thanked him for helping me, and we said goodbye. Two days later, after riding 240 kilometers to the next city, I found a hospital. As the doctor was giving me a shot of antibiotics, I was thinking, "I sure don't like shots, but at least they aren't as gross as leeches!"

---

[1] **gross:** very unpleasant to look at or think about
[2] **sucking out the pus:** drinking the yellowish liquid from the dirty cut
[3] **nodded:** moved his head up and down to say "yes"

Source: Adapted from *Why leeches influence my physical examination. (Essay).* Shetal Shah. *The Lancet* 352.9145 (Dec 19, 1998): p. 2014(1).

Now circle the best answer to complete each statement.

1. Shah was traveling through ____ when he fell off his bike.
   a. a village
   b. Botswana
   c. a desert

2. Shah's ankle was swollen because ____.
   a. the leeches bit him
   b. he rode his bicycle too far
   c. he cut his ankle and didn't wash or bandage it

3. Shah needed a hospital. He couldn't get to one soon enough because ____.
   a. he didn't have a donkey
   b. it would take too long on his bicycle
   c. his car was too slow

4. Ntemidisang tried to make Shah laugh. He ____.
   a. wanted Shah to stop thinking about the leeches on his ankle
   b. wanted Shah to like him and think he was funny
   c. was nervous and didn't know what to do while they waited

5. The leeches helped Shah because they ____.
   a. cured him by healing the infection in his ankle
   b. took away the swelling so he could bike to the hospital
   c. made him relax

C INTEGRATE READINGS ONE AND TWO

STEP 1: Organize

Read the phrases based on Readings One and Two. Write each phrase in the correct box in the chart on the next page.

- ~~To take away the extra blood in reattachment surgeries~~
- A few put on for about an hour
- Like worms—one millimeter to five centimeters long
- To cure every illness
- Put on until they fall off once or twice a day for 4-5 days
- Like chocolates but really dark green
- They suck out the pus from a dirty cut
- A small metal box
- Make the blood flow
- Lakes and rivers
- Make the veins open wide
- Include an anesthetic
- To take the pus out of his ankle so he can move it

What's Your Medicine?   **187**

	THE ENCYCLOPEDIA ENTRY	SHETAL SHAH'S EXPERIENCE
1. What do leeches look like?		
2. Where do they come from?		
3. Why are they used?	Before: Today: To take away the extra blood in reattachment surgeries	

4. How do they work?	Chemicals in the saliva:
	  a.
	  b.
	  c.	

5. How are they used?		

◀ **STEP 2: Synthesize**

Shetal Shah told the doctor he saw at the hospital about the leeches. The doctor laughed and said he was lucky. Leeches are good medicine. Shetal Shah was interested. He asked his doctor a few questions about leeches and medicine.

Complete the conversation between Shetal Shah and the doctor. Use information from the chart in Step 1.

SHETAL SHAH: Why did the traditional doctor use leeches on me?

DOCTOR: _____

_____

Shetal Shah: Where do you think he got those leeches?

Doctor: _____

Shetal Shah: Why didn't it hurt?

Doctor: _____

Shetal Shah: Why did the bite keep bleeding so long afterward?

Doctor: _____

3 FOCUS ON WRITING

A VOCABULARY

REVIEW

1 Match the statements or questions on the left with the responses on the right.

__f__ 1. Yoga is so **popular** these days.

____ 2. You get headaches a lot. How do you **treat** them?

____ 3. How can I bring down the **swelling** in my knee?

____ 4. Do you think I have a **fever**?

____ 5. Oh, I have a terrible **sore throat**.

____ 6. Ew! That's **gross**!

____ 7. You need to get some **antibiotics** for that cut.

a. No, your forehead doesn't feel hot to me.

b. Put a bag of frozen peas on it for 20 minutes. That should help.

c. I drink a big glass of water and lie down in a dark room for an hour. It works most of the time.

d. Yeah, I guess you're right. It's all red and painful.

e. I know. But what can I do? It's my job to put leeches on people.

f. I know. Everyone I know is taking classes. We all want to be healthy, I guess.

g. Would some tea with honey make it feel better?

What's Your Medicine?   **189**

2 Complete the sentences with the words from the box. Use one word more than once.

| ~~bandage~~ | blood | cure | flows | patients | saliva | shots | swollen | vein |

1. I need a new ___bandage___ for this burn on my hand. My old one got wet when I washed the dishes, and I should have a dry one.

2. Some people are very afraid of getting _____ when they go to see a doctor. One friend of mine asked me to go with her to hold her hand to help her be more relaxed!

3. Sometimes when you need a blood test, the nurse has trouble finding your _____. This often leaves a black-and-blue mark on your arm.

4. When you are hungry, your body makes extra _____ in your mouth. It's getting ready for the food that should soon be coming!

5. The Hudson River in New York _____ into the Atlantic Ocean.

6. I fell down the stairs yesterday. Today my ankle is so _____ I can't put on my shoe!

7. The doctors said they could _____ him if he took the medicine now. If he waited, they gave him six months to live.

8. Today in the United States, doctors are tired. They see twice as many _____ in a day as doctors did 25 years ago.

9. Most hospitals have something called a _____ bank. This is a place where they keep extra _____ for people who lose too much of their own when they have an accident or a long surgery.

EXPAND

Read each sentence. Circle the word or phrase that best matches the boldfaced word.

1. Last summer, I got a piece of glass in my foot. My wife washed my foot and pulled out the glass **gently**.
   a. in a way that was not hard
   b. in a way that was fast

2. If you get a bad cut, you must put a bandage on it right away. Hold the bandage to the cut **firmly**. This will stop the bleeding.
   a. in a soft way
   b. in a hard way

3. The four-year-old girl would not stop screaming. But the doctor talked to her **calmly**, and she finally sat still and listened.
   a. with a gentle, quiet voice
   b. with a loud, angry voice

4. Last summer, I broke my finger. I went to the hospital. I waited **patiently** for two hours. But after four hours, I was angry. Why did it have to take so long?
   a. becoming upset or mad
   b. without becoming upset or mad

5. The first time I met my husband's mother, I was surprised. He had told me she was not very nice and never smiled. But, instead, she greeted me **warmly** and made me feel very welcome.
   a. in a friendly way
   b. in an unfriendly way

6. He was a new doctor, so he put the bandage on **roughly**. The patient cried "Ouch!"
   a. in a soft way
   b. in a hard way

CREATE

Complete the conversation between the first-aid teacher and a student. Use as many of the words in parentheses as you can.

TEACHER: So, to review, what do you do if someone gets a sprained ankle?

STUDENT: _____
(bandage / patient / gently / swelling / swollen)

_____

_____

TEACHER: Good. Now tell me what you do when you see someone bleeding?

STUDENT: _____
(blood / veins / flow / patient / treat / firmly)

_____

_____

TEACHER: _____?
(sore throat / fever)

STUDENT: _____
(cure / popular / antibiotics)

_____

B GRAMMAR: Adverbs of Manner

1 Read the excerpt from Reading Two. Then answer the questions.

> Ntemidisang was a traditional doctor from a village four kilometers away. He looked at the cut. He pushed on it carefully.

1. How does the doctor push on Shetal's cut?
2. How do you know?

ADVERBS OF MANNER

1. **Adverbs of manner** describe action verbs. They say **how** or in what manner something happens. They are helpful when writing **descriptions**.	The doctor listened **carefully**.
2. Adverbs of manner usually come **after the main verb**.	The patient **talked slowly**.
3. Most adverbs of manner are formed by adding **-ly** to the adjective.	careful careful**ly** slow slow**ly**
4. Some **adjectives** end in **-ly** and have no adverb form.	He was a **lonely** old man. She has a **friendly** neighbor.
5. Some **adverbs** have the **same form** as the **adjective**.	**hard** *(adj.)*: The test was **hard**. **hard** *(adv.)*: She worked **hard**. **fast** *(adj.)*: He is a **fast** runner. **fast** *(adv.)*: She ran **fast**.
6. The **adverb** for **good** is **well**. CAREFUL! **Well** is also an adjective that means "in good health."	**Good** game! You played **well**.

192   UNIT 9

2 Like leeches, maggots are a kind of worm-like animal, but unlike leeches, maggots live on dead flesh[1]. Like leeches, maggots were used in the past to treat certain medical problems. Recently, doctors have started using maggots again when nothing else works.

Read the paragraph and circle the adverbs.

> The patient lay quietly on her bed. She was not feeling well. As soon as the doctor arrived, the patient felt more uncomfortable. She looked nervously at what was in the doctor's hand—a small jar with hundreds of small, white, worm-like things. And they were moving. The doctor smiled warmly at the patient. The patient felt better. She remembered that the maggots in the doctor's jar were going to help her. Parts of her left leg were dead because of an infection[2]. The maggots were going to eat the dead parts and allow the rest of her leg to heal well. It wasn't very nice to think about, but it was the best choice she had to save her leg.

Now write the adjective form of the adverbs you circled.

1. _____   3. _____
2. _____   4. _____

3 *Complete each sentence with the adjective or adverb form of the word in parentheses.*

1. Mrs. Ewing became __slowly__ weaker over the months of her illness.
   (slow)

2. If you take an aspirin, your headache will go away _____.
   (quick)

3. Please be _____. I don't want anyone to get hurt!
   (careful)

4. My doctor is so friendly and _____. You'll like her.
   (warm)

5. Alice's husband was _____ when Alice returned from the hospital. He'd
   (happy)
   missed her.

6. The nurse washed my cut _____. It almost didn't hurt.
   (gentle)

7. The baby came in the middle of a snowy night. We drove very _____ to the
   (careful)
   hospital, but we got there in time.

8. His cut was _____. It hurt a lot.
   (painful)

---

[1] **flesh:** the soft part of the body of a person or animal

[2] **infection:** a disease or sickness

What's Your Medicine?   193

4 Answer each question. Use one or two adverbs from the box in your answer.

| badly | easily | gently | painfully | quickly | slowly | well |
| carefully | fast | hard | patiently | quietly | suddenly | |

1. How do you walk when you have a sprained ankle?
   _____
   _____

2. How do you want your doctor to talk to you?
   _____
   _____

3. How do you take off a Band-Aid?
   _____
   _____

4. How do you clean a cut before you put a bandage on?
   _____
   _____

5. How do you talk to a small child who is crying?
   _____
   _____

C WRITING

In this unit, you read about people all over the world still using traditional medicine and home remedies. Do you have childhood memories of your parents or grandparents treating you with a home remedy? What happened?

You are going to **write a narrative paragraph about an experience you had with a home remedy**. First, you will describe when and where you had this experience, what your health problem was, and what remedy you (or a parent) chose. Then you will describe what happened and how it worked. Use the vocabulary and grammar from the unit.*

---

*For Alternative Writing Topics, see page 199. These topics can be used in place of the writing topic for this unit or as homework. The alternative topics relate to the theme of the unit, but may not target the same grammar or rhetorical structures taught in the unit.

PREPARE TO WRITE: Brainstorming

Brainstorming is a helpful way to get ideas for your writing. In brainstorming, you think of **as many ideas as possible** about a topic. No ideas are bad or wrong. You can brainstorm alone or in a group.

Follow the steps.

1. As a class, **brainstorm** as many home remedies as you can. Write them on the board. Ask questions about the ones that are unfamiliar to you. (For examples of some home remedies, reread Background and Vocabulary on pages 183–184.)

2. Choose one remedy that you want to write about. Make sure it is one you have experience with.

3. Make a **cluster diagram**:
   a. Write the remedy in the middle of a piece of paper.
   b. In the space around it, write any words you can think of that are related to your experience of the remedy: your health problem, the place where it happened, the people who were there, how the remedy felt or tasted, etc.

Example

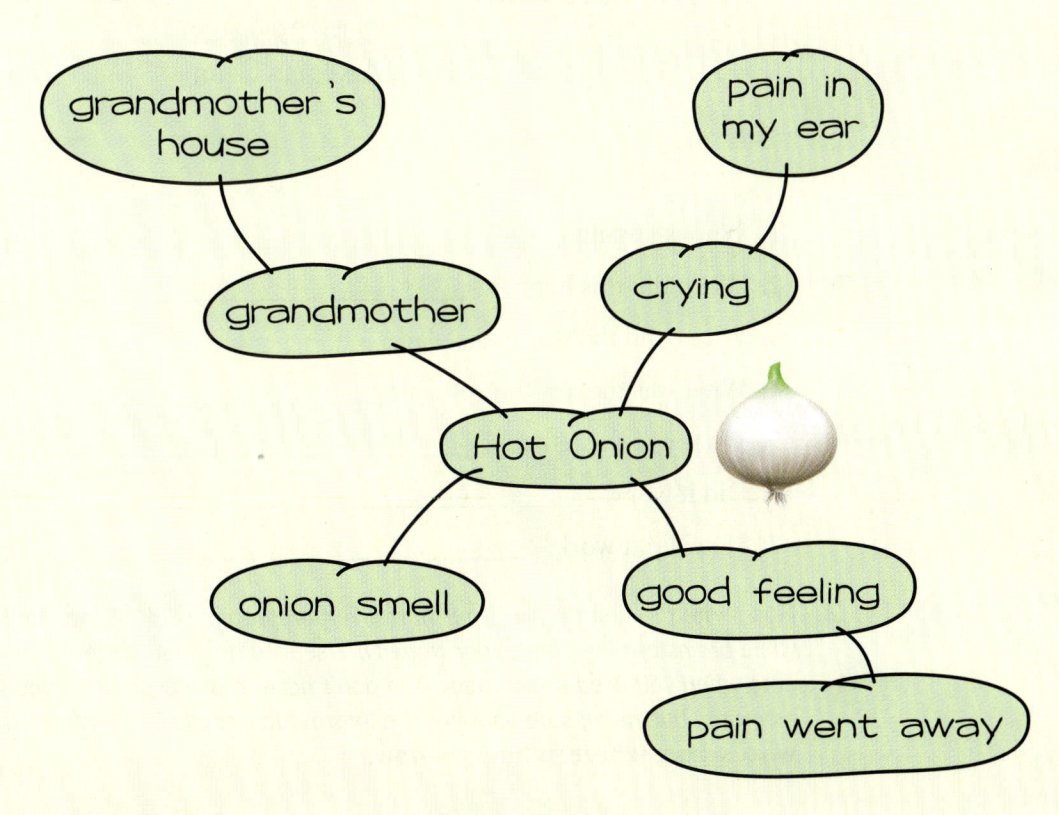

- grandmother's house
- grandmother
- pain in my ear
- crying
- Hot Onion
- onion smell
- good feeling
- pain went away

What's Your Medicine? 195

WRITE: A Narrative Paragraph

A **narrative** is a **story** about something that happened to you or someone else. It starts by telling **who** this story happened to, **when** it happened, and **where** it happened. Then it describes **what** happened and **how**.

1 Read the narrative paragraph. Then answer the questions.

> When I was about six, I went to visit my grandmother in Canada. One day, I got a really bad earache. I was in a lot of pain, and I was crying. My grandmother said she knew what to do. First, she walked calmly to the kitchen cabinet and took out an onion. Then she cut it in half and put the two pieces in a pot of water. Next, she heated the onion in the water. Soon the smell of onion filled the kitchen. After that, she took out one half of the onion and put a small piece of cloth around it. Finally, she put the hot onion carefully against my ear. The heat from the onion felt very good on my ear. After a while, the pain went away.
>
> Sally Collingsworth
> Austin, Texas

1. Who is talking? _____
2. When did this happen? _____
3. Where did the story take place? _____
4. What was the health problem? _____
5. What was the remedy? _____
6. Did it work? _____
7. How did it work? _____

2 Now write the first draft of your narrative paragraph. Look at the diagram you made while brainstorming about your remedy. Use it to help you write a story describing one time when you used this remedy. You don't have to use every item you wrote in that diagram. But, make sure you give the information needed to answer questions about **who, when, where, what,** and **how**.

◀ **REVISE: Using Time Order Words in a Narrative**

When you tell a story in the first person, it helps the reader understand the story better if you describe what happened in **time order**—this means in the order in which things happened. We show time order by using **time order words** like these:

> First, ...   Second, ...   Then, ...   Next, ...   After that, ...   Finally, ...

1 Read the two stories. Which one is clearer (**A** or **B**)? Put a check (✓) next to it. Discuss your answer with a partner.

A. ○

> When I grew up in Vietnam, all of us children frequently got head lice[1]. We didn't have chemicals or special shampoos to kill the lice. So my mother treated it the traditional way: with coconut[2] oil. My mother washed my hair with shampoo. I sat on a chair in front of her, and she combed out my hair slowly. This is one of my favorite memories as a kid: my mother singing to me while she combed my hair. I loved to close my eyes and listen to her rich voice. She poured some warm coconut oil carefully onto my hair. I loved this part. Usually we left the oil in for a few days. Mom shampooed and combed my hair one last time. My hair still looked oily, but the lice were gone.
>
> ---
> [1] **head lice:** very small insects that live in human hair
> [2] **coconut:** a very large brown nut; it is white inside and has liquid in the middle

B. ○

> When I grew up in Vietnam, all of us children frequently got head lice. We didn't have chemicals or special shampoos to kill the lice. So my mother treated it the traditional way: with coconut oil. First, my mother washed my hair with shampoo. Then, I sat on a chair in front of her and she combed my hair slowly. This is one of my favorite memories as a kid: my mother singing to me while she combed my hair. I loved to close my eyes and listen to her rich voice. After that, she poured some warm coconut oil carefully onto my hair. I loved this part. Usually we left the oil in for a few days. Finally, Mom shampooed and combed my hair one last time. My hair still looked oily, but the lice were gone.

Now read Story **B** again, and circle the time order words.

2 *The following story would be clearer with some time order words. Fill in the blanks with the appropriate time order words from the box. Make sure you use proper punctuation and capitalization.*

| Finally, . . . | First, . . . | Next, . . . | Then, . . . |

Last winter I had a bad cold. I was home from work for a week. I couldn't breathe well through my nose. I remembered an old remedy my grandmother used. _____ I put a towel over my head and put my head over the sink. _____ I turned on the hot water all the way. The towel was like a tent over the hot steamy water. _____ I breathed hard through my nose. I did this for about 30 minutes. _____ Near the end I could breathe more easily through one side of my nose. I did this three more times until I could breathe normally.

3 *Now go back to the first draft of your narrative paragraph or story and add the time order words necessary to show in what order things happened.*

EDIT: Writing the Final Draft

Write the final draft of your narrative paragraph. Carefully edit it for grammatical and mechanical errors such as spelling, capitalization, and punctuation. Make sure you used some of the vocabulary and grammar from the unit. Use the checklist to help you write your final draft. Then neatly write or type your paragraph.

✓ FINAL DRAFT CHECKLIST

- ○ Does your paragraph describe an experience you had with a home remedy?
- ○ Does it answer the questions of *who, when, where, what,* and *how*?
- ○ Does it describe what happened in time order?
- ○ Do you use time order words correctly?
- ○ Do you use adverbs of manner correctly?
- ○ Do you use new vocabulary that you learned in this unit?

ALTERNATIVE WRITING TOPICS

Write about one of the topics. Use the vocabulary and grammar from the unit.

1. In a letter to a friend, describe a strange or unusual medical treatment you (or someone you know) had. What was it? What was it for? Why was it strange or unusual? Would you (or the person who had it) agree to have it again?

2. Shetal Shah's description of his bike accident, hurt ankle, and the cure make a good story. In a paragraph or two, describe an accident you had. Where were you? What happened? How were you hurt and how did you heal?

3. Do you have a friend or family member who is a nurse or doctor? Write a paragraph or two describing why that person chose to work in medicine. Describe the person's job.

RESEARCH TOPICS, see page 229.

UNIT 10
Endangered Cultures

1 FOCUS ON THE TOPIC

A PREDICT

Look at the pictures and discuss the questions with the class.

1. These two people are from the same country: Malaysia. Why do you think they look so different from each other? What are the differences?

2. An endangered culture is a culture that is in danger of disappearing. Why do you think the person on the left is part of an endangered culture?

B SHARE INFORMATION

Indigenous people are people whose families and cultures have been in one place for a very long time. In North America, there are many groups of indigenous people (often called Indians or Native Americans)—for example, the *Cree*, the *Hopi*, and the *Shoshone*. Many indigenous cultures have disappeared. Almost all indigenous cultures today are endangered.

Discuss the questions in a small group.

1. What indigenous cultures do you know about from your country or elsewhere?
2. What do you know about them?
3. What is their life like today?

C BACKGROUND AND VOCABULARY

The map below shows where most indigenous cultures are found today. There are about 5,000 indigenous cultures in the world today; the map lists a few of them.

1 Study the map. The names in boldface refer to the indigenous cultures mentioned in the unit.

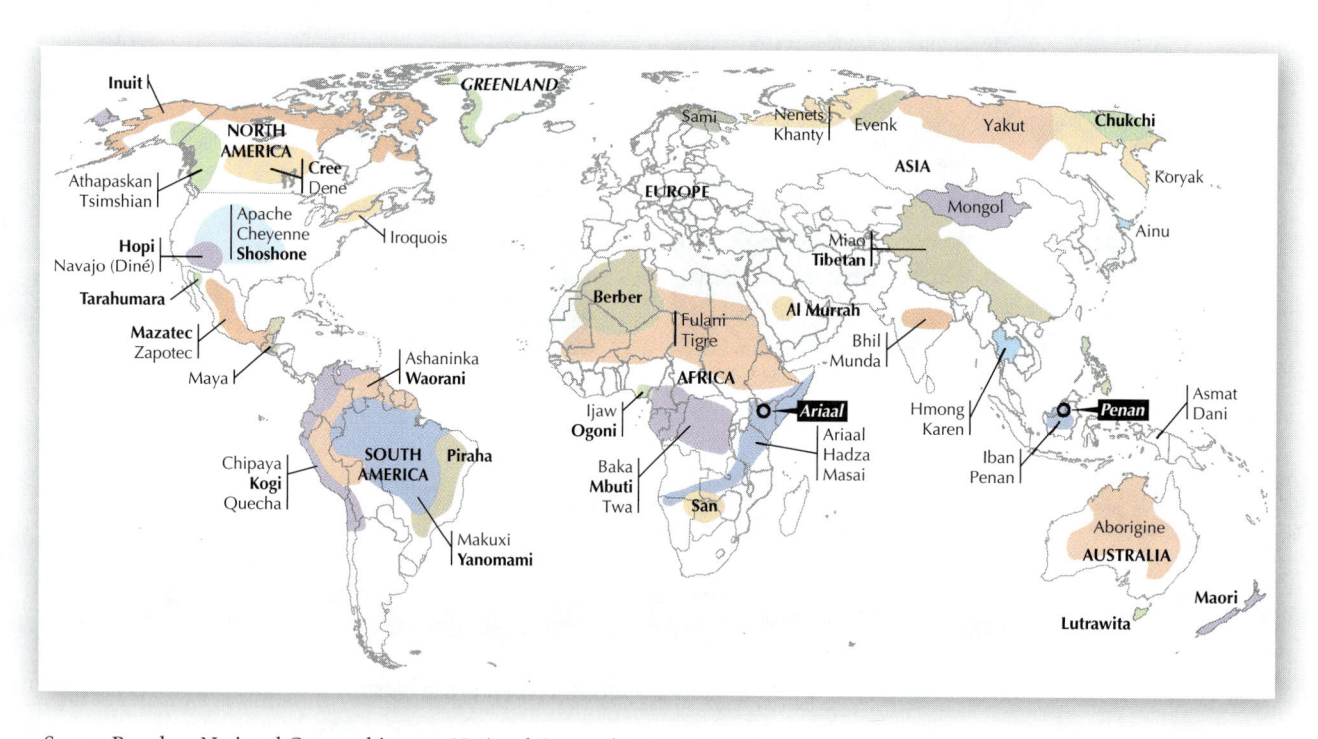

Source: Based on National Geographic map, *National Geographic,* August 1999

202 UNIT 10

Now answer the questions with a partner.

1. Where are there many groups of indigenous people?
2. Look at the coasts (places where the land meets the sea) of North America and Australia. Are there any indigenous cultures there? Who lives there?
3. Look at Europe. What do you think happened to the indigenous people of Europe?

2 Read the statements about indigenous people. Try to understand the boldfaced words without looking them up in a dictionary.

1. The *Lutrawita*, indigenous people of Tasmania, Australia, did not **survive** into the 20th century. The last Lutrawita died in 1876. Most of them died between 1803 and 1833.

2. A long time ago, when the sea was lower, a land bridge connected Siberia and Alaska. The *Chukchi* people of Siberia and the *Inuit* people of Alaska were part of one culture. As the sea rose, the land divided and the Chukchi and Inuit cultures became separate. But they started as the same culture. They share the same **roots**.

3. The *Tibetan* people of the Himalayas believe that the Dalai Lama, their leader, is **holy**. They believe that in his body lives Chenrezig, their god[1] of compassion[2].

4. The *San* of southern Africa do not **adapt** well to modern life. Life in the desert is a very important part of their culture. If they move to towns and live in buildings, they become sick and sometimes die.

5. The *Al Murrah* is a group of 15,000 people from southern Arabia. Like all **nomadic** groups, they don't live in one place. The Al Murrah travel about 1,800 miles (3,000 kilometers) each year.

---

[1] **god:** spirit or being who controls the world or part of it, or who represents a particular quality (in the belief of religious people)

[2] **compassion:** sympathy for people who are suffering

(continued on next page)

Endangered Cultures

6. Some scientists think that the New Zealand *Maori* men and women have different **ancestors**. The ancestors of the men are from Melanesia and those of the women are from Taiwan. The scientists believe that 6,000 years ago a group of women from Taiwan came in boats to Melanesia. At that point, some Melanesian men joined these women and together they came to New Zealand and stayed.

7. The old ways of life for the *Mbuti* of the Democratic Republic of Congo are in danger. Large mining companies[3] are **destroying** the land where the Mbuti live. The trees and the animals are disappearing and the water is bad.

8. The *Piraha* people of the Amazon have a **unique** language. It is unlike any other language in the world. It has no words for colors or numbers greater than two.

---
[3] **mining companies:** companies that take metals, like gold, and minerals like diamonds, from the land

Now match the words with their definitions.

_c_ 1. survive
___ 2. roots
___ 3. holy
___ 4. adapt
___ 5. nomadic
___ 6. ancestors
___ 7. destroy
___ 8. unique

a. the beginning or origin of something; the connection with a place
b. unusual, the only one of its type
c. to continue to live in spite of difficulties or illness
d. members of your family who lived a long time ago
e. to change your behavior or ideas to fit a new situation
f. traveling from place to place
g. connected to a god and religion
h. to damage something so badly that it cannot be fixed

2 FOCUS ON READING

A READING ONE: Will Indigenous Cultures Survive?

Before you read, look at the title of the magazine article. What do you think is the answer to the question in the title?

Will Indigenous Cultures Survive?

By Alex Knight

1. In northern Colombia, a four-year-old *Kogi* Indian is carried into the Sierra Nevada mountains. He will live in a small dark house for 18 years. There he will learn to be a **holy** man. In the Amazon, a *Waorani* hunter follows animals by their smell. A *Mazatec* farmer in Mexico talks to other Mazatec by whistling[1] across the valleys. These stories come from three different indigenous cultures.

2. About 300 million people, or 5 percent of the world's population, belong to indigenous cultures. These cultures have deep **roots** in their histories, languages, and the places they live. Most of these cultures have lived the same way for thousands of years.

3. Change is an important part of any living culture. To **survive**, most indigenous cultures are learning to change in small ways. These small changes help them live with the bigger changes happening in the larger world. However, recent changes in the world are too big and are happening too fast. Most indigenous cultures can no longer **adapt** to them. For example, in Brazil, a gold rush[2] brought diseases to the *Yanomami* in the early 1990s. Now one-quarter of them are dead. In Nigeria, the *Ogoni* homeland near the Niger River is full of chemicals from oil companies. The Ogoni can no longer drink the water or grow food there. In India, over 250,000 indigenous people had to leave their homes in the Narmada River valley because the government built a dam[3] on the river.

4. What happens to the people from these cultures? Where do they go? Usually they have to move away from the lands of their **ancestors**. Often they move to the poor areas outside of large cities. They have to learn a new way of living and thinking. Their children will know little about the culture they came from.

5. There are about 5,000 cultures with their own **unique** languages alive today. Some scientists predict that by 2100, 50 percent of these will disappear. There are many indigenous people who are working hard to stop this from happening to their culture. They are fighting against governments who want them to become part of the modern world. They are fighting against oil and logging companies[4] who want their land.

6. The *Ariaal*, an indigenous **nomadic** group in Kenya, have been fighting for years. So far, their culture is surviving. The Ariaal understand that some changes may help them, but other changes may **destroy** their way of life. The Ariaal are trying to stop the things that will hurt their culture and accept the helpful parts of the modern world. For example, the Kenyan government wants the Ariaal to move to villages. The government wants the Ariaal and other indigenous people to become more modern. The

---

[1] **whistling:** making a high or musical sound by blowing air out through your lips
[2] **gold rush:** a time when many people move to one area to look for gold
[3] **dam:** a wall built across a river to make a lake and produce electricity
[4] **logging companies:** companies that cut down trees to make wood and paper

(continued on next page)

Ariaal know that if they move to villages, their nomadic way of life will disappear. So they aren't moving to villages. But some Ariaal are sending their children to Kenyan schools. They decided that schools are modern things that can help their culture survive.

7   There are no easy ways to save indigenous cultures. We now know that indigenous cultures must adapt to survive. Most importantly, they must choose *how* they will adapt, as the Ariaal are trying to do. The big question is: Will the rest of the world let them?

Source: Based on information in Wade Davis, "The issue is whether ancient cultures will be able to change on their own terms," *National Geographic*, August 1999.

◀ READ FOR MAIN IDEAS

Circle the answer that best completes each statement.

1. Most indigenous cultures _____.
   a. are changing with modern times
   b. live the way they lived for thousands of years

2. Indigenous cultures are disappearing because _____.
   a. big changes are happening too fast
   b. their governments don't want them to adapt to the modern world

3. Indigenous cultures are fighting against _____ to keep their cultures.
   a. governments and big businesses
   b. other indigenous cultures

4. In order to survive, indigenous cultures must _____.
   a. listen to their governments
   b. decide how to adapt

5. For indigenous cultures to survive, the rest of the world must let them _____.
   a. have schools
   b. choose how to change

◀ READ FOR DETAILS

The article gives many examples to support general ideas. List the examples below each statement.

1. Three examples of the ways indigenous cultures understand the world and live their lives:
   a. The Kogi Indian child goes to live in a dark house for 18 years.
   b. The Waorani hunter in the Amazon follows animals' smells.
   c. The Mazatec farmer in Mexico whistles to talk across the valleys.

2. Three examples of changes that indigenous cultures cannot adapt to, and their results:

   a. _____ (result: _____)

   b. _____ (result: _____)

   c. _____ (result: _____)

3. One example of an indigenous group that is fighting to keep its culture:

   _____

4. One example of something that will hurt the Ariaal way of life:

   _____

5. One example of something from modern Kenyan culture that the Ariaal want:

   _____

◀ MAKE INFERENCES

The article mentions many groups of people who have opinions about what should happen to indigenous cultures. Three persons from these groups are listed below.

---

a government official   the president of an oil company

an indigenous group leader

Read the quotes about indigenous people and decide which person in the above list said each quote. Discuss your answers with a partner. Use information in the text to support your decisions.

1. "We are not afraid to change, but we cannot forget everything about our culture and our ancestors."

   Who said it? _____

2. "We don't want these indigenous people running around like animals. We need to teach them how to be a part of the modern culture of our country."

   Who said it? _____

3. "We are not trying to change cultures. We bought the land from the government, so it is ours. We are giving the people here good jobs. They should be happy!"

   Who said it? _____

4. "We need to learn the language of the larger culture around us. Because then we can talk with them and tell them what we want and don't want."

   Who said it? _____

(continued on next page)

5. "They're nomadic, right? They can move to a different forest. We can't. We have to work here where the oil is."

   Who said it? _____

6. "I know. I know. I don't like taking these people off their land either. But the cities need this electricity and this land is the best place to build the dam."

   Who said it? _____

EXPRESS OPINIONS

Discuss the questions in a small group. Give your opinions. Then share your answers with the class.

1. Reread the quotes in Make Inferences. With which person do you agree the most? The government official? The indigenous group leader? The president of an oil company? Explain your answer.

2. Reread the title of the article. What is your answer to this question?

3. Should governments try to help indigenous people survive? If so, what can they do?

B READING TWO: The Penan

Read the journal entry about a visit to an indigenous people from Malaysia: the Penan.

June 10

1 I am going back to visit my Penan friends after 10 years. The big ships[1] are the first things I see as I turn my boat to go up the river. They are waiting to get filled up with logs[2] from the forests where the Penan live.

2 When I arrive at the Penan village of Long Iman, my old friend, Tu'o, greets me warmly. Tu'o was born a nomad. But 30 years ago, the Malaysian government moved Tu'o to Long Iman. Since that time, thousands more Penan have moved to villages because their forest home was disappearing. The Penan fought to keep their home in the forest, but the logging companies were too powerful.

---
[1] **ships:** large boats
[2] **log:** the large thick part of the tree after it is cut down

208   UNIT 10

3 Long Iman is a sad place. The river is dirty, and there is mud[3] everywhere. There are no hospitals or schools. In the evening, children watch television, but they don't understand the language. Tu'o says he is sorry about the small amount of food at dinner. "How can you feed your guests[4] in a village? It's not like the forest where there is a lot of food. In the forest, I can give you as much as you want. Here, you just sit and look at your guests, and you can't give them anything. My house here is strong, and we have beds and pillows. But you can't eat a pillow."

4 I am here to find one of the last groups of Penan nomads. There are only about 200 Penan nomads left. The group I am looking for now lives in a national park, where the forest is safe from oil and logging companies. Tu'o says he will take me to them. We leave the next morning. After three days of traveling, we reach the nomads.

5 Asik, the leader, welcomes us. In the evening, we eat with the nomads. We eat baskets of beautiful fruit, mushrooms for soup, delicious vegetables, and two pigs—all collected or caught in the forest. Sharing is an important part of the Penan's way of life. They do not even have a word for "thank you."

6 I ask Asik about the villages like Long Iman. He says, "There are no more trees, and all the land is no good. The animals are gone; the river is muddy. Here we sleep on hard logs, but we have plenty to eat."

---

[3] **mud:** dirt and water mixed together
[4] **guests:** people you invite to your house to visit or share a meal

Source: Based on information in Wade Davis, "The issue is whether ancient cultures will be able to change on their own terms," *National Geographic*, August 1999.

Now circle the answer that best completes each statement.

1. The ships on the river in Paragraph 1 belong to _____.
   a. the logging companies
   b. the Penan
   c. the Malaysian government

2. _____ Long Iman.
   a. Tu'o was born in
   b. The government moved Tu'o to
   c. Tu'o decided by himself to move to

3. The forest is disappearing because _____.
   a. the Penan are burning it
   b. the government is building villages
   c. the logging companies are cutting it down

4. Tu'o is sorry that he doesn't have more ____.
   a. boats for the river
   b. food to feed his guests
   c. children to help him

5. There are about ____ nomadic Penan left in the forests.
   a. 20
   b. 200
   c. 2,000

6. The name of the nomadic Penan leader is ____.
   a. Long Iman
   b. Tu'o
   c. Asik

C INTEGRATE READINGS ONE AND TWO

STEP 1: Organize

The article in Reading One is about indigenous cultures in general. The journal entry in Reading Two is about the Penan, an example of an indigenous group.

Look at the chart. On the left are general statements from Reading One. Read each statement and decide how the Penan are an example of that general statement. Write the information about the Penan on the right.

GENERAL STATEMENTS FROM READING ONE	HOW ARE THE PENAN AN EXAMPLE OF THIS?
1. "These cultures have deep roots in their histories, languages, and the places they live."	
2. "Recent changes in the world are too big and are happening too fast. Most indigenous cultures can no longer adapt to them."	
3. "Oil and logging companies … want their land."	
4. "Usually they have to move away from the lands of their ancestors."	

STEP 2: Synthesize

A group called The Malaysia Project *works to stop the disappearance of indigenous cultures like the Penan. You receive the following letter from the director of* The Malaysia Project.

To Supporters of Indigenous Cultures:

As you know, *The Malaysia Project* has worked for years to help save the indigenous cultures of Malaysia. Right now the Penan are in serious danger. They need your help. Congress (or Parliament)[1] will soon vote on a bill[2]. If this bill passes, our country will send money and people to Malaysia to help indigenous groups like the Penan. We are asking you to write to your representatives. Tell them about the Penan, who they are, and what is happening to them. Your letter can help show our leaders how important this vote is. Please help us in the fight to protect groups like the Penan.

Thank you for your support.

Sincerely,

Richard Gow
Executive Director, *The Malaysia Project*

---

[1] **Congress (Parliament):** the group of people elected to make laws in the United States (in other countries)
[2] **bill:** a plan for a new law

Now complete the letter to the member of Congress (or Parliament) who represents[1] the people from your area. Use information from the chart in Step 1.

Dear _____,

Please vote for the Indigenous People's Bill. It's very important that _____
(your country)
support all indigenous people around the world. Many indigenous people are losing their way of life. The Penan in Malaysia are one such group.

Like all indigenous cultures around the world, the Penan have deep roots in their histories, language, and the places where they live.
_____
_____
_____

This wonderful way of life is in danger.
_____
_____
_____

Because of these changes, the Penan can no longer live as they did for thousands of years.
_____
_____
_____

Most of them have to move away from the land of their ancestors.
_____
_____
_____

Life for the Penan is not very good. For those in the villages, they are sad because they are losing their culture. For the few left in the forests, hunting is difficult. Please vote **YES** on the Indigenous People's Bill. It will help save indigenous cultures like the Penan.

Sincerely,

_____
(your name)

---

[1] **represents:** does things or speaks officially for someone else

3 FOCUS ON WRITING

A VOCABULARY

REVIEW

1 *Read each group of sentences. Pay attention to the boldfaced words. Cross out the sentence that does not make sense. Discuss with a partner why it does not make sense.*

1. a. The people have lived in this town for 50 years. They are **nomadic**.
   b. Many indigenous people were **nomadic** in the past, but now most of them live in villages.
   c. **Nomadic** people usually move after their animals eat all of the food in one area.

2. a. American blues music has its **roots** in African American culture.
   b. Our house is very old. Its **roots** are from the 1800s.
   c. Most people who live in the United States have **roots** in other countries.

3. a. These cups are all handmade, so each one is **unique**.
   b. McDonald's hamburgers in New York are **unique** because they are just like the McDonald's hamburgers in Los Angeles.
   c. Claire spent a year looking for a wedding dress that was **unique**.

4. a. The backpacking trip through Nepal was tough, but I **survived**!
   b. Today people who have AIDS can **survive** for many years because we have new medicines.
   c. From the time I was eight years old until I went to university, I **survived** in Canada. Then I moved to the United States.

5. a. Your hair is fine the way it is. Don't **adapt** anything.
   b. The most difficult thing for Noriko to **adapt** to when she moved to England was the food.
   c. Several people got headaches on the first day of the trip to the mountains. But after a couple of days, their bodies **adapted** to being in such a high place.

6. a. Muslims all over the world fast (stop eating and drinking) during the days of the **holy** month of Ramadan.
   b. Tibetans believe that some mountains are **holy**—a god or spirit lives in these mountains.
   c. This office building must be a **holy** place on weekdays. I bet over 500 people work here every day.

7. a. Please don't touch the photo with your dirty hands. You'll **destroy** it.
   b. I had a small accident yesterday. I **destroyed** the car a little. I'm sure it can be fixed.
   c. In Sri Lanka in 2005, the hurricane **destroyed** thousands of homes.

Endangered Cultures 213

2 Complete the article with the words from the box.

| adapted | destroy | ~~nomads~~ | survived |
| ancestors | leaders | roots | unique |

The Berbers

The *Berbers* are the indigenous people of northwest Africa. They lived there before the Arabs. At one time, they were **(1)** _nomads_, but now most of them live in towns and villages. Some Berbers are very light-skinned, and some are dark. Nobody is really sure who their **(2)** _____ were, but they probably have **(3)** _____ in both Europe and Africa.

The largest number of Berbers live in Morocco and Algeria. At one time, some Arab **(4)** _____ in those countries wanted to **(5)** _____ Berber culture. But Berber culture **(6)** _____. Berbers **(7)** _____ to the Arab environment they were in. They became Muslim, and most of them learned Arabic.

Many Berbers live like modern-day Moroccans and Algerians now, but most of them still speak Berber. They return to their villages often so that they don't forget their **(8)** _____ traditions.

◖ EXPAND

A reporter is interviewing an indigenous people's leader. Match the questions with the responses below.

214   UNIT 10

Questions

    a. Do you think you'll catch a lot of fish on your trip today?

    b. I thought this indigenous culture was against modern culture. Why is that man using a camera?

    c. What do you think of your young people who want to move to the cities and leave the old ways?

    d. What do you think will help your people to survive?

    e. Why do all the women sit on one side and the men on the other?

    f. How many children from this village do you think will attend school in the fall?

Responses

  _e_ 1. I'm not sure. It's been our **custom** for so long.

  ___ 2. I **doubt** it. I went out yesterday and didn't get anything.

  ___ 3. I **expect** we'll get a large group. Maybe 15 to 20.

  ___ 4. You're right. We hold onto our own culture very strongly. But frequently we will **adopt** a custom or tool that we find useful.

  ___ 5. I think we must learn how to **stand up against** the governments and the companies that try to take away our lands.

  ___ 6. Of course, this makes us sad. But if they want to **integrate** into modern culture, we can't stop them. We hope they will bring to the modern world all that they learned in our world.

CREATE

You are interviewing a leader of one of the indigenous groups mentioned in this unit. Complete the interview. Use at least nine words from the box. Use different types of questions.

adapt	destroy	integrate	roots
adopt	doubt	leader	stand up against
ancestors	expect	nomad	survive
custom	holy	nomadic	unique

You: What is the name of your culture? _____

Leader of indigenous group: _____

(continued on next page)

Endangered Cultures

You: What are some of the customs of your culture?

Leader of indigenous group: _____

_____

You: _____

Leader of indigenous group: _____

_____

You: _____

Leader of indigenous group: _____

_____

B GRAMMAR: Expressing Predictions and Future Plans

1 Read about Asik's trip to the capital city. Underline the verbs that refer to the future.

> Asik is traveling to the capital city in three days to talk with people in the government. He is going to bring along three young Penan who speak Malay. They will help him and the people he meets understand each other. He is going to meet the president of the Rainforest Action Network (RAN), and then he is giving a short speech to the Parliament. He is not going to meet with experts from the logging companies. They said, "Are you going to tell us anything new? The land is ours. We bought it, so there is nothing to discuss. Nothing will change." The president of RAN will try to help. The members of Parliament will listen to him politely. But Asik wonders, "Will anything change?" He hopes so, but he is not sure.

Write an example of each of the three different forms used to talk about the future.

1. _____
2. _____
3. _____

EXPRESSING PREDICTIONS AND FUTURE PLANS

There are **different ways to talk about the future** in English.

1. Use *will* + **base form** of the verb for **predictions**.	They **will listen** to him politely, but they **won't do** anything. **Will** anything **change**? No, nothing **will change**.
Do not use *will* + base form of the verb for plans made before now.	INCORRECT: I can't go to the capital with you because I will get married.
2. Use *be going to* + **base form** of the verb for **predictions**. Use it also for **plans made before now**.	They **are going to listen** to him politely, but they **are not going to do** anything. *(prediction)* He **is going to bring** along three young Penan. *(plan made before now)* **Is** he **going to meet** with the president?
3. Use the **present progressive** (*be* + *-ing* form of the verb) for **plans made before now**. Future time is indicated by future time words or by the context.	Asik **is giving** a short speech to the Parliament *next Tuesday*. When **is** Asik **coming** back?
Do not use the present progressive to make predictions.	INCORRECT: The Penan are surviving in the future.

2 *Complete Asik's speech to Parliament. Use a future form of the verbs in parentheses. For each blank, two forms are possible; choose one. Use each of the three ways of expressing the future at least once.*

The government says that it is helping us. The logging companies say that the Penan people ___will make___ lots of money. But the jobs _____
                          1. (make)   2. (disappear)

with the forest. When the forest is gone, there _____ any more jobs.
                                                      3. (not be)

Why do we need jobs anyway? My grandfather didn't have a job. My father didn't have a job. They lived off the forest. But there _____ any more forest
                                                                              4. (not be)

to live off in a few years—for anyone.

The people from the government say that they _____ schools
                                                                                5. (build)

and hospitals for us in the next few years. They say they _____ us
                                                                                                       6. (help)

learn to be part of modern Malaysian culture when the schools are finished. But we

don't want to be part of modern Malaysian culture. We _____ the
7. (stay)
way we are. We _____ from the forest.
8. (not move)

My aunt moved to a government village 20 years ago. She says, "This logging is like a big tree that fell on my chest. I wake up every night and talk with my husband about the future of my children. I always ask myself, 'When _____?'"
9. (it / end)

My elderly grandmother went to live with that aunt a year ago, but she _____ back to the forest. "I _____ soon," she says. "I
10. (come)   11. (die)
_____ in that government village. My spirit _____
12. (not die)   13. (never rest)
there."

3 *Write six questions about the future of the Penan and other indigenous cultures. For items **1–3**, use the words given. For items **4–6**, write your own questions. Make sure you use appropriate forms.*

   1. Penan culture / disappear?
      _____

   2. How many / Penan nomads / be alive / in 50 years?
      _____

   3. anyone / speak Penan / in 100 years?
      _____

   4. _____
   5. _____
   6. _____

4 *Work with a partner. Read the questions your partner wrote for Exercise 3. Then write answers to your partner's questions. Make sure you use appropriate forms for talking about the future.*

   1. _____
   2. _____
   3. _____
   4. _____
   5. _____
   6. _____

C WRITING

In this unit, you read about endangered cultures in general and about one culture in particular, the Penan of Malaysia. Do you think the Penan will survive the next 100 years?

You are going to **write a paragraph to make a prediction about the survival of the Penan**. You will give reasons for your prediction. And you will support your reasons with facts from Readings One and Two or any facts you know from your general knowledge. Use the vocabulary and grammar from the unit.*

PREPARE TO WRITE: Taking Notes from a Reading

Taking notes from a reading is an important tool for writing. To take useful notes, you must first decide what your opinion on the topic will be. Then go back to the reading and take notes on the **parts that show that your opinion is the correct one**. When you take notes, don't write in full sentences—use **short phrases** or one word.

1 Read the article about the Tarahumara culture. Do you think the Tarahumara will survive? What is your opinion?

The Feet Runners

1 The *Tarahumara* people live in the mountains of Mexico. The high mountains make it difficult to know how many Tarahumara are living today. But most people agree the number is close to 50,000.

2 The Tarahumara call themselves the *Raramuri*. This means "feet runners" or "those who walk well." In fact, they are known for being very strong runners. Because their villages are far apart, the Tarahumara run long distances all the time.

(continued on next page)

---

*For Alternative Writing Topics, see page 224. These topics can be used in place of the writing topic for this unit or as homework. The alternative topics relate to the theme of the unit, but may not target the same grammar or rhetorical structures taught in the unit.

Endangered Cultures   **219**

3   The Tarahumara have resisted[1] the modern world since the 1700s. They refuse to adapt to the changes of modern Mexico. They run away from change. Whenever an outside group gets too close, the Tarahumara move higher into the mountains. They want to keep their people and their culture away from modern Mexican culture. The Tarahumara still dress, farm, and live like they did long ago. They teach their children to love their customs, their language, and their way of life.

4   The Tarahumara have survived 400 years since the Spanish first came to Mexico. But what about the next 400 years? In general, the Tarahumara live in the mountains called Copper Canyon. This area is very interesting to mining companies. There is gold and silver deep in the mountains of Copper Canyon. Also, logging companies are slowly destroying the forests of this area. These big companies will destroy the land and the water if they come to get the trees and the gold and silver. Will the Tarahumara be able to survive? The world will have to wait and see.

[1]**resisted:** not allowed something to change you

2 Imagine you believe the Tarahumara will survive. Check (✓) the notes that support your opinion.

___ known for being strong runners
___ have resisted modern Mexico since 1700s
___ call themselves Raramuri
___ still dress and farm like they did years ago
___ new people get too close, they move higher
___ live in Copper Canyon
___ 400 years of change have not killed them

3 Imagine you believe the Tarahumara will not survive. Go back to the reading and make two notes that support this opinion. Remember: Use short phrases.

NOTE 1: _____

NOTE 2: _____

4 Decide if you think the Penan will survive the next 100 years or not. Then reread Readings One and Two and take notes on the facts that show why your opinion is correct.

WRITE: A Paragraph Based on an Outline

An **outline** is another useful tool for writing. An outline helps you **organize your ideas** before you start writing.

1 Read the outline about the Tarahumara.

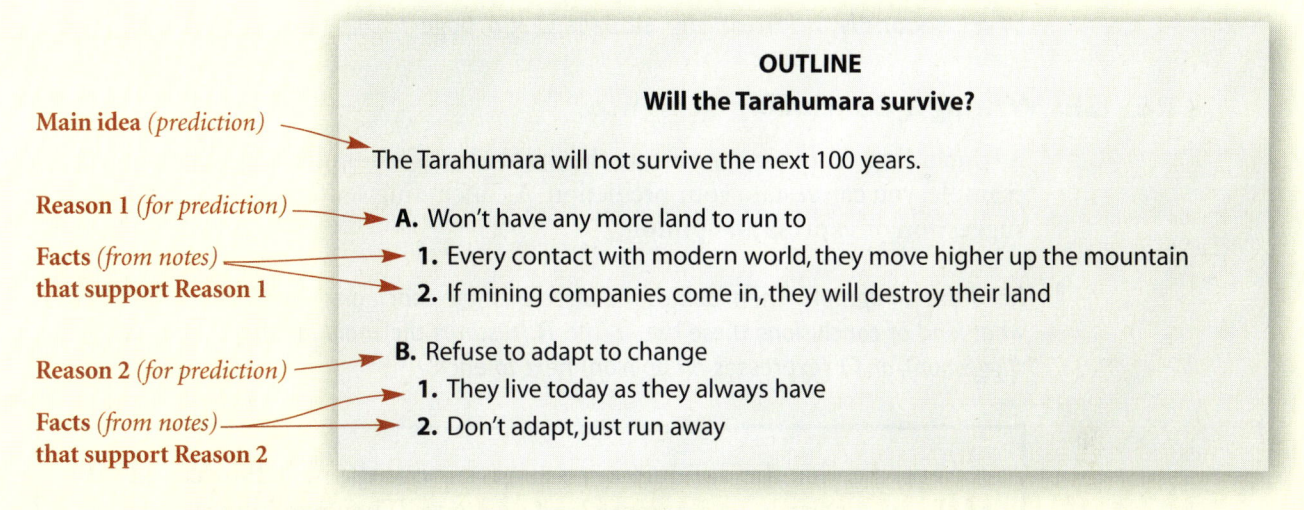

OUTLINE
Will the Tarahumara survive?

Main idea (prediction) — The Tarahumara will not survive the next 100 years.

Reason 1 (for prediction) — **A.** Won't have any more land to run to

Facts (from notes) that support Reason 1 —
  1. Every contact with modern world, they move higher up the mountain
  2. If mining companies come in, they will destroy their land

Reason 2 (for prediction) — **B.** Refuse to adapt to change

Facts (from notes) that support Reason 2 —
  1. They live today as they always have
  2. Don't adapt, just run away

2 Read another outline on the Tarahumara. Complete the outline by choosing the best reasons for **A** and **B** from the lists below.

OUTLINE
Will the Tarahumara survive?

The Tarahumara will survive the next 100 years.

A. _____
  1. Still dress, farm, live as did 400 years ago
  2. Teach children to love customs and language

B. _____
  1. 50,000 living today

The Best Reason for A

1. They are interested in changing their culture
2. They work hard to stop their culture from disappearing
3. They haven't changed anything in their culture for 400 years

The Best Reason for B

1. They have a small number of people
2. They have a fairly large population
3. We don't know exactly how many are living today

Endangered Cultures

3 Write an outline about your prediction for the Penan. Your prediction will be your main idea. Provide at least two or three reasons for your prediction. Use your notes for the facts that support your reasons.

4 Now write the first draft of your paragraph, based on your outline. Remember to help your reader identify your different ideas by using order of importance words such as **first of all**, **secondly**, **additionally**, etc. (see Unit 6, page 130).

◀ REVISE: Writing a Concluding Sentence

A **concluding sentence** can **restate the main idea** of a paragraph. In this case, for example, you can restate your prediction. A concluding sentence can also **make a suggestion** or **express an opinion**.

1 Read the paragraph. Then look at the three possible concluding sentences below. Decide what kind of conclusions these are. Write **R** (restates the main idea), **S** (makes a suggestion), or **O** (expresses an opinion) next to each.

> I predict that the Tarahumara will not survive the next 100 years. First of all, they won't have any more land to run to. They won't be able to move higher into the mountains every time modern people get too close to them. Also, if mining companies come in, they will destroy the mountains where the Tarahumara live. Secondly, they refuse to adapt to change. They dress and farm the same way they did 400 years ago. To survive, indigenous cultures must adapt. The Tarahumara have only run away. Soon, they won't be able to even do this.
>
> _____
> _____
> _____

Concluding Sentences

_____ 1. This is why the Tarahumara will not survive another 100 years.

_____ 2. In my opinion, if the Tarahumara can't adapt to change, they'll disappear forever.

_____ 3. To save the Tarahumara, I think the Mexican government should stop the big companies from destroying the Tarahumara's land.

2 *Read the paragraph. Write a concluding sentence. Share it with a partner.*

> I predict that the Tarahumara will survive the next 100 years. First of all, the Tarahumara work hard to hold onto their culture. They still dress and farm the same way they did 400 years ago. Also, they teach their children to love their customs and their language. Secondly, the Tarahumara have a fairly large population. There are about 50,000 Tarahumara living today.
>
> _____
>
> _____
>
> _____

3 *Now go back to the first draft of your paragraph and write a concluding sentence.*

EDIT: Writing the Final Draft

Write the final draft of your paragraph. Carefully edit it for grammatical and mechanical errors, such as spelling, capitalization, and punctuation. Make sure you used some of the vocabulary and grammar from the unit. Use the checklist to help you write your final draft. Then neatly write or type your paragraph.

✓ FINAL DRAFT CHECKLIST

- ○ Does your paragraph clearly predict if the Penan will or will not survive the next 100 years?
- ○ Does it show clear reasons for your prediction?
- ○ Does it use facts from the readings or from your general knowledge to support your prediction?
- ○ Do you use the proper verb tenses when making your prediction?
- ○ Do you use the tenses correctly?
- ○ Do you use a concluding sentence?
- ○ Do you use new vocabulary that you learned in this unit?

ALTERNATIVE WRITING TOPICS

Write about one of the topics. Use the vocabulary and grammar from the unit.

1. What will the world be like if most indigenous cultures disappear? Write a paragraph about your predictions.

2. Is it a good idea to try to save indigenous cultures? In a letter to an editor, explain why or why not. Give examples.

3. Some indigenous cultures have become modern cultures. In a paragraph or two, write about one of these cultures, and tell how it adapted. How different is that culture today from the way it was before?

4. Find someone who is from an indigenous culture. Ask him or her about that culture and write a paragraph or two about it. Write about how that culture thinks and lives. Be sure to use examples in your writing.

RESEARCH TOPICS, see page 230.

RESEARCH TOPICS

UNIT 1: Finding the Ideal Job

Work in pairs. Interview someone who wants to change careers. This person might be a classmate, a teacher, a neighbor, or a relative. Follow these steps:

Step 1: With your partner, prepare a list of questions for your interview. You could start with the following questions and then add some questions of your own to the list.

1. What is your name?
2. What is your career now?
3. What do you do?
4. What are the good and bad things about your career?
5. What is your ideal career? Why?
6. Why would you like this career better than the one you have now?
7. _____
8. _____

Step 2: You and your partner interview the person. One of you asks the questions, the other one takes notes.

Step 3: After the interview, you and your partner write a report. Describe the job that person has and the job that he or she wants. Explain why he or she dreams about a different kind of career. Use any ideas you learned from the readings to help you write.

Step 4: Share your writing with another pair. Read the other pair's report.

UNIT 2: Country Life or City Life?

What is it like to live on a farm? Find out. Follow these steps:

Step 1: Interview someone who at one point in his or her life lived on a farm. Ask this person to tell you about the day-to-day activities on the farm. You could start with the following questions and then ask questions of your own. Take notes.

1. When did you live on this farm?
2. Where was the farm?
3. What time did you usually wake up?
4. What did you do before breakfast?
5. When did you eat breakfast?
6. What was the hardest thing you did on the farm?

Research Topics   **225**

7. What did you like best?

8. _____

9. _____

Step 2: Write a paragraph using the simple past tense to describe one usual day in the life of the people living on that farm. Use the information you collected.

Step 3: Share your writing with a partner.

UNIT 3: Making Money

Find out how banks look for counterfeit money and what they do when they find it. To get this information, your class will write letters to several banks. Follow these steps:

Step 1: In a small group, prepare a list of questions for your letters.

Step 2: In pairs, write your letters. In the letter, follow these steps:

1. Address the letter to the Bank Branch Manager.
2. Introduce yourselves. Explain that you are writing this letter for a class assignment, and that you want to learn what banks do about counterfeit money.
3. Ask your questions.
4. Give your teacher's name and the school's mailing address so someone at the bank can send you an answer.
5. Thank the branch manager for taking the time to read your letter and answer you.

Step 3: Choose several different banks to send the letters to. The banks can be local—or can even be in other countries.

Step 4: Before you send your letter, share it with another pair. Read the other pair's letter and make sure it is correct.

UNIT 4: A Different Path to Justice

As a class, you will interview victims of crime to find out how many of these people might be interested in a restorative justice program. You will write a short summary of your research results. Follow these steps:

Step 1: Interview the victim of a crime. The crime doesn't have to be violent. You might ask about car thefts or robberies. Find out what took place during the crime and what happened with the justice system following the crime. Use these questions to help you:

1. Where did the crime happen?
2. What did the offender do?

3. What did you do?

4. What happened to you?

5. Did the police come? What did they do?

6. Was the offender caught? If so, was he or she arrested? Sent to prison?

7. Did you go to court?

Step 2: Describe restorative justice to the person you are interviewing. Ask the person: "Do you think a restorative justice program could work for this kind of crime? Why or why not?"

Step 3: Share your information with your classmates. Use the following list to help you organize all the information from the whole class.

- Type of crime: _____
- Types of reactions by victims to the crime: _____
- Percentage of offenders caught: _____
- Percentage of caught offenders sent to prison: _____
- Percentage of people who think a restorative justice program could work for this crime: _____

Step 4: Write a paragraph summarizing the class data.

UNIT 5: Subway Etiquette

With a partner, choose a place that you both want to travel to. Choose a place that you don't know very well. Research this culture's rules of etiquette. Follow these steps:

Step 1: Choose the place that you would like to go to.

Step 2: Divide your work so that each of you researches different categories of etiquette. Some of the categories you might research are:

- eating
- traveling
- doing business
- dating
- being a university student
- meeting new people

Step 3: Interview people in your class to see if anyone knows anything about this place. You might ask the following question:

What rules of etiquette for (eating) are different from here?

Step 4: Search on the Internet about "etiquette in _____". You will find a lot of information. Try to find the etiquette rules that are mentioned several times in several websites.

Step 5: Make a list of the rules that you need to remember if you go to this country. You might want to list them by category.

Step 6: Share your results with the class.

Research Topics 227

UNIT 6: Serious Fun

As a class, make a buyer's guide for serious games. The guide will include information to help people decide what game they might want to play or buy. A buyer's guide is different from a review because it includes several games. A buyer's guide can just be a list of information that is easy to read. It doesn't have to be written with complete sentences. If you are not able to research computer games, choose some board games to research. Follow these steps:

Step 1: With a partner, choose a game to research. Find out the following information:

1. its title and what it teaches
2. its cost and where you can buy it
3. what ages it is good for
4. how long it takes to play
5. the goal of the game
6. your rating of the game (How many stars? Five stars is the best rating; one star is the worst.)
7. the reasons for your rating, in note form (if you and your partner disagree, you can include both opinions)

Step 2: As a class, arrange all of the information so that it is easy to read. You might want to make a chart with one column for each game in your research. Write the name of a game at the top of each column, and list the information below.

UNIT 7: The Best Produce There Is

Work in a small group. You are thinking about opening a restaurant that serves only local food. Find out what is available in your area. Follow these steps:

Step 1: As a group, choose several vegetable markets where you can do your research. Farmers markets are best for finding local produce, but "health food" stores or vegetable markets might also carry local produce.

Step 2: At the market, make a list of which local vegetables are in season at different times of the year. You might also list local foods that are not vegetables, such as meat and cheese. You will need to ask the person selling the vegetables which items are local. You can also ask him or her what is available at different times of the year.

Step 3: As a group, make a list of the ingredients that you will have available at different times of the year.

Step 4: Find dishes that you will be able to make with these ingredients.

Step 5: Think of a name for your restaurant and make sample menus for each season.

UNIT 8: "I'll take the train, thanks."

To be a good travel agent, you have to be able to help people with special needs, like people who do not want to fly. Could you be a good travel agent? To find out, follow these steps:

Step 1: Work in a small group. Choose a place to travel to that people usually go to by plane.

Step 2: Research other ways to travel to that place. Each person in the group should find out about one way of getting there.

Step 3: Organize your information in a chart. Categories could be:
- way of traveling
- stops or overnight stays
- round trip cost
- time for one-way journey
- advantages
- disadvantages

For each way of traveling you will fill in the information for these categories.

Step 4: With your group, decide which way of traveling to this place is the best. Write a short report based on the information in your information sheet. If possible, draw a map showing the route(s) of the journey.

UNIT 9: What's Your Medicine?

Compare health practices around the world. Follow these steps:

Step 1: Work in a small group. Choose a common illness.

Step 2: Research traditional ways of curing this illness. Interview people, look on the Internet or find information at the library. How many different ways can you find to treat the same illness?

Step 3: For each different way that you find, record the following information:
- What is the name of the illness?
- How common is the illness?
- What are some interesting facts about the illness (unusual beliefs about what causes the illness / almost nobody gets this illness / the illness is unusually common in this culture, etc.)?
- What medicine is used to treat this illness?
- What else is done to treat the illness?
- How long does it take to work?
- How successful is the treatment?

Step 4: Write a summary of information.

Step 5: Put the summaries of the whole class together to create a resource for your school library.

Research Topics

UNIT 10: Endangered Cultures

Could you be a good reporter on an endangered culture or people? Work in pairs. Follow these steps:

Step 1: Choose an endangered culture / people from the map on page 202.

Step 2: Go to the Internet or to the library to do research about this group of people. Information to look for:
- name
- population
- location
- traditional customs
- relationship to modern culture
- future predictions for these people

Step 3: Write a short report about this endangered culture / people. Expand on the information in your information sheet.

Step 4: Share your report with the class.

GRAMMAR BOOK REFERENCES

NorthStar: Reading and Writing Level 2, Third Edition	Focus on Grammar Level 2, Third Edition	Azar's Basic English Grammar, Third Edition
Unit 1 Descriptive Adjectives and Possessive Adjectives	**Unit 5** Descriptive Adjectives **Unit 12** Possessive Nouns and Possessive Adjectives; Questions with *Whose*	**Chapter 1** Using *Be*: 1-6 **Chapter 2** Using *Be* and *Have*: 2-5 **Chapter 6** Nouns and Pronouns: 6-2
Unit 2 Simple Past Tense	**Unit 3** The Past of *Be* **Unit 20** The Simple Past: Regular Verbs—Affirmative and Negative Statements **Unit 21** The Simple Past: Irregular Verbs—Affirmative and Negative Statements	**Chapter 8** Expressing Past Time, Part 1
Unit 3 Comparative Form of Adjectives	**Unit 40** The Comparative	**Chapter 16** Making Comparisons: 16-3
Unit 4 *Should, Ought to,* and *Shouldn't* for Giving Advice	**Unit 38** Advice: *Should, Shouldn't, Ought to, Had better,* and *Had better not*	**Chapter 13** Modals, Part 2: Advice, Necessity, Requests, Suggestions: 13-1
Unit 5 Imperative Sentences	**Unit 17** The Imperative	**Chapter 13** Modals, Part 2: Advice, Necessity, Requests, Suggestions: 13-6

NorthStar: Reading and Writing Level 2, Third Edition	Focus on Grammar Level 2, Third Edition	Azar's Basic English Grammar, Third Edition
Unit 6 Expressing Habitual Present with *When-* Clauses	**Part IX** **From Grammar to Writing:** Time Clauses with *When*	
Unit 7 *Wh-* Questions in the Simple Present Tense	**Unit 7** *Wh-* Questions **Unit 10** The Simple Present: *Wh-* Questions	**Chapter 3** Using the Simple Present: 3-11, 3-12, 3-13
Unit 8 Superlative Form of Adjectives	**Unit 43** The Superlative	**Chapter 16** Making Comparisons: 16-4
Unit 9 Adverbs of Manner	**Unit 41** Adverbs of Manner	**Chapter 14** Nouns and Modifiers: 14-10
Unit 10 Expressing Predictions and Future Plans	**Unit 30** *Be going to* for the Future **Unit 31** *Will* for the Future; Future Time Markers	**Chapter 10** Expressing Future Time, Part 1: 10-1, 10-2, 10-6, 10-7

CREDITS

Photo Credits: Page 8 (**top**) Brand X/Jupiterimages, (**middle**) Shutterstock, (**bottom**) Larry Williams/Corbis; **Page 26** Little Blue Wolf Productions/Corbis; **Page 29** Mary Kate Denny/PhotoEdit; **Page 36** Mike Grandmaison/Corbis; **Page 39** (**top left**) Animals Animals/Earth Scenes, (**top right**) E.J. Tarbuck, (**bottom left**) Demetrio Carrasco/SuperStock, (**bottom right**) Mark Turner/Jupiterimages; **Page 45** (**top**) Dorling Kindersley, (**bottom**) Shutterstock; **Page 50** David Young-Wolff/PhotoEdit; **Page 52** Shutterstock; **Page 54** Shutterstock; **Page 93** Mike Segar/Reuters/Corbis; **Page 94** Chris Sanders/Jupiterimages; **Page 97** Dave Krieger/Getty Images; **Page 99** Shutterstock; **Page 100** (**top**) Chad Ehlers/The Stock Connection, (**middle**) Stock4B/Jupiterimages, (**bottom**) Jupiterimages/Creatas/Alamy; **Page 113** Ausloser/zefa/Corbis; **Page 119** www.food-force.com; **Page 133** Jeff Greenberg/Omni-Photo Communications, Inc.; **Page 137** Rubberball Productions; **Page 157** (**left**) Kris Timken/Jupiterimages, (**middle**) Ariel Skelley/Jupiterimages, (**right**) Radius Images/Jupiterimages; **Page 160** Christina Hotz Kopernik-Steckel; **Page 163** CBS/Photofest; **Page 183** Shutterstock; **Page 201** (**left**) Robert Holmes/Corbis, (**right**) Eric K. K. Yu/Corbis; **Page 203** Rob Howard/Corbis; **Page 205** Maria Stenzel/National Geographic Image Collection; **Page 208** Robert Holmes/Corbis; **Page 211** Paul Chesley/Getty Images; **Page 214** Jean Du Boisberranger; **Page 219** Robert Harding Picture Library Ltd/Alamy.

Illustration Credits: Ron Chironna, **Page 64;** Aphik Diseño, **Pages 58** (**top**), **59, 134, 135, 195;** Paul Hampson, **Pages 71, 126, 169, 179, 180, 198;** Hal Just, **Page 155;** The Mapping Specialists Limited, **Page 140;** Derek Mueller, **Pages 58** (**bottom**), **60, 78, 138;** Dusan Petricic, **Pages 1, 16, 23, 24, 53, 72, 186;** Gary Torrisi, **Page 124.**

Notes